POLICE REPORT

POLICE REPORT

A View of Law Enforcement

JERRY WILSON

Little, Brown and Company • Boston • Toronto

FIRST EDITION

T 05/75

LIBRARY OF CONGRESS CATALOGING IN PUBLICATION DATA

Wilson, Jerry.
  Police report.

  Includes index.
  1. Police — United States.   2. Police administra-
tion — United States.   3. Crime and criminals — United
States.   I. Title.
HV8138.W634 1975   363.2'0973   74-23557
ISBN 0-316-94493-9

Designed by Susan Windheim

*Published simultaneously in Canada
by Little, Brown & Company (Canada) Limited*

PRINTED IN THE UNITED STATES OF AMERICA

*With appreciation to Snoopy, whose supine
example stirred me from years of procrastination*

Introduction

SPECIFIC ISSUES within police administration, just like issues within society in general, tend in some cases to appear and then to disappear, and in all cases will vary in magnitude of importance from time to time.

Around 1920 the great issue in public administration was unionization of police. In the context of those times, shortly after the Revolution in Russia, when many thoughtful observers believed capitalism to be in danger of extinction, police unionization was viewed as a grave threat to the American system of government. Today, police unions are quite common and are increasing in number and in strength. Even in cities without formal unionization, police executives commonly negotiate with spokesmen for the subordinate ranks of the department. The administrator may find the union to be a challenge to his prerogatives, but no one any longer perceives the police union as a force for violent revolution.

During the middle and late 1960's, the principal issues of police administration were first, the urban riots, and shortly thereafter, the antiwar and campus disorders. These, too, were seen by some observers as precursors of impending violent revolution. As late as 1970, I experienced the shock of having a ranking member of Congress say to me in great seriousness that hiring large numbers of black policemen was a dangerous policy because "we won't have anyone to protect us from blacks if there is a revolution."

But as police learned how to respond to the urban and the antiwar disorders, and as the issues which generated those problems were eliminated, and as the participants simply grew tired of them, the disorders no longer were viewed as symptoms of revolution, but merely as another troublesome phase of history through which the police have been challenged and have responded.

As a matter of fact, of course, the early efforts at unionization of police in World War I days and the mass disorders of the last half of the 1960's were, indeed, potentially revolutionary movements. A fortuitous combination of responses at the time, both by the government in general and by the police in particular, somehow translated those potentials for revolution into simply beginnings of evolution. Different handling at any point in the process might well have brought different results. In crises such as these and in other situations of less remarkable magnitude, police officers and police administrators frequently find themselves serving as bearings at the pivot point of history. A quick emergency judgment by a patrolman on the beat can have greater long-range implications than he could possibly imagine, and the decision of a middle-level police manager may very easily have an impact upon the course of national history.

But it is rarely in the context of the continuum of history that police management decisions are made. Because of the pressures to produce immediate solutions to problems of the moment, most police administrative decisions are made to accomplish results which will be perceptible within that day, that month, or at least that year, with relatively little consideration for the longer term of history.

Decision making for the present rather than for history is a logical response to the constantly shifting public consensus of what is important for the police to do. The reduction of armed robberies may be highly important, but if the police respond effectively to this priority, thus reducing armed robberies, other lesser problems like purse snatchings may become predominant in the public mind. If the police then respond by reducing purse snatchings (and armed robberies don't go up while their activities are diverted), public interest may shift to a few spectacular murders. If the police solve the murders and resolve that problem, public priority for police activity may shift to traffic enforcement or even to enforcement of garbage regulations. It is a great hazard to attribute continuing importance to any aspect of police administration, for the priority will surely change as time passes.

This phenomenon of transitory issues applies not only in major operational areas, but also in technical staff areas; decisions made at one point may prove to be either right or wrong as time passes. As late as 1928, radio manufacturers were saying that there was insufficient market in police work to make development of police radios practical; even in the late 1950's, police communicators were arguing against the practicability of portable radio sets. Even as late as the middle 1960's, some very progressive police administrators were making decisions *not* to establish computer systems within major law enforcement agencies. At the time, none of these decisions was all that conservative; only history has shown them to be erroneous. And for the individual police administrator, who makes or breaks his reputation within the span of a few years, who in the short run must make his agency operate, who in the short run must live within his budget, the temptation always is to make decisions which will produce short-run effectiveness and to let the long run take care of itself.

The constant shifting of problems, the continuing variation in priorities, makes police administration both frustrating and interesting. Frustrating because before the police administrator can relax and enjoy recognition for having resolved one problem, criticism for some new problem is already developing; interesting because each new problem, each new priority, brings with it a challenge which keeps the job from becoming dull and routine.

As with all management, administration of a police department is much more art than science. There is no *only* way or *best* way to accomplish objectives. What works at one time or in one situation may fail in some other context. Special projects and programs which produce and need dramatic results in their early stages often lose their effectiveness after the shine of newness wears off and they become bureaucratized.

For all of these reasons, the reader is cautioned that this is not a "how to do it" book. Many of the issues discussed are subjects of

current importance, and in some cases, controversy, in police administration. But except for crime control, each of these issues is likely to
diminish in importance with the passage of time.

Most of this book is written in depersonalized style. I have purposely avoided making this an autobiography. From 1961 on, I was
an influential staff official of my department. In that capacity I
supported some of the viewpoints and policies which I now suggest
were faulty. In some instances I thought at the time that the policies
were correct, and supported them for that reason; in other instances, I
thought the policies were incorrect, but was unable to persuade my
superiors to change their views.

This confession is not an apology. I would stress that what may be
a correct action at one time may be incorrect at another, and that
hindsight perceptions of error should never be for criticism but only
for instruction.

This book avoids the hardware and technological aspects of police
administration for two reasons. First, the state of the art of technology
is so fast changing that treatment in any book will be soon outdated.
Second, hardware and technology must be specifically designed for
local needs, taking into account work load, space availability, budgetary considerations, and political attitudes. It is patently nonsense to
include a design for a universal police station or a universal communications system.

There are two themes in this book which are likely to find some
agreement but a lot more disagreement in police circles. The first and
most important of these is that the police should be held responsible
for control of crime.

It is a fact that the police alone cannot control crime if they have
no support from the remainder of the criminal justice system and
from the community. But if the police are permitted to hide behind
that fact, then no one is left responsible for crime control.

Police administrators should be held accountable for crime control,
given the resources to perform their part of the function, and encouraged to complain publicly of deficiencies in the remainder of the
criminal justice system. If the courts are not doing their part of the
job, the police administrator should say so; there is no reason why
the police chief should be reticent about criticizing poor sentencing

policies. But shortcomings of the courts should not be an acceptable reason for crime increases.

Throughout the 1960's, when higher court rulings were reducing the authority of police in matters of searches and confessions, the response of supporters of those rulings was that increased constraints on convenience of operations of the police should be offset by increased numbers of police. But the police never collected that debt. Crime in the large cities of America increased threefold from 1960 to 1972, while the number of police officers was increased by less than one-third. To some extent this reflects the attitude of police, and of mayors and others, that the police are not the mainstay of crime control.

This is not to minimize the complexity of crime control. But it is to make the point that someone must be given the burden, and in most systems of local government the police chief is the only readily available possibility. In most cities he controls the greatest proportion of resources of the criminal justice system; he usually has a capability within his records system to monitor what is occurring throughout the system, and he ordinarily has sufficient public exposure to bring public pressure to bear on clearly faulty performance in the remainder of the system.

Objection to the notion of police responsibility for crime control will also come from those who argue that holding the police responsible for crime control will force police tampering with crime statistics. This obviously is a hazard. To some extent it can be offset by requiring open police records systems which are subject to monitoring by the media. To some extent it can be offset by both internal and external auditing processes.

Inevitably, though, even in the best audited system, if there is pressure on the police to reduce crime, some pickpocketing offenses or stolen hubcaps are likely to end up in lost property reports — if for no other reason than that it is impossible to determine whether or not a crime has occurred.

At great risk of being misunderstood, with full realization that some critics will seize upon this statement as proof that reported crime decreases were obtained by statistical tampering — I would suggest that the cost of an absolutely pure crime reporting system, if purchased by relieving the police of direct responsibility for crime prevention, is too high a price to pay.

Crime statistics are sketchy measures at their very best, and more often mislead than enlighten the public. Given that public safety is nearly as much a matter of public mood as of statistical fact, it is possible, even probable, that a city is better served by a police agency which grossly underreports crime and talks in positive terms of its low crime rate (as one large city did throughout the 1960's, until the state planning agency which dispensed Law Enforcement Assistance Agency grants installed a system of crime report audits) than by a police agency which has a relatively low crime rate but miscasts its increases as the important factors (as Washington did in the 1950's). The value of positive thinking as a crime deterrent is inestimable!

For even without reliable statistics, when crime becomes really bad that fact will be obvious. This occurred in Washington in 1968–1969, when those who had doubted the validity of statistical increases suddenly were aware of too many personal friends having been robbed. This occurred throughout the nation when the heroin problem, for which there is a paucity of meaningful data, became so severe as to be obvious to any careful observer.

The best alternative, of course, is to have a reasonably rigid and reliable crime reporting system while at the same time keeping pressure on the police to reduce crime. This actually is what occurred in Washington, combined with massive commitment of resources for the police in particular, for the criminal justice system in general, and for other anticrime measures such as street lighting and narcotics treatment.

But the basic principle of crime reduction is to get the police interested in reducing crime. Make it clear that retention of prestige assignments and advancements to higher ranks will depend on performance in crime reduction. Make field supervisors so interested in crime reduction that they will carefully review every crime; for every borderline case they can declassify in an audited system, they are likely to find ways to redeploy resources so as to prevent fifty crimes: it is far better than having them not caring about crime or caring but not accepting responsibility for doing something about crime.

The second theme likely to evoke more disagreement than praise is that the police craft need not and perhaps should not be comprised entirely of what some would characterize as physically and mentally "superior" individuals.

It already has been demonstrated that exclusion of women from police work was unjustifiable discrimination; it will be shown that exclusion of shorter than average persons has been the same.

An even greater threat than the sexual and physical discrimination of the past is the growing trend toward intellectual discrimination. The proposals for universal requirement of college education as prerequisite for appointment as a police officer will exclude some individuals who are able to do college work but lack college degrees. But an even greater loss will result from exclusion of many highly talented and useful individuals who perform well in the practical world of work but are neither scholastically nor intellectually equipped to do college work.

The police service needs both of those groups and society needs their presence in the police service. I firmly believe that the police service should strenuously avoid unequivocal educational requirements for either appointment or promotion, and should strive instead for an accommodation similar to the military services, which give much emphasis to college education for the commissioned officer corps but which still make it possible for highly capable non–college graduates to proceed to high rank.

In this same theme I suggest that police officers should avoid the snobbery of "professionalization" and instead take pride in being master craftsmen. For several decades the police have been striving to make themselves professionals, with much emphasis on educational courses which mostly are superfluous to the work of a patrol officer on the street.

The incipient trend of the 1970's toward increased unionization of the police may save policemen from their own snobbery, giving them the pride and pay of master craftsmen instead of questionable status as professionals and ending with their having the training they need rather than less functional educational courses.

Both of these themes are discussed in greater detail in this book.

Contents

POLICE REPORT

1

Measurements of Criminal Activity

SHOULD INTERPLANETARY TRAVEL bring to Earth social analysts from other solar systems, they undoubtedly will be surprised to find that in the United States the statistical measure of crime is almost as often a controversy as is crime itself.

This phenomenon is not surprising when one realizes that measures of crime are highly imperfect at best, and that these imperfect measures must be and are used in both support and derogation of a wide range of law enforcement, social, and political purposes. Social scientists have been trying for two hundred years to develop accurate, meaningful indices of crime, of criminals, and of underlying causes leading to their occurrence. Their effort has produced little agreement on anything other than that crime statistics are perhaps the most difficult to obtain, the least accurate, and the most likely to be misinterpreted of all social indicators. Most police administrators wholeheartedly agree with that conclusion.

To discuss a problem or to deal with a problem, however, it is necessary to define the problem in language terms and to measure the problem in statistical terms, however imperfect these definitions and measurements may be.

The legal definition of a crime is essentially "any act committed or omitted in violation of a public law forbidding or commanding it which the government notices as injurious to the public and punishes in a proceeding in its own name." For law enforcement purposes, a careful distinction is usually drawn between criminal wrongs committed against the public and civil wrongs committed against an individual; the recourse of the public is to arrest and prosecute, the recourse of the individual is to institute civil suit. In recent history, however, that distinction has been diminished by legislation in such fields as housing, civil rights, and consumer affairs, where wrongful acts which formerly were only civil matters have been declared to be criminal offenses.

In complex modern society, all kinds of actions are called crimes. To the list of such ancient crimes as murder, robbery, arson, and theft have been added puritan-ethic offenses such as obscenity, profanity, Sabbath breaking, and many technological crimes reflecting modern times. Included now are not only numerous motor vehicle and traffic offenses, but also such crimes as income tax evasion, unlicensed use of the radio spectrum, violations of building, licensing, and zoning codes, and criminal law constraints against discrimination based on race, sex, religion, or national origin. The modern criminal law is far more complex than the natural law.

For a variety of reasons of public policy, relatively few of these myriad prohibitions are regularly enforced by the police, and many are rarely enforced through criminal prosecution by any government agency. Selection of those criminal prohibitions to be a continuing responsibility of the local police varies between jurisdictions and from time to time. The responsibility of the police for prevention or enforcement of the proscriptions against any stated offense will depend on past usage of the community, citizen attitudes influencing policies and priorities of enforcement, and the extent to which either the government or private interests have provided resources outside the police department for prevention of a given type of crime.

The variations in how local jurisdictions handle specific crimes are many. For example, most jurisdictions never aggressively investigate or prosecute sex offenses committed in private between consenting adults, even though such acts often are declared felonies by statute; indeed, although adultery is still a criminal offense in many jurisdictions, it is unlikely that an irate spouse could ever obtain a criminal warrant and prosecution for that "crime." In many jurisdictions, enforcement of license laws is assigned to some special agency of government, and the police do not become involved at all except perhaps in the service of a criminal warrant obtained on oath of the licensing agent.

Many jurisdictions have established separate classes of employees to enforce parking regulations, sometimes placing them under control of the police department and other times placing them under control of some different agency of local government.

There are many proponents, both within and outside police departments, of a policy to relieve police departments from traffic control chores and traffic enforcement by assigning these functions to a special traffic agency. Traffic experts often like this idea because in recent years, as crime reduction has attracted high priority in cities, police administrators and police officers have tended to de-emphasize traffic enforcement; police officers often like the idea because traffic enforcement is the most unpopular of the functions they perform, especially among the "noncriminal" majority of Americans to whom the police look for moral support.

But opponents of such a change make the argument that both crime prevention and traffic enforcement must rely on a large patrol force operating around the clock throughout the city, and it would be uneconomical to maintain separate forces for each of these functions. Also, police officials observe than many criminal arrests result from police contacts initiated as part of traffic enforcement. The purpose here, however, is not to persuade the reader what agency should enforce the traffic laws, but only to demonstrate the complexity of determining exactly what the police are responsible for at any given place and time.

Other examples of bureaucracies, separate from local police, which deal with prohibitions of criminal acts are the special police agencies (sometimes merely guard forces and sometimes full-powered police agencies) which provide police service for industrial plants, for governmental installations, for transit systems, and for private businesses. In some jurisdictions, whatever action is taken against shoplifting is taken by the local police agency, but in most cities the large stores employ their own security forces, and the municipal police do not construe special efforts to control shoplifting as one of their major functions, if they consider such effort as their function at all. Thus, because the combination of modern-day shoplifting and employee theft constitutes a numerical majority of all traditional crimes committed, a large part of the crime problem is eliminated by definition before arriving at basic areas of police responsibility.

The police traditionally have given scant attention to such white-collar crimes as embezzlement by employees and consumer fraud by merchants. In the case of embezzlement by employees, the police have neither access to the records nor auditing resources and expertise to "police" activities within private business houses. Employers, therefore, customarily have dealt with these problems through their own auditors, and in the rare case where they desire a criminal prosecution, the police are involved only in service and processing of a warrant obtained by the employer.

The police have given little attention to consumer frauds primarily because, where the government has taken an active interest in policing private industry in its exchanges with the public, the responsibility for enforcement of constraints against businessmen more naturally has fallen under the responsibility of a separate city licensing department; too, until very recent times public policy has not assigned high priority to criminal prosecution of consumer frauds, with the consequence that both the police and the public have viewed such activities more as civil torts even though such fraudulent actions are prohibited by criminal statutes.

As can be seen, then, local police have a general authority and at least a theoretical responsibility for enforcing all criminal codes and for arresting all criminal offenders, but through a combination of tradition, public policy and perception, and variations in governmental bureaucracies, the local police usually are held accountable for only a very few categories of crime; these tend to be the common law, non-business-related offenses.

Statistical measures of crime in America both reflect and influence public and police priorities in crime control. The most common measure of criminal activity has been the Crime Index, devised in 1958 and based on the Uniform Crime Reporting program. The UCR system was devised in the late 1920's by the Committee on Uniform

Crime Records of the International Association of Chiefs of Police and is administered by the Federal Bureau of Investigation, which serves as a national clearinghouse which receives voluntarily submitted reports from state or local agencies and which publishes consolidated data for the United States.

Because of local variations across the United States in definitions of crimes, the Uniform Crime Reporting program has been developed around a system which categorizes each offense according to the UCR classification, without regard to what that offense may be called by local statute. For example, in many jurisdictions the offense of pickpocketing is classified by statute as larceny, while in other jurisdictions it is classified as robbery; for the statistical purposes of the UCR reporting, however, all jurisdictions tabulate pickpocketing as a larceny, even though they may prosecute it as a robbery under the local statutes.

The Crime Index, the principal measure of crime in America, consists of the first seven crime classes: Criminal Homicide, Forcible Rape, Aggravated Assault, Robbery, Burglary, Larceny, and Auto Theft.

Selection of the categories to be included within the Crime Index is based on several different premises, each of which is sufficiently correct to make the index useful in measuring gross changes in crime trends, but each of which has enough exceptions, variations, and other faults to make the index questionable when measuring subtle changes.

The basic assumption for a crime to be included in the Crime Index is that the victim is likely to be aware that the offense has occurred and is likely to make a report to the police.

This premise holds up reasonably well for classifications such as Robbery and Auto Theft. The victim will usually know with certainty that the offense was committed and likely will make a report to the police — in the case of robbery, because of anger; and in the case of auto theft, because of anger as well as desire to recover his vehicle. There are exceptions, though, which make accuracy less than absolute. The victim may be too drunk to realize that he was robbed or to remember the details of the robbery, or he himself may be engaged in illegal activity such as gambling or narcotics traffic or in a personally embarrassing activity such as utilizing the services of a prostitute, which he does not want to come to the attention of the police or to be put into a public record. Conversely, examples of overreporting of robbery occur when an individual involved with a prostitute has his wallet stolen through an act of larceny but then (because he must account for his credit cards and other paraphernalia) reports to the police that it was stolen on the street in an act of robbery, or when a husband loses his weekly pay at gambling and reports to the police that he was robbed so he will have an acceptable story for his wife, or when an employee of a small shop, or a delivery truck driver, steals the day's receipts and reports to the police that he has been robbed in order to account for the money to his employer. These variations from accurate reporting by citizens occur often enough that even the statistics for robbery, which is considered by many police officials as the best indicator of crime trends, though they are valuable for measuring significant changes, do not record subtle variations in crime levels.

There probably are fewer citizen errors in reporting auto theft than in any other crime index classification. Because any automobile likely to be stolen is a valuable piece of property, and also because the owner bears civil liability for damage done during its operation *with* his permission, there is strong incentive for the owner to make a report to the police whenever his car is stolen; and there are few reasons for an owner to report a car stolen when it is not. The infrequent exceptions are such instances as when a car is taken, used for a joyride, and returned intact to its original location before it is missed by the owner, or when an owner falsely reports his car stolen in an effort to avoid responsibility for a hit-and-run accident. Those kinds of variation, however, are statistically insignificant; more prevalent are the cases where a tourist or other stranger to a city is mistaken about where he parked his automobile and consequently makes an erroneous report to the police; these errors, though, are usually discovered quickly by the officer on the beat and the report declared unfounded before final statistical tabulations are made. Auto theft, therefore, has a high degree of reliability in reports of the offense by citizens to the police, and would be a good indicator of crime trends except that it is such a specialized type of crime, in most cases involving temporary use of the automobile for joyriding or transportation rather than being a theft for permanently depriving the owner and for profit by the thief. Its disability of being a specialty means that reliance on auto theft alone as a gauge of overall criminal activity would be pointless.

Categories other than robbery and auto theft involve much greater variables in citizen reports to the police. Criminal Homicide, for example, is not so often reported to the police as it is *discovered* by them, and the proportion of all homicides correctly diagnosed as such by the police will depend on the efficiency of the homicide investigators and the competence of the medical examiner. From the standpoint of statistical analysis, however, criminal homicides constitute such a small proportion of total crime index offenses that inaccuracies in reporting of this category have little real impact on assessments of overall crime rates or crime trends. The category of criminal homicide is included in the crime index not so much because it is an offense presumed to be consistently reported to the police, as because its gravity as a crime and as viewed by the general public makes it an offense with which police administrators must be concerned. While a statistical reduction in the number of criminal homicides seldom can placate public fear during a period when other Crime Index offenses are sharply increasing, a series of spectacular homicides can always arouse public concern even during a period when other index crimes are declining.

The classification of Forcible Rape is believed to have the highest variation in accuracy of victim reporting to the police. On the one hand, a few incidents are reported as forcible rapes which cannot bear either the scrutiny of the term "forcible" nor otherwise meet the criteria of a prosecutable criminal offense. On the other hand, confessions from multiple rapists have demonstrated time and again that one-half to two-thirds or more of all rapes are never reported to the police. This undoubtedly is a product of embarrassment of a victim at the prospect of discussing this crime with the police, or of being subjected to attempts at impeachment of testimony at the criminal trial if the offender is apprehended. (There is some speculation, however, that the liberalized sexual mores and the more open discussion of sexual acts in recent times has lessened the embarrassment of victims at reporting this crime, perhaps accounting for some of the statistical increase in this offense in the late 1960's and early 1970's.) As with criminal homicide, however, the category of forcible rape is included in the Crime Index not so much because of supposed accuracy of victim reporting to the police as because of its importance as a serious offense and a matter of consistent public concern. And, again similar to criminal homicide, the number of reported forcible rapes is so small a portion of the total Crime Index that variations in this category ordinarily have little impact on total Crime Index statistics.

The UCR category Aggravated Assault is more misunderstood by the general public than any other of the Crime Index classes. Also, this category, over the years, has been subject to variations from city to city and from time to time because of police reporting policies and practices.

More often than not, the average citizen seeing a listing of Crime Index offenses misconstrues the Aggravated Assault category to represent mostly assaults committed on innocent bystanders, passersby, or others in public places; in fact, however, the typical aggravated assault under UCR standards will be the outgrowth of a domestic quarrel within a private home or, if it occurs in a public place, more often than not will be a fight between friends or at least between drinking or gambling acquaintances. Aggravated assault is not very often a stranger-to-stranger crime; stranger-to-stranger offenses are usually counted in the more serious categories of robbery or forcible rape.

Because aggravated assaults so often result from domestic quarrels, these crimes are not consistently reported by victims to the police nor, in some jurisdictions, correctly tabulated by the police. A high proportion of those aggravated assaults which are reported to the police derive from serious injuries which come to the attention of the police through calls for emergency ambulance service or through medical reports by hospitals and doctors; in many of these cases, the victim has no real desire to prosecute nor to make a report of the event, and does so reluctantly. Some other cases are reported to the police primarily for the purpose of getting the offender (usually the husband) out of the home for the evening and thereby ending the quarrel (at least for that night).

In the overwhelming majority of aggravated assaults where the victim makes a report to the police and asks that the offender be arrested, by the time the case comes to trial and tempers have cooled, the probability of prosecution is doubtful. This experience of repeated aborting of prosecution is the factor leading in the past to much underreporting of this offense by police agencies; many agencies have engaged in a practice not authorized by UCR guidelines, of not making any formal report of an aggravated assault (except in case of a very serious injury) until after the victim has obtained a warrant showing a desire to prosecute the offender.

Although Burglary is often misreported through citizen error, this category can be ranked second to robbery as an important classification for interpreting general crime trends. This classification, like robbery, is usually a property-oriented crime (without the specialty nature of auto theft), is usually a stranger-to-stranger offense, and occurs in sufficiently large numbers to be of statistical significance.

In middle-class and in upper-class communities and in business districts, reporting of burglaries to the police is highly accurate; in those environments, premises are usually well enough secured and living styles are well-ordered enough that the occurrence of a burglary is likely to leave noticeable traces, be reported to the police, and be verifiable as a burglary for police reporting. However, the great majority of nonbusiness burglaries occur not in upper- or middle-class residential areas, but in high-crime areas where poor people live, where locks on windows and doors frequently are unworkable, if they exist at all, and where informal life-styles may result in so much coming and going of unrelated or loosely related individuals that a reported burglary may be indistinguishable from a larceny or vice versa. Still, if this factor of reporting error is discounted, and it is recognized that the burglary total is at best a sampling, then this category is highly useful for interpreting and evaluating crime trends and effectiveness in combating them.

A most serious defect of the Crime Index occurs in the Larceny-Theft category, numerically the largest category in the Index. This category imposes a great error rate in citizen reports to the police and in reporting by the police. Lacking the motivations of anger as in robbery, desire to protect the home or business premises from future attack as in burglary, or probability of recovery of property as in auto theft, the victims of common larcenies often simply do not bother to report theft of bicycles, of items stolen from their automobiles, or of items taken by thieves from other places with access to the public. Error also results from the fact that many larceny-thefts are not clearly distinguishable as criminal offenses; for instance, many a pickpocketing offense is mistaken by both the victim and the police to be simply a lost wallet, and a wide variety of other thefts are mistaken by victims to be absentminded misplacement of their property.

The largest majority of larceny-thefts in any city almost certainly will be the combination shoplifting offenses and employee thefts. Yet these crimes cannot feasibly be reported on a crime-by-crime basis, as most of these thefts are never perceived as such but show up as a consolidated "inventory shortage" of many items. Shoplifting, therefore, is seldom reported except in the very small proportion of these crimes where the offender is caught; employee thefts seldom are reported at all.

To reduce the effect of these "minor crimes" on "serious crime" statistics, the UCR Committee originally excluded from the Crime Index all larceny-thefts of property with a total value of less than $50. This approach seemed logical, but serious problems developed from having an index based on valuation.

First, there is the influence of inflation; over a period of years, increases in the number of reports of larceny-theft of property valued at $50 or over just as likely may reflect the effects of inflation as increases in the actual number of criminal offenses.

Second, trend changes in offenses such as purse snatchings, thefts of bicycles, or thefts of property from parked automobiles, which have relatively high priority in the public mind and also are crimes which police activity is especially suited to prevent, often were not reflected in the Crime Index because the value of property taken is often under $50.

Third, there is a serious difficulty in assigning a reasonably fair market value to used stolen goods. Victims have an understandable tendency to assign the highest believable value to their stolen property, both for tax and insurance purposes, and because victims perceive their losses in terms of what replacement goods will cost them. Police, however, try to reflect a fair market value, often translated by them into market value of goods on the street.

To overcome these valuation deficiencies, the UCR Committee in 1973 revised the Crime Index to include all larceny-theft offenses, regardless of valuation of property stolen. Although this change has significant impact in the *number* of offenses counted in the Crime Index, its effect on long-term *trends* of offenses is not substantial.

To some extent the effect of minor larcenies on the Crime Index is offset by the separation of the index into "Violent Crimes," which include murder, rape, robbery, and aggravated assault, and "Property Crimes," which are burglary, larceny, and auto theft. But however subdivided, any significant grouping of crime data will always include so many diverse kinds of offenses that judgments based on minor fluctuations of the total must be made with great care and some element of skepticism.

The basic rationale of crime reporting, then, is that crime trends are measured from the index constructed of offenses rationalized as being those crimes most likely to be reported to the police on a consistent basis, with the crimes of criminal homicide and forcible rape included because of their seriousness.

Excluded from the Index are such important categories as the organized crime offenses — narcotics, gambling, prostitution, extortion, and fencing of stolen goods. These kinds of crime are unsuitable to an index of crime occurrence because the "victim" seldom makes a report to the police. Instead, such crimes are usually discovered only through police investigations; thus, statistical data for these categories may reflect shifting absence or presence of police effort rather than crime trends. Also excluded are such serious crimes as kidnapping and arson, both excluded because of their relative rarity and their not fitting neatly within any of the seven Crime Index categories.

An important fault of the Index is that such problems as vandalism, hooliganism, and similar disorderly acts cannot be adequately reflected. These offenses carry relatively light criminal penalties, but nonetheless are of consequence to the quality of life in a city, and therefore are problems which need to be taken into account in police resource allocation.

Failure of victims to report crimes to the police is only a part of the problem faced in trying to achieve reliable crime reporting data. Victim error is compounded by the difficulty of devising accurate but economical police reporting systems for capturing and auditing crime data.

Police chiefs and their subordinates are, *or should be,* under continuous heavy pressure to reduce the level of crime, or at least to keep the level of crime from rising. There is nothing wrong with having this pressure to control crime imposed on the police, but police administrators may respond to the pressure by tampering with the crime reporting system or the crime statistics instead of by actually controlling crime.

The history of crime reporting is filled with instances of this kind; indeed, it is doubtful than any large city has continuously participated in the Uniform Crime Reporting program since 1930 without there having been some purposeful, major defection from UCR standards at some time during that period. The methods of evading the system are numerous and sometimes imaginative. In some instances, reports of major crimes are turned over to detectives to be held out of the records system until submitted for statistical tallying only if the culprit is apprehended; or a crime such as robbery is reported as a minor larceny. A common evasion of the system has been to hold reports of auto thefts for as long as a week or more before tallying them, and then to count them as stolen automobiles only if they are not recovered during the interim (as most automobiles are stolen for joyrides or temporary transportation, most are recovered and therefore go untallied in such an arrangement). As already noted, aggravated assaults may be kept out of formal reporting systems by a police policy of not making a report unless a warrant of arrest is obtained by the victim.

Efforts have been made frequently by progressive police departments to avoid these defaults and to devise crime reporting systems which produce both accurate statistics and effective reporting procedures for follow-up investigations. However, these efforts have generated numerous problems, not the least of which is the deluge of data-gathering paperwork thrust upon police officers whose time could be better spent in crime prevention patrol.

A common complaint among citizens is that it takes the police too long to respond when they are called in an emergency. Concern for rapid response to emergency calls is a valid interest which police administrators across the nation share. One cause of this service delivery problem is that far too much time of the police patrol officer is spent gathering information and preparing police report forms, many of which will serve no significant purpose other than as basis for statistical data.

The more care the police administrator takes to devise a completely auditable reporting system, the greater the problem of imposing wasteful paperwork on line police personnel, particularly patrol personnel. Elsewhere in this book is a discussion of the misuses of police officers in clerical and other jobs suitable for performance by lower-paid civilians. While such permanent misassignments are a significant problem in many departments, a much greater problem in every department is the temporary but repeated taking of time of the patrol officer for field paperwork and related data gathering. Diversion of police time to paperwork is much more difficult to cope with when it occurs in the line function than in the staff function.

Staff function paperwork ordinarily is done at a time convenient to the administrator; he sees the need, decides when the work will be done, and assigns someone to do it for that period of time. Line paperwork, on the other hand, mostly has to be done at the time of the event. And because events in police work tend to occur spasmodically, with sharp peaks and valleys of work load, the police administrator is likely to be faced from time to time with having all patrol units out of service on emergency assignments. If too extensive a data-gathering and reporting requirement is imposed on those units, the unavailability of units will occur frequently.

Some authorities on police reporting systems argue that to produce valid UCR statistics, a police department must require a written report on every dispatch, even though the responding officer finds that the call to the police was erroneous or false. If the call were false, the report would be tallied as an offense reported but then eliminated from statistical trends as an unfounded report. The problem with such a system is that the majority of calls for police service are not even related to crime, but are complaints of obstructed driveways, barking dogs, and traffic accidents; further, between 25 percent and 50 percent of the calls pertaining to supposed crimes are either false or erroneous for one reason or another. Some who argue for statistical perfection from the moment the telephoned complaint is received by the police would require a written report from the field for every dispatch; others claim a need for a written report from the field only for every dispatch alleging a criminal offense.

The Uniform Crime Reporting instructions recommend that if police receive a telephone call reporting a burglar climbing through a window, but on arrival at the scene find that the supposed burglar is the home owner who accidentally locked himself out, then a report must be filed on a reported burglary (to be deducted as unfounded before reporting actual offenses). Similarly, the UCR handbook would require a written report, tallied as unfounded, for the tourist who misplaces his automobile. Some purists argue that even burglar alarms, which have only about 5 percent accuracy, should be subject to complete written reports and then tallied as unfounded when appropriate.

Although some small cities with very low crime rates have followed the practice of making a written report on every telephone call and dispatch, large cities found the requirement impractical even before crime increases of the 1960's added so substantially to their work loads; efforts to devise a workable system have produced a variety of compromises between perfected statistical gathering and less demanding systems of report writing.

In some cities the dispatchers closely screen the calls before sending a patrol unit, thereby reducing by one-quarter or more the number of assignments given to patrol units, making it more likely that their assignment is a valid one, and making it more logical as well as reasonably practical for the patrol unit to submit a written report of every assignment. There are problems with this system, however. Many callers for police service are not articulate; they may express themselves in street slang or a jargon which is difficult to understand in face-to-face conversation and nearly impossible to comprehend in telephone conversation; this creates a hazard that the telephone complaint clerk may mistake a kidnapping complaint for a neighborhood squabble, a burglary complaint for an unwanted guest, or a forcible rape for a common-law domestic quarrel, errors much less likely to be made by an officer dispatched to the scene. A second problem with dispatcher screening is that police dispatchers also get very busy during peak work load periods; consequently, unless the complaint clerk–dispatcher function is given personnel considerably in excess of predicted peaks, a dispatcher performing a screening function will be unable even to answer all telephone calls during peaks. Unlike the case with patrol personnel, overstaffing of dispatchers cannot be easily diverted to productive use during slack periods.

The most common dispatch-reporting system requires dispatch of a police officer to the scene of virtually every incident reported by a citizen to the dispatch center, with the dispatcher screening out only calls such as a citizen requesting services of another government agency. In these systems, some form of paper record is made of the dispatch information, and of the disposition reported by the patrol officer upon return to service. Usually, these systems will permit an officer returning to service from an unfounded call to give a disposition of "no report necessary," which then ends the matter. On the other hand, if a crime actually has occurred, the officer comes back with disposition of a crime report made, and obtains a serial number of the radio dispatch card for later matching and auditing.

This system has the advantage of producing a copy of dispatch complaint form for later audit. With an effective inspection staff auditing this system, the department should be able to produce reasonably consistent statistics, for measuring both crime levels and significant changes in trends and for deploying their resources.

Clearly though, both because of the citizen error already discussed, and because of honest, understandable officer error in analyzing what has happened in questionable situations, even the best reporting systems will be only a sampling. Every research sampling of victims indicates that actual crime levels are several times higher than indicated by UCR statistics.

Besides tabulations of offenses reported, there are two other important kinds of general crime data tabulated and published under the UCR system; these are *clearances of offenses* and *arrests of persons*. The clearance of an offense refers to the solving of the case followed by the arrest of the offender. There are UCR guideline provisions for exceptional clearances in such cases as a deathbed confession or where an identified offender is unavailable for arrest because of being in prison on another conviction, but these are not statistically significant; generally, the marking of an offense as cleared means that the case has been solved and the offender arrested. Only about one of every five Crime Index offenses is cleared by arrest, ranging from a high clearance rate of eight out of ten criminal homicides to a low of only about fifteen of every one hundred auto thefts being solved.

Distinctly separate from the data on clearance of offenses are the data on arrests of persons. Although there ordinarily must be some person arrested in order to declare an offense cleared, there are many instances where a single offense is cleared but several persons are arrested, as when a gang of several men rob a supermarket and all are arrested. There are numerous other instances where a single individual is arrested and charged with the commission of numerous crimes, as when a professional burglar may be charged with dozens of burglaries committed by him, all of which are cleared by the single arrest.

From this conglomerate of clearance and arrest statistics, as with most data in the criminal justice system, the speculator can conclude almost anything. It can be supposed that the 20 percent clearance ratio means that only one out of every five criminals is ever caught; or, given the observable high rate of multiple crimes by single offenders, and assuming that this rate is surely even higher than provable cases show, one might as easily conclude that most persons who commit Crime Index offenses are eventually caught, but on the average are caught for only one out of five of their criminal acts.

Where the truth lies between these two extremes is very hard to judge. Undoubtedly many individuals have committed one or a few Crime Index offenses, then stopped committing crime, without ever being caught. However, without question a great many of the unsolved Crime Index offenses were committed by criminals who have avoided detection in the unsolved crimes but have subsequently been charged with other offenses.

Beyond the arrest data (and related analyses of sex, age, race, and similar social data on persons arrested), the compilation of crime statistics is moved out of the purview of the police and passes out of the Uniform Crime Reporting program. Thereafter, data on criminals are the responsibility of other agencies of the criminal justice systems. The trail becomes harder to follow.

It is the notorious crime, such as a celebrated murder or rape case which the public reads of in the newspaper, that forms the public impression of how crime is handled by prosecutors and courts. The impression is an erroneous one; for just as the police investigate a murder or vicious rape more thoroughly than they do run-of-the-mill robberies or burglaries, prosecutors and courts treat these significant crimes differently from the bulk of crime that forms the greater part of their work load. This differential treatment is born of necessity, for if either the police, the prosecutors, or the courts tried to handle every larceny case as they do a murder case, the entire system would bog down in impotence.

The system is kept going through many compromises and accommodations of convenience which confound efforts to define statistically exactly how the average criminal is treated. Just as the police measure their effectiveness in terms of offenses reported and in clearances of those crimes reported, prosecutors measure their success in terms of the proportion convicted of those persons charged, and courts measure one aspect of their success in terms of keeping down the backlog of cases pending.

Certainly no police, prosecution, or court agency in America measures its success *only* in terms of such simplistic statistical indices. Police are bound to measure their success in other terms than just offenses reported or offenses cleared; they must also think of themselves in a context of community relations, in terms of how well they handle demonstrations and disorders, in rates of traffic fatalities and traffic accidents, and other indicators outside the criminal statistics system. Prosecutors must think of themselves in other terms than conviction rates; they must consider how well they do with the celebrated murder or rape cases, which though few in number are what influence public confidence in the criminal justice system; the prosecutor also must take care not to obtain convictions through unethical or unfair conduct, and not to convict innocent individuals simply to bolster his conviction rate. And the courts, above all else, must take care to render justice to those before them and also, hopefully, justice for the public.

There is a long-recognized need for a comprehensive data system for tracing criminal careers through the criminal justice system and for relating various parts and subparts of the system to one another. Computerization promises at some time in the future to fill this need, but historically the data collection of the separate elements of criminal justice have served more to confuse than to enlighten subsystem relationships.

The discontinuity begins at the prosecutor's office, where prosecutorial screening of cases sharply reduces both the number of persons charged with crimes and the number of crimes charged against the persons remaining. The two common purposes of this screening are to facilitate plea-bargaining to make the system workable and to eliminate cases which are difficult to prosecute, so that time will not be wasted on fruitless effort and also so that loss of these cases in court will not affect conviction rates.

Even the most aggressive law-and-order prosecutor's office can find numerous good, practical reasons for charges to be dropped or reduced. Family assaults, for example, contribute heavily to nonprosecution rates; the police officer responds to a call for a "cutting," finds either the wife or husband injured by the spouse during an argument, and because the offense is a felony (and also to preserve the peace temporarily by separation of the antagonists), the officer arrests the offender; typically, the victim either fails to appear at the prosecutor's pretrial conference, or, upon appearing, refuses to prosecute and claims marital immunity from testifying. The prosecutor has no practical recourse except to drop the charge.

Or an officer apprehends a stolen automobile with several occupants, arrests them all because there is no practicable way for him to sort out and verify their alibis on the street, often in the nighttime; yet, by the time of the prosecutor's pretrial conference the next day, it is found that all or some of the occupants other than the driver have verifiable or at least plausible stories how they came to be in the car without knowing it was stolen (for example, hitchhikers); the prosecutor is left with no choice but to drop charges against them.

A third frequent occurrence is the multiple offender who comes before the prosecutor charged with a half-dozen (or even twenty or thirty) crimes such as robberies or burglaries; for a variety of reasons, some of these cases will be much easier to prove in court than others; also to be considered is that proving each case in court would be a wasteful use of resources of the prosecutor's office and the time of crowded court dockets, and also would impose an inconvenience on victims, each of whom might have to spend several days at court waiting to testify as witnesses; the usual result is the selecting of a few of the better cases for prosecution and dropping the remainder. And when a prosecutor considers proceeding with every single offense charged against the individual in the context of the frequent policy of courts of handing down concurrent sentences, it is clear that the advantage to the government lies in trying to obtain a plea of guilty to a few of the charges with an agreement by the prosecutor to drop the remainder; it is this plea-bargaining system which keeps major court systems from falling even further behind in their dockets.

It is more difficult to generalize about statistics emanating from the courtrooms than about any other data in the criminal justice system. Judges have a great deal more personal, individual latitude than do other participants in the system. Some judges are strongly pro-prosecution, others are strongly pro-defense; some judges hand down harsh sentences, others hand down lenient sentences; between these extremes are the vast majority of judges, who try to be fair to all sides and therefore cannot be categorized. But for either the moderate or the extreme, there is very little direct control over the actions of the individual judge except appeal to a higher court in the specific case. (However, there now are a few jurisdictions with commissions on judicial conduct and tenure and growing sentiment for such institutions.)

Not only are courtroom data unsystematic because of judicial independence, but useful courtroom data are generally unavailable because court systems strenuously avoid collection of data which might show individual judges in a bad light. As a consequence it is extraordinarily difficult to obtain meaningful information to relate what happens in the court to the remainder of the criminal justice system. The lack of data is compounded by the confusion regarding what the data may mean; by the time a strong-arm robbery reaches the stage of conviction, it may have been reduced through plea-bargaining to a simple assault; then a six-month sentence on a misdemeanor appears harsh to those who don't realize that the conviction is for a brutal crime which may carry a maximum penalty of ten or more years.

Also complicating understanding of sentencing data are indeterminate sentencing laws and community correctional policies. In many jurisdictions these have shifted from the courts to the correctional authorities much of effective authority over length of sentences. The initial diminishing of judicial authority over sentences grew out of the indeterminate sentencing statutes, which are based on the notion that a judge, who has seen the defendant for only a few days during the trial and has the further insight of only some secondhand probation officer reports, is less capable of determining what sentence will better serve the purposes of society and of the offender than are correctional officials who have the offender under close observation for months or years. The premise that correctional officials rather than the judge should determine the actual time to be served is reinforced by the idea that power by the correctional officials to either lengthen or reduce the period of incarceration can be a positive force in rehabilitation.

There is little argument against the logic of sentence review after a period of incarceration, with the observations of correctional officials included as a part of the review; but there should be a requirement that any reduction in the actual sentence be authorized by the court, rather than by correctional officials. Regardless of what official does the amending of sentences, systems need to be devised for keeping both the public and other officials of the criminal justice system aware of the extent to which original sentences are actually carried out or are shortened. Criminal justice data on length of sentences imposed by judges are meaningless without companion data showing to what extent those sentences are actually served.

The newest development in correctional programs, which completely confounds analysis of sentencing data, is community correctional programs under which offenders serve some, even much, of their sentences in the community.

These programs began with what were initially known as "halfway houses." These subinstitutions have been justified to the public with the argument that there is little sense in taking an individual from several years of institutionalized prison environment and, at the expiration of his sentence, turning him out on the streets without any opportunity for him to acclimate to an unregimented existence and to find a niche in the community which will keep him from crime. The persuasive argument was made that this deficiency of the system should be remedied by the halfway-house concept, whereby individuals incarcerated for several years would spend the last few months before release in the quasi-institutionalized environment of community-based facilities where they would be permitted absence during the day for work, then in the last few weeks or days of sentence would be permitted merely to report to the halfway-house supervisor on some occasional schedule.

No one could disagree with these very sensible arguments (except neighborhood groups which object to location of halfway houses near their homes or businesses) until police officials suddenly perceived a high number of crimes committed by inmates of these institutions, inmates who had been committed for long-term sentences only months before. Examination of the programs in the District of Columbia showed that not only were convicted offenders going into the halfway houses very early in their sentences (rather than in the final months, in the fashion proposed by program justifications), but that some offenders, convicted of serious crimes, actually were serving sentences imposed by the court while living, not even in halfway houses, but in their own homes in the community. The rationale for this system of noninstitutionalized corrections was that the sentence by a court puts the individual in custody of the director of corrections and that the director of corrections can thereafter maintain such "custody" in such place and in such manner as he sees fit, including mere theoretical "custody" of a requirement for occasionally telephoning the "corrective" office.

From all this discussion of how the system works in practice, the reader can understand how complex and how easily misleading are much of the data relating to the criminal justice system. Anyone can conclude almost anything, and can prove or disprove almost any theory from the wide range of statistical tabulations available. Most tabulated data reflect little of what actually is happening.

Police chiefs have long complained that they are the only officials of the criminal justice system who give regular, well-publicized accounting to the public of their activities, referring here to the periodic UCR publications of offenses reported. Police chiefs argue that this is wrong, that the other elements of the system should be required to make similar, comprehensive reports to be released together with the crime trend data.

These arguments reflect an understandable desire of police chiefs not to be held solely accountable for crime in their communities. After all, the other elements of the system — the prosecutors, the courts, corrections — all play a part in crime control. Why then should the crime statistics reflect primarily on the police?

In one sense these lamentations are correct; in another sense they are wrong. Comprehensive data should be compiled for all activities within the criminal justice system. There should be regular public accounting of such matters as plea-bargaining dispositions, of conviction rates measured against both charges made by the police and charges approved by the prosecutor, of length of delays to trial, of court backlogs, of sentencing data, of time actually served before release, of the status and character of individuals released to community correctional programs, of recidivism. These kinds of *performance* data are needed to keep officials of the criminal justice system and the public aware of what actually is occurring within the system and of what needs to be done.

But to the extent that the *objective* of the criminal justice system is to prevent crime and instill a sense of safety in the public mind, none of these are *objective* measuring statistics (nor are police *performance* statistics of clearances, of arrests, of response time, of hours on patrol). There is no firm assurance that any of these activities actually achieve the objective.

To the extent that the purpose of the criminal justice system is to prevent crime and instill a sense of safety, the *objective* measuring data are only two groups: the statistics of crime occurrence and the polls of public attitudes. All other data measure *performance,* which is presumed but not proven essential to achieving the *objective.* High clearance rates, speedy trials, long sentences, and effective corrections are meaningless if crime levels are unaffected.

Paradoxically, even low crime rates or reduced crime rates, as measured by Crime Index reports, are meaningless if a general feeling of safety does not prevail in the public consensus. The primary objective, the responsibility of government, is not only to make the public *be* safe, but also to make the public *feel* safe.

This primary objective is especially difficult to achieve in our government systems, which require that problems be defined, be described, and be serious in order to justify budgetary, legislative, or judicial remedies. Because public attitude is such a real and important part of public safety, some spokesman for public safety is needed who has sufficient sophistication, who has enough public visibility, and who has significant authority to cause things to happen within the criminal justice system. In most large urban jurisdictions, where the criminal justice systems are diffused, the office of chief of police is uniquely situated to serve as such a spokesman.

What would be better, but nowhere exists, is a publicly visible line official with authority and responsibility over all elements of the criminal justice system, excluding only the trial judges and their immediate assistants but including court administration. But this alternative is unlikely to be achieved. For a variety of reasons public-safety directorships, where they exist, never achieve this ideal. And the proliferation of criminal-justice planning agencies, which at least do serve the useful function of publishing increasingly comprehensive statistical reports on system operations, have neither the visibility nor the line authority to require fundamental changes and be responsible for their success and failure.

Chiefs of police, at least those in significant urban jurisdictions, must reconcile themselves to being the principal reporters to the public of the state of criminal justice and public safety. The under-taking of this reporter function inevitably carries with it both advantages and disadvantages. The advantages are that the reporting activity gives the chief of police an opportunity to lobby for changes and improvements throughout the criminal justice system.

Although they sometimes chafe at the spokesman role, chiefs of police, with much support from both liberal and conservative quarters, have done a pretty effective job — perhaps too effective a job — of persuading the public that factors of the criminal justice system other than police were responsible for the crime increases of the 1960's. Polls usually show that the public believes leniency of courts to be at fault.

The disadvantages of the spokesman role are two. Vocal criticisms of other elements of criminal justice by the police usually produce counterattack criticisms of the police. And public spokesmanship confers a public stewardship, a responsibility to be constructive and, ultimately, a responsibility to be productive.

The role as main reporter of public safety is perhaps the most important function of a chief of police. The duty should not be shirked.

2

Crime in America
since 1960

FOR NO PARTICULAR REASON, other than attachment through habit to
the decimal system, it is popular to think of decades as cycles, such as
the Gay Nineties, the Roaring Twenties, the Depression Thirties,
and the placid Fifties. The change of decades does also happen to be
when the United States census is taken, which will result in reappor-
tionment of the Congress a couple of years later.

Calendar years are cycles, because the seasonal variations affect
crime rates (and most other sociological rates susceptible to seasonal
influences); fiscal years, terms of politicians, the term of each Congress, all may be cycles with respect to social trends because of
influential policies of local and national leaders. But decades really
have no influence to endow them with cyclic effect.

Having thus rejected the notion that the decade is a cycle or that
anything specific occurred in 1960 to influence crime rates thereafter,
it bears explaining that 1960 has been selected as a cutoff point only
for convenience. It was a couple of years after 1960 that the crime
problem began ascending as a priority issue in America; it was the
1964 presidential campaign before crime became a national political
platform issue, it was mid-decade before the really dramatic increases
in crime trends began, it was 1967 or later that narcotics addiction
was to be perceived as a very serious problem in all segments of

society, and it was 1970 before there was the slightest cause for optimism that crime might be brought under control. Even though not a cycle, the decade of the 1960's was a period which produced what may prove to be most of the major law enforcement issues of two generations.

The Uniform Crime Report data and graphs in the Appendix demonstrate how Crime Index trends in America dipped downward in the middle 1950's, then began an upward trend in 1956 which, except for one slight dip in 1959, was not abated until 1972.

There are faults with American crime reporting. These deficiencies are sufficient to make careful thinkers wary of accepting crime data at face value. Nonetheless, imprecise though the data may be, most authorities will agree that the magnitude of the crime problem is reasonably well represented by graphs based on UCR data — that index crime began a gradual upward trend in the mid-1950's and that the upward trend was sharply accelerated after the mid-1960's.

Those who were involved in law enforcement, particularly in large central cities, can easily recall the occurrences and influences which led to the early increases and, then compounding one another, resulted in ever-sharper upward crime rates.

The process began with the suburbanization of America and the pernicious result suburbanization had on the central cities as middle- and upper-class whites and later (when civil rights laws finally made it possible) as middle- and upper-class blacks moved out of the central cities into suburban jurisdictions. This increasingly distinct separation of classes seemed to magnify the already higher crime-producing factor of the less affluent groups left in the central city.

At the same time, there was an acceleration of the historical movement of Americans from rural to urban areas, so that many of the large cities of America were increasingly becoming only core units of relatively vast metropolitan areas.

Any large city has usually had some older, run-down slum section or sections, containing much of its social ills and consequently producing much of its crime. And just as the metropolitan areas were enlargements of cities, many central cities with fixed boundaries became in some ways essentially the enlarged run-down area for the enlarged "city."

To fully understand the impact of urbanization on national crime rates, it is necessary to know that urban areas have always had much higher rates of crime than rural areas, with a direct correlation between size of city and crime ratio, and that most crime in America always has occurred and still is occurring within the cities.

In 1961, the rate of violent crime in cities over 250,000 population was six times the rate of small towns and rural areas; by 1967, the large city rate was ten times the small town and rural rate.

Even with the suburbanization of America, and the development in the suburbs of such targets of crime as shopping centers, banks, and of course, more residences, even by 1970 nearly 45 percent of American Crime Index offenses and 61 percent of all violent crimes were committed in 55 cities of one quarter million or more persons, which altogether accounted for less than 25 percent of the nation's population.

Although crime became an increasing problem in suburban and rural areas since 1960, and may become even more of one as suburbanization continues, the problem of very high rates of incidence of crime is likely always to be concentrated in the heavily urbanized cities. Certainly this will continue to be true so long as combined social factors persist in concentrating in the cities the low-income, socially depressed classes of persons.

A second factor contributing to the sharp increase in crime during the 1960's was the arriving at the age of high criminal propensity of the children born during the baby boom following World War II.

Time and again, studies have shown that the years of adolescence, and early manhood, are the crime-prone years — especially in terms of Crime Index offenses and violent crimes.

Biographical sketches of notorious criminals often mislead the public to think of crime as being mostly the work of professional criminals who enter a life of crime at a very early age and continue in crime throughout all or most of their lives. Criminals such as these do exist, of course: master burglars who travel around the country committing major crimes throughout all of their lives (except for periods of time spent in prisons); carefully scheming holdup men who concentrate only on large jobs; master forgers who steal hundreds of thousands of dollars before they are caught.

But as a part of the total number of Crime Index offenses committed each year and of the total number of persons committing them, these professional criminals and their crimes constitute such a small proportion as to be statistically insignificant. Virtually all of the crime index offenses in America are committed not by a relatively few lifelong criminal types, but by large numbers of quasi-amateurs, most of whom fall into crime during their middle or late teens, commit a few or dozens or hundreds of crimes each, and then pass out of the criminal picture as they begin to mature in their early and middle twenties.

More than one-half of all Crime Index offenses generally, and more than one-half of violent crimes specifically, are committed by persons fifteen through twenty-four years of age, and about three-quarters of such offenses are committed by persons under thirty.

Between 1958 and 1967, while the total population of the nation increased by 14 percent, the population in the age group fifteen to twenty-four years increased by 42 percent. Taking this fact into account, along with the high level of criminal productivity during the years of youth, it can be surmised that a substantial part of the crime increases of the 1960's could be attributed simply to the coming of age of a spurt in the population trends.

Other factors contributing to the crime increases of the 1960's were the increasingly restrictive court rules which impinged on both the police and the courts, and were compounded by the advent of enforced statutory and court requirements for furnishing meaningful defense counsel for persons accused of crime.

The Supreme Court ruling in *Mapp vs Ohio* in 1961, which extended the Fourth Amendment exclusionary rules regarding searches and seizures from the federal courts, to which the rules had always been applied, to state and local courts as well, was a first step in a chain of events which was to have heavy impact on the ability of police to effectively apprehend and successfully prosecute criminal suspects. The procession of Supreme Court decisions extended from *Mapp*, restricting search and seizure, through *Escobedo* (1964) and *Miranda* (1966), both restricting the police in obtaining confessions, to *Wade, Gilbert,* and *Stovall* (all 1967), closely circumscribing eyewitness identifications and police lineups.

Simultaneously, law schools and bar associations in major cities, under prodding from the courts, began developing programs to insure more effective legal representation of indigents. The basic objective of these programs was commendable, but there was a very serious side effect. Highly principled young legal interns went into already congested court systems and began to give factual legal representation, demanding full trials, for hundreds of defendants who formerly were pleaded to lesser offenses by the coterie of lawyers known as courthouse regulars. The result was that judicial systems, which had been built (or had grown topsy-turvy) on foundations of compromise and plea-bargaining, began to fall apart.

This is not to suggest that all of these changes — the court decisions, the programs for proper defense of the accused — were totally wrong or should never have happened. It is possible to argue with persuasion that some of these decisions and programs went too far in favor of the criminal, but their basic purposes would be hard to dispute, since they essentially were efforts to extend to a wider range of Americans rights and protections which everyone always thought they had (at least until they were unfortunate enough to be caught up in the system). Proponents of these decisions and programs argued, with some justification, that the basic rights which were strengthened by these changes are important enough that increased costs of police investigations and of court operations is not too high a price to pay for their insurance. In most cities, however, commensurate increases in police personnel and court facilities were never provided. Moreover, in retrospect it is unfortunate that the criminal justice system was subjected to the impact of these changes at a time when its work load was being heavily affected by crime increases resulting from other causes. And the courts were diminishing the ability of the police to deal with crime through such tools as vagrancy arrests, at a time when America could least afford a tampering with police effectiveness.

But such is how the process has always worked. Invariably, the criminal justice system moves from one extreme to another, with pendulum-like effect, moving first too far to the left, then too far to the right; it is interesting to speculate that if improvements could be introduced on a gradual basis, during carefully selected periods of minimum crisis, the ultimate gains might be far more rapid and much more satisfactory.

A fourth factor contributing to the heavy increase in crime in the late 1960's was the combination of increased black activism and of urban disorders during that period. During the middle and late 1960's, many American cities underwent racial strife, tensions, and outbreaks of disorders. These events struck first in large cities, then, as the large cities became immunized to the phenomenon of riots (both because the riot targets were diminished and because the cities learned techniques for preventing and for dealing with disorders), riots on proportionally lesser scales occurred in medium-sized cities and then even in very small cities and towns.

Although the riots themselves consisted mostly of large numbers of individual crimes such as burglaries, larcenies, robberies, and arsons, many of which would fall within categories of the Uniform Crime Reporting system, the actual occurrence of a riot is not an event which can be reasonably translated into the normal statistics of the UCR classifications. As an intellectual exercise in crime reporting theory, it would be possible to argue that every separate entry by a looter into a business place is a separate burglary, for example, and that any major riot is made up of many thousands of offenses; countering that is the argument that the procedure of tallying a single offense when two or more persons join together in commission of one criminal act should be used, and that a riot is simply hundreds or thousands of persons engaged in a single crime of rioting, then all the crimes in the riot should be tallied as one offense. Without regard to either of these intellectual exercises, most jurisdictions simply resorted to the practical procedure of making a report regarding each premises looted or burned, primarily for insurance rather than for statistical purposes, and didn't worry all that much about their crime statistics for the month during which the riot or riots occurred.

Discussion of how crime statistics are handled for the event of a riot is, however, a digression. The impact of the urban disorders on ordinary crime patterns was longer-lasting and more significant than simply the number of offenses reported during the period of rioting. The deeper problem was the mood developed from the rhetoric and the attitudes which preceded, accompanied, and followed the actual disorders.

It became fashionable to advocate vigorously such notions as that crime results almost exclusively from sociological root causes and that the criminal therefore is not personally responsible for his crimes, and that ghetto merchants and landlords obtain their money almost exclusively by cheating the poor and therefore it was all right for the deprived to take the money back through robbery or theft. No reasonable person would argue that root causes have nothing to do with crime or that ghetto merchants never take advantage of the poor, or that these factors should never be considered. But the persistence and vigor with which concepts such as these were argued and repeated, often by government and community leaders, did much during the last half of the 1960's to rationalize and even to dignify the actions of the ordinary criminal at a time when the example of urban disorders was already giving many youngsters a stimulation toward unlawful conduct.

An even more direct effect which urban disorders had on the criminal justice system was the impact, primarily on the prosecution and court systems, of hundreds and even thousands of riot-related arrests, which had to be assimilated into already overburdened dockets. It usually was deemed politically unfeasible to dismiss riot-related cases en masse immediately after the disorders occurred, and while further disorders were imminent. This was so even though the ultimate result was predictable: that most of the rioters would be found to be previously law-abiding, relatively responsible citizens who would be deserving of and would get probation for their offenses, a probation which might just as well have been administered informally by the prosecutor at a hearing without trial. But the political and practical realities at the time more often than not forced a full processing of the riot arrests through an already clogged machinery.

Another consequence of the urban disorders was that police often found it temporarily advisable and sometimes even necessary to abate enforcement of public order regulations and to reduce emphasis on aggressive programs such as those for stopping and identifying suspicious persons. This occurred both because so much police officer time was diverted from normal patrol functions to training and operational details for riot control and because of the practical fact that in a highly tense situation, the immediate benefits to be obtained from enforcement of a minor regulation or from a "stop and frisk" may not be worth the cost of precipitating a disorder.

Flexibility and improved police-community relations became the watchwords of the police. Again, as with the rhetoric of crime coming from social root causes, the problem was not that the watchwords were wrong, only that they were shouted too loudly and often to the exclusion of other important considerations. In 1970, the head of a large city police department, where crime was then an epidemic problem, sent a senior assistant to interview each of his area commanders and ascertain what they regarded as their priority functions; almost all of them designated police-community relations as having high priority, and only a few even mentioned crime suppression as a consideration at all. To some extent they may have only been saying what they thought their boss wanted to hear, but it is always that process by which policies are ultimately implemented.

The remaining major factor contributing to the sharp increase in Crime Index offenses during the last half of the 1960's was the explosion of heroin use at all levels of American society.

Statistical data reflecting the illegal importation, sale, and use of drugs rank among the most sketchy and incomplete of crime indicators. It is because there is no reliable method of measuring illegal narcotics activities that these crimes are omitted from the Crime Index. Because these are not crimes usually reported to the police by the victims (or the nonvictims, if one chooses to classify narcotics offenses as victimless crimes), the only solid data which police have relating to illegal narcotics traffic are arrest statistics, which may reflect presence or absence of police effort but not necessarily presence or absence of narcotics traffic. Other, also unreliable, indicators are interviews or urine samplings of persons arrested for various crimes made to determine whether or not they are narcotics users; these indicators, like arrest statistics, are useful for telling if the narcotics problem is minor or major, but are not very practical for discerning or measuring trends between those extremes.

The reason for this discussion of the unreliability of narcotics data is to make clear that — and why — police and other government authorities were unable to perceive the growing problem with hard narcotics in the late 1960's until the problem had gotten almost completely out of hand, and that — and why — even from an historical perspective it is difficult to identify with precision when the sharp upward trend began and exactly what factors precipitated the change in the nature of the problem.

The general perception of police officials is that a significant change in the nature and the dimensions of the narcotics problem occurred around 1967 or 1968. Assumptions long held by police of what kinds of persons were likely to be heroin users and what kinds of crimes such users might commit to support their habits were supplanted after 1968 by different notions born from the experience of a new era of narcotics use.

Before 1968, it was widely assumed that the typical user of heroin was a slum resident from the lowest socioeconomic strata, in his twenties or thirties, so heavily addicted to drugs as to be unable to hold gainful employment, supporting himself and his habit through nonviolent property crimes; it was an article of faith among police that the male narcotics addict would sustain himself primarily from larceny, perhaps from burglary, but would never be involved in robbery or other violent crime.

By late 1968 and early 1969, however, police officials would observe that there were no longer any "typical heroin users"; by then, users could be found in all socioeconomic levels of society, in all age groups ranging from as young as late elementary school, through middle age, with many habitual but unaddicted users supporting themselves largely, if not exclusively, through gainful employment of all kinds. Perhaps most of the new breed of users supported their habits by work; however, users contributed heavily to the Crime Index. And gone was the assumption that heroin users avoided crimes of violence; samples of arrestees in Washington, D.C., showed that upward of one-third or more of all Crime Index offenses, ranging from larceny through robbery, rape, and murder, were being committed by persons who used heroin. The crime of robbery, previously shunned by narcotics users, came to be regarded as a characteristic "addict" crime.

No verifiable explanation has been discovered of exactly what it was that generated these vast changes in the number and the nature of narcotic users and their crimes. One reasonable assumption is that the epidemic was related to the increases, beginning in the middle 1960's, of American troop strength in Southeast Asia, where narcotics were readily available and inexpensive. This premise assumes that returning American veterans included large numbers of young men who had developed heroin habits while in Asia and who upon return home infected many of their friends with the practice. More difficult to explain is what combination of circumstances opened the gates of America to an influx of sufficient heroin to sustain the epidemic. Theories, all of which have at least a modicum of plausibility, range from the notion that returning veterans supplied themselves through contacts made while overseas, to the idea that political changes in one or more foreign countries facilitated increased heroin traffic, to the theory that some changed policies of domestic organized crime eliminated traditional proscriptions against dealing in heroin. Whatever happened, the growth of the problem was greatly facilitated by the disorganization of American society in general and of American law enforcement in particular during the period.

A final factor among the components contributing to crime increases during the 1960's relates to the attitude of government officials generally and of police officers specifically toward crime and toward crime-inducing problems during the period. Already described in this chapter are many explanations of why crime could be expected to increase during the 1960's. These reasons are now discussed through a historical perspective; but it is important to realize that they also were discussed in a contemporary context by various social analysts, both liberal and conservative, at the time. Most of these reasons were expounded over and over again by various analysts.

There were plenty of exponents in the early and middle 1960's of the analysis that, although there might have been an increase in the actual number of Crime Index offenses reported, there was no increase in real crime rates; this argument was the premise that conversion of the gross numbers into rates based on the urbanization of the population and on the increased proportion of the population in the crime-prone age groups showed that the levels of crime, at least in proportion to those factors, were substantially unchanged. The synthesis of this argument is that, if people are going to live in cities, and if there are going to be a lot of adolescents and young adults around, a higher level of crime must be expected than if people live on farms or if the age distribution of the population is different. In other words, learn to tolerate urban crime just as you tolerate traffic deaths in order to have efficient transportation.

By the middle and late 1960's, however, as crime in some cities had increased so much that it was no longer acceptable to argue that people should just "learn to live with it," and as in fact people did begin in a sense to learn to live with it by moving into fortified apartment complexes or closed communities, traveling to and from work in sanitized corridors, avoiding going out at night, doing their shopping in suburbs, putting extra locks on their windows and doors, and by foregoing the "luxury" of being able to ride buses or taxis without correct change, the arguments were converted from the notion that a relatively high level of crime is to be expected to an argument that crime really is unacceptable but, being the product of such root causes as poverty, unemployment, and racial discrimination, can be effectively reduced only by eliminating those root causes. Those were the "liberal" arguments.

Concurrently, the "conservatives" were arguing that crime essentially grows out of the permissiveness of society, the permissiveness of the courts, and the special permissiveness of the Supreme Court and the appeals courts which eroded the authority of the police to deal with criminals. These points, especially the argument that higher courts were eroding police ability to apprehend criminals, were disputed by "liberals" who said that the police would simply have to improve their methods, through upgrading of personnel, through better training, and through better administration, in order to perform effectively under the new laws.

Throughout the 1960's, a great deal of emphasis was placed by "liberals" and "conservatives" alike on the need for improved administration, equipment, and training of police. It was a decade when emphasis, in police agencies across America, was being placed on administrative surveys, reorganizations, computerization, community relations, and training.

None of the various analyses of why crime was increasing was entirely wrong; none of the emphasis on the need for improving the police was entirely wrong.

Among the great failings of the so-called criminal justice system are the facts that, for one thing, it is not a system at all, and for another, neither a single organizational entity nor any single official within the system has full authority over all aspects of criminal justice and, concurrently, full responsibility for criminal justice and for crime prevention.

Although a prosecutor is often self-described as "the chief law enforcement officer" of the jurisdiction, it is rare if ever that a prosecutor has sufficient resources or influence over the total criminal justice system to have a truly broad impact on crime. Typically, the prosecutor who wants to make a name for himself as a crime fighter will simply concentrate his efforts on one or two segments of the crime problem, usually on segments which attract current public interest and thus have publicity appeal. For example, he may concentrate on racketeering, on consumer crimes, even on a persistent street-crime problem such as a band of holdup men, using his power of subpoena and of grand jury investigations to bring the major figures to court. But in the broader picture, in the context of the reality of mass-produced crime and mass-produced justice, the prosecutor is going to be dependent on the police department to bring cases to him for prosecution.

The courts have perhaps the most ambivalent of all the functions in the criminal justice system. Most judges undoubtedly are motivated by a desire to see crime prevented, repressed, and reduced. But judges are bound by their duty to take care that their desire for good law and order does not outweigh their responsibility to insure that the accused before them has a fair trial and, if he is convicted, that his sentence at least takes into consideration the interests of the accused as well as the interests of society. But no matter how the individual judge views his duty, the court even more so than the prosecutor, faces the crime problem on a case-by-case, instance-by-instance, basis. Thus, even though the courts can and do from time to time adopt "get tough" policies with regard to specific crime problems, the court — by consistently low sentences, by failure to deal with backlogged calendars, by poor bail policies — can have severe, adverse effects on law enforcement; except in a relatively limited way, it would be difficult to hold the courts primarily responsible for overall crime suppression.

The final element of the criminal justice system, the correctional, is often as ambivalent as the courts in self-interpretation of its role. It can be presumed that, just like judges, correctional authorities are usually in favor of crime suppression and reduction. But professionals in corrections often see the primary objective of their role as being the rehabilitation of offenders committed to their institutions. During recent years, experimentation has increased with concepts such as indeterminate sentencing by judges, community-based correctional centers, furloughs for prisoners, and even systems under which some prisoners served their sentences while living at home. These concepts have vastly increased the potential impact of correctional policies on overall crime rates. Even with this increased potential for correctional decisions to influence crime, however, and even with the fact that some past correctional policies have been shown to be dangerous, it is unlikely ever to be demonstrated that correctional officials have sufficiently broad impact on crime to be held primarily responsible for prevention and reduction of crime rates. (Additionally, correctional authorities usually are insulated from community sentiment about crime by the fact that community sentiment, at least in the large cities, tends to be directed to local officials, while correctional authorities in felony cases usually are state officials.)

Absolved, then, from effective accountability for crime control and reduction are the prosecutors, the courts, and the corrections officials. What of the police? Is it reasonable to hold the police primarily accountable for crime rates? It has in the past been thought to be reasonable. Inherent in allocation of most criminal justice funds to the police is the presumption that these resources will directly prevent crime.

This implied presumption that the police, through deployment of patrols, through solving cases, and through arresting offenders, can literally prevent crime, almost independently of what goes on in society and the remainder of the criminal justice system, needs some scrutiny and some modifications.

For one thing, in no jurisdiction in America are there sufficient police officers to provide a thorough patrol coverage on a continuing basis. Secondly, continual presence of a police officer is not necessarily a certain guarantee against a commission of a crime, for many places are robbed despite the presence of an armed, uniformed guard or a passing uniformed police officer. And a high rate of success in solving cases, coupled with a high rate of arrest of offenders, may be effective in reducing and preventing crime, but effectiveness of those actions can be seriously diminished by bail, prosecution, court, or correctional processes.

Reasonable thinkers understand that much crime occurs off the streets, outside the reach of police patrols, that it is impossible for the police to solve every single case, and that the police are dependent upon the remainder of the criminal justice system for support in dealing with those who are apprehended. But even with this rather complicated, half-clear understanding of the realities of crime and criminal justice, it has been traditional in America for the politicians and the public to complain to the police and about the police when serious crime problems crop up and are not promptly dealt with. A criminal court judge may get a spate of nasty letters because of a decision he makes or a sentence he hands out in a highly publicized case. The prosecutor may feel political pressure to gain a conviction or at least to make a good showing in the trial of a notorious criminal. But when there is a rash of murders, or rapes, or robberies, or burglaries — in short, when people begin to fear rising crime rates — they traditionally have demanded action from their police. When crime gets out of hand, it is the chief of police who receives the mail and the delegations of citizen contingents demanding action. And it is then that the police chief becomes the spokesman for law enforcement.

The more practical reason why the public demands that the police keep crime down or reduce crime is that, within limits, the police can deal effectively with some crime problems and through their action or inaction can have a direct effect on overall crime rates.

For example, when a rapist commits a sufficient number of crimes, the police, recognizing his modus operandi, realize that they are dealing with a special problem (instead of an isolated pattern of unrelated crimes, which are much harder to deal with) and concentrate special efforts to apprehend him. These efforts may include such things as increased uniformed patrols to deter his operations, establishment of nonuniformed patrols or stakeouts to apprehend him, singling out his crime for special efforts by investigators, repeated analysis of his modus operandi and of physical evidence from the scene of his crimes, and commitment of manpower to long, tedious, and often fruitless manual search of fingerprint files in an effort to match even partial prints. Efforts such as these to apprehend a special criminal, efforts which would be economically unfeasible for ordinary crimes, are often successful either in deterring the individual from committing crimes or in eventually apprehending him if he repeats his crimes.

The police can also have an impact on more complicated problems than the single, special criminal. When an area of the city is plagued with some specific crime problem, for example, a persistent problem of purse snatchings, the police can respond by shifting uniformed patrols or by establishing nonuniformed patrols at the locations and times when the criminal activity is most persistent. Or when a pattern develops of holdups of some special kind of businesses, the police can deter this activity by requiring uniformed patrolmen to make regular business checks at the establishments or by staking out the businesses in the path of the pattern until the holdup men are apprehended, or both.

There are numerous other examples of ways in which the police can directly affect crime rates when they are motivated to do so. And the principal motivation historically has been the public sentiment which held the police accountable for crime in the community.

Unfortunately, much of this public sentiment of police accountability for crime control was lost in the rhetoric of the 1960's. The predominant talk of politicians shifted to root causes, community control, police-community relations, finding ways to promote policemen on the basis of how well they relate to the community rather than on how many arrests they make; from the conservative end of the political spectrum, the oratory was of how powerless police are to do anything in a permissive society, and of how the police are rendered ineffective by court decisions. Obviously, none of this rhetoric was consistent with any notion that the police are basically responsible for crime control.

Given these kinds of signals from their political leaders, it is not surprising that aspiring young police officials, when they talked to the men at roll calls and in informal situations, stressed the new values that were being thrust upon them. And it is not surprising that ever-higher crime rates came to be accepted, even in police circles, as an inevitable part of urban life. Just as with the politicians, perhaps even more so, it is easier for the police to talk of root causes, community relations, court restrictions, and new directions for computerization, management, and training than it is to fight crime.

The foregoing suggestions of why crime rates rose for seventeen straight years would be difficult to prove valid through scientific verification. Even more difficult to explain is what factors resulted in the leveling off of crime rates in 1971 and the decreases which occurred in 1972.

Almost anything that is said about the factors which contribute to crime rates will be at least partly true. Crime producing and crime preventing processes are very complex. Indeed, it may be that the processes are so complex as to be controllable only by simple solutions. The worst failure of the American crime control system occurred immediately after the participants in the system were informed of how complex is the problem they face.

As shown by the Appendix graph, crime increased steadily but not drastically, from the middle 1950's through the middle 1960's. Those analysts who attributed this increase to a natural result of urbanization and population factors may not have been too far from wrong. But crime became a political issue in the 1964 presidential campaign. The outgrowth of that politicizing of crime was the appointment of a presidential commission in 1965, followed by two years of study and a report in 1967 describing in a bookshelf of publications exactly how complex is the problem.

Inherent in a rational contemplation of the complexity of the problem is the realization by the participants in the system that they are powerless to effect noticeable results — concurrent with this realization is the notion that they must also be without responsibility to achieve noticeable results. The sharpest increase in crime came on the heels of the thoughtful and complete analysis of the parameters of the problem!

What, then, caused the leveling of crime in the early 1970's? For one thing, perhaps America forgot exactly how complex the problems of urbanization could be, and turned to singular solutions. Because national will and national politics tend to develop from the same roots, it is difficult to separate what resulted because of changed national attitudes from what came because of presidential leadership.

Whatever the reason, there is no dispute that beginning in late 1969 or early 1970, there was a cooling of the temperament of America.

Major urban disorders became a thing of the past (this statement excludes the antiwar demonstrations, which were a totally different phenomenon from the riots). Crime rates had reached such heights in major cities that the clamor for effective action was overwhelming. Gone was most of the antipolice rhetoric of the 1960's, and what remained found no receptive ear at the national level, where the talk was of increased support for the local police, and little reception at local levels, where citizen interest was directed more toward control of crime than control of the police.

Public support for the police became evident in several ways. Police salary increases began to attain priority. The recruiting difficulties of the middle 1960's were gone; by 1972 the only major recruiting problem of large city police departments was in complying with court-ordered minority recruiting. Former police officers began running for mayoralties of large cities — and winning.

Although the polls showed that the public still blamed the crime increases primarily on the courts, mayors of large cities began to hold their police departments responsible for achieving crime reductions.

The Law Enforcement Assistance Administration began to fund impact city programs aimed directly at achieving noticeable crime reductions in robberies and burglaries rather than unobjective "management improvements."

The federal government mounted a massive attack on the heroin problem. Foreign production and smuggling facilities were abated through diplomatic efforts. Federally funded treatment programs for addicts were established. Joint federal and local strike forces centered their efforts on major narcotics dealers. By 1972 cities such as New York and Washington, which had experienced epidemic use of heroin, noted perceptible improvements in the situation. (Marijuana use, however, continued to flourish, but this drug never produced the crime index offense problem which was related to heroin use.)

President Nixon went out of his way to demonstrate that he considered the police to be the indispensable element of crime control. Not only did he make special efforts in this regard in the District of Columbia, he also made opportunities to visit police officers in other cities, to invite groups of police chiefs to the Justice Department and to the White House to discuss their problems; messages from the

President were sent to police chiefs in cities where crime reductions were achieved.

Releases of national crime statistics began to connote a more optimistic, positive view. FBI statistics for more than a decade had been regularly released amid statements with the tone of doomsday forecasts. In January, 1971, Attorney General Mitchell personally released the FBI statistics with emphasis on the fact that, while the totals were up, reductions had been achieved in twenty-three cities; he also commented on the "paper crime wave" of the late 1960's which had grown out of improved crime reporting by police departments seeking to justify LEAA financing.

The emphasis finally was on the positive, and as successes were achieved there was a growing consensus that something could be done about crime. Crime Index offenses declined 3 percent in 1972, the first decrease in seventeen years; there were decreases in thirty-two of the fifty largest cities that year.

But that decrease left 1972 crime at three times the level of 1960. The polls at the end of 1972 showed that one-fifth of the residents of large cities rated crime as the worst problem in their communities.

As he entered his second term, President Nixon made clear his intention to keep crime reduction as a national priority and to find ways of bringing honest Americans out from behind the bars and locks they had installed to protect themselves from criminals in the streets.

But then, in 1973, the series of disclosures known generically as "Watergate" began to unfold. As one after another of the Nixon team came under criminal indictment, it became unfeasible for the administration to speak out in persuasive tones against crime and in support of strong law enforcement. By midsummer, crime rates were showing increases in numerous cities across the country. There was a 16 percent increase in the index for the last quarter of 1973 and a similar rise for the first half of 1974.

The important pre-Watergate lesson to be learned from the Nixon administration seems to be a clear demonstration that strong interest and leadership by a President and his cabinet can effectively influence national crime rates. (The Watergate lesson, of course, seems self-evident.)

3

Crime Control
in the Nation's Capitol

BECAUSE OF ITS UNIQUE FORM of government and the special characteristics of its geographic, economic, and social environment, the District of Columbia can hardly be used as an example of a typical American city. Yet, in many respects, the nation's capital did typify the crime problems of many large cities during the 1960's.

Beginning in the late 1950's and continuing through the 1960's, Washington, D.C., lost many of its middle-class and working-class residents to suburbia. (Working-class refers here to what in most cities would be called blue-collar workers, a term inappropriate to Washington's industry of government.) As with many cities during the early years of suburbanization, the outflux was mostly of the white population; but as antidiscrimination laws of the later 1960's opened suburban housing to blacks, there also was a growing loss of middle-class and working-class Negroes. This suburbanization process left Washington, which before had contained a majority of the population of its metropolitan area, as a proportionally diminishing core of an ever-expanding metropolitan complex.

As in the case with many core cities, Washington of the 1960's housed a majority of the welfare recipients, a majority of the public housing residents, most of the blacks, most of the unemployed, most of the underprivileged of its metropolitan area. And, not surprisingly, among the social ills concentrated in the city was crime, crime which was ever-increasing.

Crime in Washington had reached a low point of post–World War II years in June, 1957. From 1957 onward through 1969, the Crime Index of Washington was practically always upward. The increase was gradual through 1962, then from 1962 to 1966 there was a virtual doubling of Crime Index offenses, followed by another doubling from 1966 through the end of calendar year 1969. The 62,921 Crime Index offenses reported for 1969 were more than quadruple the 15,019 such crimes of 1962.

These increases in crime can be ascribed to several causes, none of which is easy to analyze nor to verify. A reason for some of the increase in crime undoubtedly was the growth of the metropolitan area and the concomitant change in the nature of the central city, which has already been mentioned. Even though Washington's resident population actually decreased from 1950 through 1970, its daytime commuter population and its out-of-town tourist population significantly increased. Further, the lower socioeconomic "slum" areas of the city, areas which typically have higher crime rates than other parts of the city, were gradually expanding, somewhat in proportion to the metropolitan area as a whole, so that they constituted a great portion of the central city itself. In the late 1950's, the police department noted that urban renewal projects, which had eliminated some large slum areas, had displaced the slum residents, with their crime and other police problems, to many other areas of the city. This scattering made it more difficult to concentrate police efforts on the crime and effectively deal with the problems. (Similar difficulty of controlling criminal activity displaced by renewals of slum areas has been noted in other cities. The assumption, however, is that this short-run effect will be overcome by long-term advantages.)

For nearly a full decade official police department policy was to attribute the crime increase primarily to the Supreme Court *Mallory* decision of 1957, which, together with subsidiary opinions by the United States Court of Appeals, severely limited questioning by police of criminal suspects before their arraignment. Also blamed, but with less public vigor since it was an action of the executive branch superiors of the chief of police, was the 1962 order by the board of commissioners prohibiting police from making investigative arrests (essentially, arrests on suspicion), a practice of long tradition in the department, which a committee of lawyers had determined was not authorized by any law.

Both of these attributions could be, and were, illustrated by statistical graphs which showed that the previously downward trend of crime turned noticeably upward the month following the *Mallory* decision and illustrated an even sharper upward trend following the banning of investigative arrests.

There is a subtle but very important significance to the attribution of wholesale crime increases to difficulty in closing cases and making arrests, for this implies that the most important objective of the police is not to prevent crime, but to catch the offender after a crime has been committed. As noted in the chapter on measurements of criminal activity, the catching of criminals is *performance*, but the prevention of crime is the *objective*. Presumably the performance contributes to attainment of the objective, provided the remainder of the criminal justice system supports the function of prevention. But police departments need to be conscious of the difference between performance and objectives, and the important question is: where will the emphasis be placed?

During the 1940's and 1950's, the emphasis within the Metropolitan Police Department seemed to be on clearance of cases. The *Police Manual* stated that "the prevention of crime [is] the most important object in view." Washington police chiefs said that the patrol officer was the backbone of police work, but the pride of the department was its clearance rates and the way to quick promotion was to become a detective.

The blaming of some of the crime increase in Washington on the *Mallory* decision is probably correct, although not necessarily for the reasons suggested at the time by the police department. The experience of the Metropolitan Police Department in trying to obtain legislation to overturn *Mallory* exemplifies the dilemma of the police executive when he takes a strong public position in an effort to bring changes in the criminal justice process.

The immediate reaction of the chief of police when he learned of the *Mallory* decision was that the rule "put handcuffs and shackles on the police," a phrase which would be the shibboleth of efforts in ensuing years to have the rule invalidated by legislation. But the department made no immediate changes in its procedures to implement the rule and the rule by itself was not all that great a change from earlier decisions in *McNabb* and *Upshaw* (later, subsidiary rulings were, however, much more restrictive); the upturn in crime immediately following the decision, if related to the ruling at all, likely resulted from the fact that policemen, and perhaps criminals too, were impressed by the notion that policemen were now "handcuffed and shackled" more than from anything else. A precinct commander no longer had to worry about his crime rate, for increases were the result of *Mallory;* a detective no longer had to worry about his clearance rate, for everyone understood that investigations were hampered by *Mallory.*

A police chief, when faced with some major problem such as the *Mallory* restriction, knows that to obtain legislative or other remedy to cope with the problem, he must construct a strong, logical, well-publicized argument that the problem is unusually adverse to police effectiveness. This is especially so when the problem involves issues such as *Mallory* or other rulings constraining police from searches, seizures, and questioning of subjects, where the case for changing the rule has to be made against strong counterarguments from proponents of the rule.

But if the chief of police makes repeated public statements that some continuing condition is crippling police effectiveness, then criminals and potential criminals may come to believe that the police are ineffective. Worse yet, much of the police force and perhaps even the chief of police himself may come to think of their efforts as rendered ineffective by that one condition; relying on that single factor as blameworthy for all crime increases, it then is possible for the police to become complacent at continuously increasing crime, or even to be pleased at seeing substantiated their theory of their own ineffectiveness.

Retrospectively, the city of Washington would almost certainly have been much better off during the 1960's if, in 1957, the police department had taken a different position with regard to the *Mallory* decision. The department could have said that, while the ruling represented an undesirable trend in constraints on the police, it really was not all that different from the earlier *McNabb* and *Upshaw* rulings and that, with careful retraining of police officials and detectives, together with some increases in the size of the police force, the department could continue to operate effectively despite the ivory-tower notions of the Supreme Court. (In 1956 the department had just been increased in size to become one of the larger per capita police departments in America, and neither then nor later encountered any substantial difficulty in getting whatever police manpower it requested; therefore, the notion of obtaining increased manpower to cope with new investigative problems was not at all out of the question.)

A position such as this, analogous to the proposed policy of police operational guidelines discussed in Chapter 4, might well have changed the history of the city. Had the police department shown a good-faith effort to implement and comply with *Mallory,* the subsequent, much more restrictive and much more unreasonable rulings of the United States Court of Appeals might have been forestalled. Had the police department not assumed the convenient excuse of *Mallory* as the reason for increasing crime, it likely would have been much less willing to accept the ever-upward crime trends thereafter. Had the supporters of the police, among both government officials and the general public, not been distracted by the belief that *Mallory* made the police force impotent, they might have kept pressure on the police to keep crime in check.

The retrospective notion that the city might have been better served by police acceptance of *Mallory* as a fact of life is an interesting and instructive concept. But before that idea is accepted as the *best* way for the police department to have approached *Mallory,* another facet of history needs to be considered. Using the "handcuffs and shackles" watchword, and the argument that law enforcement effectiveness was seriously reduced by *Mallory,* the chief of police and his supporters came within a hair's breadth of obtaining Congressional amendment of Rule 5(a) of the Federal Rules of Criminal Procedures to vitiate *Mallory;* bills were enacted in 1957 by both the House of Representatives and the Senate to amend the Rule and were lost only on a point of order because of inconsequential discrepancy of wording between the bills of the two houses.

It also needs to be considered that *Mallory,* especially as interpreted by the United States Court of Appeals for the District of Columbia, was an ill-advised opinion, a serious misinterpretation of Congressional intent, which should have been overturned. The purpose here is not to criticize the efforts to obtain remedial legislation, but to demonstrate the difficulty an organizational leader faces when trying to balance public calls for improvements with maintenance of the morale of his subordinates.

The real lesson may be not that it is a mistake for a chief of police to aver impaired police effectiveness in an effort to remedy a situation, but only that it is a mistake for him to so aver if in the end he fails to obtain the remedy.

An interesting contributor to the increase in *reported* crime in Washington was, of all things, a program designed to improve the management of the department by distributing patrol division manpower among the fourteen police precincts in direct ratio to the police work load of each precinct.

The adjective "reported" is used here purposely, for in the middle 1950's, the crime reporting system of the Washington Police Department, although better than that of many, many other cities at the time, was far from perfect. The crime reporting system of Washington had been thoroughly overhauled in 1948 as a result of newspaper discovery of a great deal of concealment of major crimes. Included in the revision was a system for serially numbered, multicopy crime reports, which, theoretically, should have prevented hiding of any except the most minor crime.

In the early years following the overhaul, compliance with the system was reasonably consistent throughout the department, but there was no central inspection staff; and as interest in accurate crime reporting waned during the first half of the 1950's, the system gradually deteriorated, with accuracy in any given precinct dependent more on the interest of the precinct commander than on any other factor. The importance of this deterioration of the crime reporting system was that, when the department began in 1958 to distribute patrol division manpower on the basis of police work load factors (with very heavy weighting of Index crimes reported), precinct commanders were given strong incentive to begin forwarding to headquarters records of all crimes reported by the public, for only in this way could they obtain an equitable proportion of available man-power. And since the department did not stress crime reduction as a major objective (after all, crime increases were the product of court decisions adverse to police effectiveness), there was no counter-balancing incentive for precinct commanders to avoid the appearance of having crime increases.

The third milestone in the upward crime trend was the 1962 order by the board of commissioners, who then governed the city, prohibit-ing investigative arrests. Just as with *Mallory*, that order was lamented and criticized by the police, even though one of the attorneys on the panel recommending the order was a staunch supporter of the police and had been personal attorney to the chief of police.

Well into the 1960's, the preoccupation of the department admin-istration continued to be with efforts to obtain some favorable legis-lation to overturn the effects of *Mallory*, legislation which was never forthcoming until 1968, when the Omnibus Crime Act established that delay in arraignment alone should not be cause for excluding a confession from trial. But in the decade since *Mallory*, new decisions such as *Escobedo* and *Miranda* and changes in other statutes and processes had so amended the laws that the issue of delay in and of itself was no longer significant.

The fourth milestone in the escalating crime trends of Washington was, again paradoxically, a major effort to improve the situation and to reduce crime.

The 1964 presidential campaign had made crime in America gen-erally, and in the District of Columbia particularly, a national issue. Senator Goldwater referred in his campaign to the issue of crime in the District of Columbia and to proposals for dealing with the prob-lem. Goldwater's surfacing of crime as a significant issue had the effect of causing the Johnson administration to recognize crime as a problem and to undertake massive efforts to deal with it. The liberal camp, however, was not ready to admit that crime was a real prob-lem, since their thinkers, authors, and officials were attracted to the-ories that crime should be tolerated as a part of the price of urban-ization or, alternatively, to the notion that crime was no problem at all, but was only a symptom of much deeper, root cause social prob-lems. For this set of mind, it was clear that the need was not for a frontal attack on crime itself, but for study of the problem, or study to determine whether or not a problem really existed; the result was establishment of two commissions, the national President's Commission on Law Enforcement and Administration of Justice, and the local President's Commission on Crime in the District of Columbia.

The foregoing tongue-in-cheek commentary on how the commissions came into being is not intended to denigrate their work. Both commissions worked very hard at their assigned tasks; both produced useful studies and some useful recommendations. But all of the studying and public attention may have produced more crime than was prevented.

As a part of the work of the President's Commission on Crime in the District of Columbia, the International Association of Chiefs of Police, under contract to the commission, undertook a complete survey of the management and operations of the Metropolitan Police Department. The IACP recommendations, which were endorsed by the commission, proposed complete reorganization of the department and numerous internal changes.

The history of the IACP survey and the ensuing reorganization furnishes a useful lesson for police administrators. In 1965, partially in response to the rhetoric of the 1964 presidential campaign and partially in response to growing local apprehension with the ever-increasing crime rates of the city, the Senate Committee on the District of Columbia undertook special hearings to seek remedies for the problem. During the course of those proceedings, the committee asked the police department to submit a list of programs and items needed to improve local law enforcement. In developing that list, a representative of the police department inquired of the IACP, which in the early 1960's had entered the field of management consulting to police departments, about the cost and potential benefits of a full management survey of the organization and administration of the department. The IACP response was an expression of willingness to undertake a full survey if that were what the department desired, but the IACP view was that quick, broad-brushed, extensive surveys were generally less effective than IACP contractual staff assistance performed over a relatively extended period of time. But neither a survey nor staff assistance was included on the list of needs finally submitted to the Senate District Committee. The department thought it had sufficient capacity within its ranks to accomplish whatever changes were needed (which it did not), and that it would have time to exercise whatever talents it did possess (which it would not). The eventual result was thrusting of a full-scale survey on a recalcitrant department.

In July 1965, Executive Order Number 11234 was issued to establish the President's Commission on Crime in the District of Columbia. In November 1965, the commission approved a contract for the IACP to perform a complete management survey of the Metropolitan Police Department.

Parenthetically, it should be noted that one of the rituals of an IACP contract is that the IACP, being primarily an association of chiefs of police rather than a management consultant firm, declines to perform any management study of a police department without the written approval of the chief of police. What usually happens as a practical matter, of course, is what occurred in the District of Columbia; the chief of police had already made a decision earlier that year not to use contractual services of IACP for a management study; but under pressure from his appointing authority, he did formally approve a management survey contract.

This practical process is a continuing cause of friction at meetings of the IACP board of officers. On the one hand, the IACP in the early 1960's developed from what previously had been primarily a social organization with secondary emphasis on its profession, into a primarily professional organization with secondary emphasis on social interchange. Almost all of the board of officers and the executive committee are highly professional law enforcement officers who recognize that police agencies need continuous improvement if they are to stay abreast of changing times, and who also recognize that those chiefs who most strenuously object to change (for example, an IACP survey) usually head the agencies which need change the most. Added to this is the fact that the IACP, because of its nature, its membership, its staff qualifications, is unquestionably the best of the management firms doing overall (as opposed to specialized) organization and management studies of police agencies. On the other hand, the IACP is an organization of chiefs of police, and it is somewhat incongruous with that fact for the IACP staff to engage in critical evaluations of the organization and management techniques of an IACP member against his will. This dilemma has led to the ritual of requiring authorization by the chief of police before a survey is made of his department, with the predictable result that some chiefs privately object that they approved the contract only under pressure to do so from their political superiors.

Regardless of the dynamics of approval of the IACP study of the Metropolitan Police Department, once the survey was published in July 1966 with an accompanying report including forty-one major commission recommendations, the chief of police adopted the commission report and the IACP survey and report as policy documents of the department. Plans were undertaken to implement rapidly as many as possible of the proposed changes; the only exceptions were a few relatively minor recommendations which the department decided not to adopt and some significant recommendations which could not be implemented without congressional legislation.

To the credit of the chief of police, it has to be said that the decision for full implementation was not necessarily the easiest course. There were numerous senior and middle-level officials of the department who opposed findings and recommendations impinging on their areas of responsibility; furthermore, it was clear from the outset that there would be strong community opposition, most of it coming from community elements normally supportive of the police, to the proposed consolidation of the fourteen police precincts into six geographical police districts.

From the perspective of hindsight, it can be seen that a more gradual reorganization of the department, accomplishing the changes over a period of several years, or perhaps a complete reorganization of the department at some more stable point in the history of the city, would have been preferable. Hindsight shows that the major shakeup was ill-timed, when crime was to increase severely, when an epidemic of illegal drugs was imminent, and when, shortly, the assassination of the Reverend Martin Luther King would generate a major riot and a period of several months of lesser disorders within the city.

Management decision, unfortunately, must be based on what is known and what is expected at the time, not on what later history will show.

An organization has three possible approaches to a recommendation for reordering its administration; one approach, taken by the Metropolitan Police Department with a 1954 survey which presented major conclusions somewhat similar to those of the IACP more than a decade later, is to let its senior officials review the survey, have them count up their cumulative years of service in the organization, then say that on the basis of their hundreds of years of accumulated experience (disregarding that some of them may have had one year of experience served twenty times over), they have concluded that no changes need to be made; a second approach is to adopt the survey as an intermediate goal of the department, establish a timetable for accomplishing individual items so that the accepted recommendations will be implemented over a period of the next several years; the third method is to do as the Metropolitan Police Department did, adopt the survey and those recommendations which are acceptable to the leadership of the department and move forward with implementation as rapidly as possible.

The first approach speaks for itself; the second approach has the advantage of avoiding the massive disruption of an instantaneous reorganization, but has the disadvantages of prolonging, ad infinitum, the in-house arguments against doing those things still to be done, and of prolonging the impact on morale of employees who become hesitant about making improvements in a current operation which they know eventually will be changed and who are uncertain of the effect of pending changes on their personal careers; the third, the quick-and-dirty approach, while it has the disadvantage of being very disruptive for a short period of time, has the advantage that employees at all levels are rapidly shifted to their new tasks, are fairly quickly reconciled to the notion that the status quo of the past is gone, and are motivated to begin immediately reconstructing their careers to conform to the new working condition.

During the period of the middle 1960's, a chance occurrence unrelated to the reorganization served to increase significantly reported crimes within Washington. This event was the discovery in at least one police precinct in 1966 of systematic underreporting of serious crime. The discovery came to the attention of the chief of police as a result of confessions of a professional burglar who had burglarized many homes throughout the city. When detectives began the process of verifying his confessed crimes against crime reports of the police department, they found that many of his crimes in one precinct were not reported in the files of the department. Further investigation revealed the startling fact that those crimes had been reported to the police precinct, but that no reports had been sent to headquarters, even in cases where identifiable items, many with known serial numbers, were taken. These crimes were found listed (along with many other similar crimes) on incidental books maintained by the precinct, with no reports being forwarded to headquarters for either investigative, pawn-identification, or statistical purposes. This discovery led to an Internal Affairs Unit follow-through survey of reporting practices in all police precincts. Although most precincts were properly reporting offenses such as major burglaries with identifiable items, there had for years been some slippage in reporting nonmajor crimes such as thefts of items of small value, pickpocketing, and rolling of drunks; these offenses often were listed as "complaints" on precinct "complaint books," instead of being reported to headquarters as crimes. The predictable result of the Internal Affairs Unit inquiry into reporting procedures was an upward swing in crime statistics.

Prior to the IACP survey, the department had no inspection system to provide staff-level supervision for insuring compliance with department orders and policies such as crime reporting procedures. The department did have an Internal Affairs Unit, organized in 1962, but the objectives of that unit were directed at corruption or other criminal or quasicriminal activity of policemen, not at administrative management or noncompliance with procedural directives; thus, it was only as an accidental by-product of a criminal investigation that the chief of police had brought to his attention a widespread noncompliance with crime reporting procedures, a condition which, incidentally, was well known to many of his middle managers. (There is no reasonable explanation for the noncompliance with reporting procedures in 1966, as there was no great pressure on precinct commanders to reduce crime; promotions above the civil service rank of captain were then made almost exclusively on the basis of seniority.)

The need for an administrative inspections unit to insure compliance with departmental directives and procedures was noted by the

IACP survey, and such a unit was established in the reorganization of January, 1967. Also as a part of the reorganization, the records system of the department was thoroughly overhauled, with the effect of closing most minor loopholes in the crime reporting system. Although the 1967 establishment of a Field Inspections Division and the overhaul of the records system strengthened future integrity of crime reporting, it is likely that the 1966 discovery of the systematic underreporting and the Internal Affairs Unit follow-through of that discovery were the basic change agents which generated an apparent upward trend of crime.

Thus, from 1957 through 1967, there were at least two specific internal pressures which would encourage precinct commanders to be much more honest in crime reporting than had been the case before 1957; the first of these pressures was the 1958 establishment of statistical work load factors as the basis for allocating manpower among the precincts, and the second was the 1966 Internal Affairs Unit pressure to conform to the prescribed reporting system, a pressure which was continued by the new Field Inspections Division.

This leaves the unanswerable question of how much of the crime increase was real and how much of it was merely better reporting. Theoretically, when a single new factor is interjected into a crime reporting system, any changes of trend resulting therefrom should be completed during the first twelve months after its introduction.

As a practical matter, however, external factors such as those discussed here are never all that clear-cut. Some precinct commanders (those better at mathematics) would realize before others that the heavy statistical weighting of crime in manpower allocations meant that they could obtain manpower increases by simply reporting more crime; others might recognize the magic of the mathematics, but elect not to improve their crime reporting simply because they did not care to have more manpower, were afraid to have it discovered that they had previously been underreporting, or were simply indifferent to the whole thing. Therefore, it might take two or three years for the effects of that factor to become nearly complete; the 1966 discoveries of underreporting verify that the factor of manpower allocation was never altogether effective in forcing accurate reporting.

Similarly, the indefinite, subtle manner of reinforcing the reporting system in 1966 meant that the effects of that factor may have spread over much more than a single year. For example, although precinct commanders were under pressure after 1966 not to list serious crimes on precinct "complaint books," it was late 1969 before specific orders were issued prohibiting the existence of such books. In any event, no matter how it is analyzed, crime in Washington was significantly underreported in both 1956 and in 1966, perhaps by factors of as much as 10 to 20 percent. (There is ample reason to believe that the Washington experience with increased crime *reporting* occurred in other cities during the last half of the 1960's. Crime commission studies and public interest forced many police departments into management improvements which often began with records system overhauls. Technology played a part also; computerization of statistics almost invariably required better records, which made it more difficult to hide crime reports. And to obtain LEAA funds, a department needed a crime problem.)

Without doubt the foregoing commentary on improved reporting of crime between 1956 and 1969 will be misinterpreted by some, and sooner or later misquoted to imply that the highly publicized upsurge of crime in Washington and nationally during that period was largely a reflection of improved police reporting processes. This actually is not the case, however, as any who lived in Washington through the period well know. During the early 1960's, as already noted, there were some observers of the crime trends who suggested that the increases merely reflected a combination of better reporting and of normal urbanization increases; but by the end of the 1960's, crime was clearly so out of control, irrespective of statistical measures, that everyone recognized that there was more to the problem than merely better reporting. One observer who in the early 1960's had questioned whether the crime increases were real or imaginary, put it this way in 1969, "I now personally know too many people who have been robbed."

A couple of reasonably good indices of what was going on in Washington during the period can be found in the reported rates of robberies and of auto thefts, for both of these offenses were pretty accurately reported by the Metropolitan Police Department throughout the 1950's and 1960's. Robberies were ordinarily accurately re-

ported because this offense required the sending of a lookout for the
culprit, which required records division serial numbers, which required accurate reports; also, robberies often involve businesses, cab
drivers, or other constituencies which tend to follow through with
reports to their insurance companies. Likewise, automobile thefts
were almost invariably reported because these, too, required sending
a lookout, and because insurance company follow-up was likely. As
shown in the tables in the appendix, robberies in Washington increased nearly twentyfold from 1956 through 1969, while automobile
thefts increased sixfold.

While these two types of crime were fairly accurately reported by
the police, they have a deficiency as indices of total crime trends in
Washington during the period. Robbery has the deficiency that the
character of the holdup man totally changed between 1956 and 1969;
in 1956, the typical holdup man was relatively mature as criminals go,
perhaps in his middle twenties; holdups then were rarely committed
by juveniles and virtually never by narcotics addicts. But by the late
1960's, as narcotics addiction had become a serious problem in the
city, and as addiction spread to new groups, particularly to younger
persons, the experience of the past that narcotics users committed
only burglaries and thefts became invalid; narcotics users shifted to
robbery as a source of income.

But auto theft has the deficiency as an index of total crime of being
a crime by juveniles or other young offenders. As noted in the chapter
on measurement of crime, auto theft is more often for either joyriding
or immediate transportation than for profit. There simply is no single
crime that is a "best" indicator of total crime trends; but these two
categories, robbery and auto theft, are mentioned here only because
they were reported by the police with a fairly high reliability
and clearly show the sharply increased crime problem of Washington
during the period.

Equally susceptible to misinterpretation is the notion suggested
earlier that the police came to accept every increase in crime as
inevitable and perhaps even desirable. The entire process was a great
deal more complex than such an oversimplification could ever communicate. There were numerous efforts by the administration of the
department to find more effective ways to reduce crime trends; on a

couple of occasions during the 1960's, all members of the force were encouraged to "volunteer" for extra duty twice each week for special crime patrols; use of one-man scout cars to utilize available manpower better was instituted, and a special tactical branch was organized, employing both uniformed patrol saturation and old-clothes decoy procedures. Then, when the studies of the Crime Commission and of the IACP were completed, the police department went faster and farther in implementing the recommendations of those studies than any other major agency of the criminal justice system, all on the assumption that crime reduction would be the ultimate result of their adoption. Several precinct commanders and numerous subordinate officials engaged in special programs of their own aimed at trying to combat problems within their individual areas. But somehow, the essential esprit de corps was eroded; the tone of thinking of the average officer was more negative than positive.

Some indications of the tone of the department during that period can be perceived from various small indicators. For example, when the city government was reorganized in late 1967 and Patrick Murphy was appointed public safety director, one of his first questions was, "Doesn't a precinct commander ever lose his command for failing to hold crime in check?" The answer was that none ever had. The monthly crime releases of the department usually were stated in negative rather than positive tones, stressing crime increases more than any occasional decreases, a pattern carried over from the past decades of seeking to justify amendments of the rules of criminal procedure. A recurrent complaint of residents, particularly white middle-class residents living in integrated neighborhoods, was that when they reported a burglary or theft to a police officer and complained to him about high crime in their neighborhood, they would get a response such as, "What do you expect, living in a neighborhood like this?" Other residents complained about a perceptible attitude of officers that all they were interested in was devising some way of obtaining a disability retirement (a perception somewhat verified by the clear increase in abuses of disability retirements during the period). The ultimate indicator was the November, 1969, staff meeting, discussed later in this chapter, when I stressed to my district commanders their responsibility to reduce crime within their areas and heard as a response a parroting of my own speeches about the problems of the bail reform releasing felons to the street and of crimes committed by untreated narcotics addicts.

These attitudes were an understandable outgrowth of the times, however. Policemen during the 1960's saw many new constraints on their authority — the *Miranda* and *Escobedo* rulings, a ruling by the corporation counsel restraining their use of the disorderly-conduct statute against loiterers, a United States Court of Appeals ruling restricting authority to arrest persons for cursing policemen, and appeals court rulings virtually abolishing for practical purposes the vagrancy statute. At the same time, the police, as the most visible element of local government, were the target of numerous groups, including some groups financially supported by the government, who were seeking to improve the lot of minority and underprivileged groups by increasing their activism in and against government. The liberals said that crime came from root causes, and therefore police could not do anything about controlling crime and should concentrate instead on community relations; the conservatives said that the courts did not properly support the police and therefore the police could not do anything about controlling crime. Why, then, should the police believe that they could control crime?

It was not the most delightful period of the century in which to be a police officer.

The final blow to crime control in Washington came in April, 1968, with rioting following the assassination of the Reverend Martin Luther King. The immediate effects of those riots were extensive looting, millions of dollars in property damage, and several deaths. But there also were longer-term effects reflected in changed attitudes toward compliance with the law, especially among youth. A serious side effect was that the thousands of arrests made during the riots further clogged the already-backlogged court systems.

Following the riots there was a perceptibly increased brazenness among the criminals, who became far more open and far more careless in committing crimes. A significant, observable phenomenon was the increased number of very young offenders committing serious crimes; for example, offenders as young as eleven and twelve years of age were committing armed holdups. This mood of brazen misconduct carried over into other socially undesirable behavior such as baiting of police officers, truancy from school, and disorderly conduct within the schools.

There was more than one significant disorder in Washington during 1968. Following the April riots, short disorders occurred during the summer and fall of 1968 as a consequence of such varied events as a police officer shooting a crazed woman who attacked him with a butcher knife, the closing down of Resurrection City of the Poor People's Campaign, and a rumored assassination of a popular rock singer. And during the summer of 1968, in the midst of a climate of turmoil, the police were required to divert from crime control a considerable amount of attention and manpower to handle activities of the Poor People's Campaign. That activity, while it could generally be described as peaceful, was continually threatening to escalate to nonviolent civil disobedience or outright disorder and therefore required heavy police manpower commitments to standby readiness. The peak of antipolice attitudes occurred in July, 1968, when the Black United Front, an umbrella of organizations which included both militants and respectable black leaders, issued a public statement describing the murder of a police officer as "justifiable homicide."

In a way, perhaps the adversities of the period led ultimately to strengthening of the police department. The reorganization of the department; the rhetoric against the police; the generally more active life of policemen, with headquarters and administrative personnel frequently called back for standby or active duty in dealing with potential disorders; the emphasis on change and accommodation rather than the status quo: the combination of these things unquestionably forced into retirement many police officers and police officials who might have drifted along to much later retirement in more stable times. The loss of their experience, and their replacement with younger, inexperienced men, undoubtedly reduced the immediate per capita efficiency of the force; in the long run, however, it is likely that the force was strengthened by the change.

The experienced men who left were mostly officers who had come into the department in the 1940's and early 1950's. The police department then was oriented toward service of a predominantly white population; the lines of racial segregation within the force were clearly drawn, even to the extent that orders detailing policemen for presidential details specified "Send white officers only"; investigative arrests were a standard procedure, and abuses of the procedure were tolerated; detentions and interrogations in violation of the Federal Rules of Criminal Procedure were not only tolerated by the department but were supported by the prosecutors and the courts. A police officer who serves one or two decades in such an environment deserves understanding more than blame if he is psychologically unable to accept fully the transition to a police force serving a predominantly black population, where racial segregation in the department is prohibited and where some reverse discrimination is observed, and where his police authority is constrained by often-changing but ever-tightening limitations.

It is well and good to say that police officers are employees of the government, and therefore must serve whatever lawful objectives that government may from time to time adopt. But police officers are also people, and people are slow to accept change. It is tempting to generalize that police officers, because the nature of their work tends to be to preserve the status quo, are more slow to accept change than are most other persons. But generalizations about police officers suffer from the same deficiencies as do generalizations about any group. Some police officers seek and actively support change in policies and practices, others are willing to accept or learn to accept changes thrust upon them, and it is only some who cannot deviate from practices of the past. During periods of significant change, police departments are usually improved by separation of this latter group through resignations or retirements and replacement, with new police officers hired during and for the new era (an era which will prove for some of them, as they reach middle age, to be their own status quo). This need for continual transition to new policies and practices over long periods of time may be a more important justification for police pensions that permit early optional retirements than are the traditional concepts that physical requirements of the job justify liberal retirement policies.

The police force unquestionably was improved, in the long run, by the infusion of young men attuned to the realities of urban police work of the late 1960's, and also by the fact that a high proportion of those youngsters were black, softening the image of the police as an "occupation force" in the city. Paradoxically, the morale of the force also was in some ways improved by the occurrence of the disorders of 1968 and the numerous details of police officers to the Poor People's Campaign (and also by the occurrence of antiwar demonstrations in 1969 and subsequent years).

These events forced the department into training, organization, practice drills, and the actual experience of massive, unified team efforts unlike the ordinary single-officer or partner-pair operational organization of police work. These events also put senior officials into direct, highly visible contact with the rank and file of the force, a common occurrence under the methods of the Metropolitan Police Department in handling special events and emergencies, but an uncommon occurrence in everyday police operations. Together, these factors led to a strengthening of relations and understanding between senior officials and subordinate personnel of the department.

Added to these factors was the high degree of success obtained by the department in dealing both with the riots and with the later disorders and potential disorders. This is not to say that any of the events was handled perfectly, for it is an uncommon situation when any major event is handled with no error. But the department learned from its experiences and, amending its operations to avoid repeating its mistakes, was able to attract high praise for its operations which considerably strengthened the confidence and morale of the force.

However, by late 1968 crime in Washington could accurately be described as almost completely beyond control. Even more than in the 1964 presidential campaign, the crime problems of the nation in general and of the District of Columbia in particular were major issues in the 1968 presidential race.

Soon after the inauguration of President Nixon, it could be seen that his administration took seriously its vow to make a frontal assault against crime in Washington, the only jurisdiction in America where the federal government has control over local law enforcement. By the summer of 1969, the incumbent chief of police had been retired, a new chief of police was appointed, and the Department of Justice had undertaken the task to develop a legislative program for improvement of criminal justice in the city. At the same time strategies were being developed for coping with the growing problem of narcotics use and narcotics-related crime.

There also was a noticeable change in 1969 in the attitude of the local community toward both crime and the police. Respectable black leaders had become careful to dissociate themselves from organizations with militant spokesmen. Militant calls for "community control" of the police found little support in any quarter. Calls to the chief of police from community groups, from both middle-class and poor areas, were for more, not less, police activity. Whatever it is that influences community consensus had convinced the community to support their police and to emphasize crime reduction as a priority.

By late summer, readied for transmission to Congress was legislation which would (1) amend the bail reform act of 1966 by a provision of controlled pretrial detention of dangerous criminals, (2) provide legislative authority for no-knock warrants, (3) eliminate the bifurcation between the United States District Court and the local superior court of jurisdiction over local criminal offenses, (4) expand the resources of the superior court, and (5) transfer appeals jurisdiction over local criminal matters from the ultraliberal United States Court of Appeals for the District of Columbia to the District of Columbia Court of Appeals and thence direct to the Supreme Court.

Civil libertarians were incensed, argued vigorously against the pretrial detention and the no-knock provisions of the legislation, and were successful in amending the pretrial detention sections so that the enacted provisions were practically useless. For some reason, the opponents of the legislation failed to take strong issue with the shift of appeal jurisdiction from the United States Court of Appeals, a change which in the long run is likely to have much more important effect on law enforcement in the District of Columbia than either the pretrial detention or the no-knock sections of the legislation.

President Nixon made it forcefully clear that his legislative objectives for dealing with the problem of crime in the District of Columbia were more than mere notions to be debated among members of his own administration or simply halfhearted proposals to be pigeonholed by some Congressional committee. On October 9, 1969, to stress to the Congress his personal interest and commitment on the subject, the President invited to a White House briefing on District of Columbia crime the leadership of the two houses of Congress together with the committee chairmen concerned with District of Columbia affairs and with judiciary affairs. As the only senior official of the city government who unequivocally supported the President's legislative proposals, I was selected as the principal briefing officer for the session and was the only spokesman from the city government present, a clear signal that the President expected support for his decisions, once made.

But as the proposed changes followed the path through the legislative process, crime in the city continued upward, and it became increasingly evident that some immediate remedy had to be found.

Throughout the late summer and fall of 1969, while busily engaged in settling down the organization around myself and the new senior officials I had appointed, I also was persistently lobbying for enactment of President Nixon's anticrime legislation. This latter activity, which involved repeated public appearances before Congressional committees, citizens' associations across the city, and television appearances, is mentioned here because the experience is a classical example of the constant dilemma of the police administrator in trying to obtain needed changes without diminishing the effectiveness of the police force.

The process of justifying a change is very simple. One states what the problem is, argues that the problem is very serious, proposes a solution, and demonstrates that there is no more reasonable alternative than the proposed solution. For the legislative proposals to deal with crime in the District of Columbia, this involved describing the problems of persons arrested for serious crimes being released on personal recognizance before police officers had their paperwork finished, of extraordinary court backlogs, of unconscionable reduction of charges through the abused plea-bargaining system, all compounded by rampant narcotics addiction with no effective treatment programs.

But as every month brought added increases in crime, it became clear to me that, even with all of these adverse factors, the crime trend should have reached a new level and stabilized. With this in mind, on November 3, 1969, I called a meeting of my field operations staff, including the district commanders, and informed the group of my view that, with the manpower and other resources available to the department, it was unreasonable for crime to continue to rise, with each month bringing increases on top of increases on top of increases. Soliciting their views of ways to abate crime, I was dismayed to hear several of them repeat the points from my own speeches — criminals out on personal recognizance, court backlogs, plea-bargaining charge reductions, untreated narcotics addictions — one articulate official espoused correction of root causes as the only way to control crime.

The meeting was adjourned without any valuable effect having been produced. I left the meeting knowing that I had not convinced my command officials that fundamental responsibility for crime control rested with the police. The command officials left believing, as before, that crime was a legislative and social problem, which the police were powerless to control effectively.

That experience reinforced my realization that some system had to be devised to make middle-managers of the department accountable for crime control. Remembering the question of the former public safety director, "Doesn't any precinct commander ever lose his command for failing to deal with crime?," it became clear to me that the one point in the hierarchy of the organization where I could best apply pressure for crime reduction was at the level of the district commanders. The six district commanders controlled two-thirds of the manpower of the department, including most of the uniformed patrol, generally accepted as the backbone of police operations, and a majority of the detectives.

Because each district commander was responsible for a specific geographical area of the city, it was easier to establish accountability for their results than for other units, such as the special operations division or the criminal investigations division, both of which operated citywide.

More important than anything else, the district commanders were an ideal group of officials to hold accountable. Holding the rank of inspector, they were at a level in the hierarchy where it was possible to remove one of them from his command without penalizing him by loss of rank and pay for failure to accomplish an extraordinarily difficult task (reduction of crime in his district). There were at the time twenty-one inspectors in various assignments throughout the department; therefore, there were ample opportunities for shifting various inspectors into and out of districts until strong leaders, capable of reducing crime, were placed in those six vital spots.

Until that time, although no added rank or pay was involved, a district command was a coveted assignment for an inspector; this was primarily because of the extraordinarily large number of men working under a district commander and also because of the prerogatives of his territorial imperative. Later, however, after responsibility had clearly been put on the district commanders to reduce crime, I would encounter difficulty in finding inspectors who would voluntarily move from staff jobs to district commands; this development was counteracted by retracting the authorization for most staff inspectors to use police vehicles for transportation to and from their residences, by establishing the district commanders as a board to recommend which captains would be promoted to inspector, and by making it clear that promotions to the rank of deputy chief would almost invariably be made from among the district commanders.

Having concluded that the chief of police alone could not lead the force to reduce crime, and that the district commanders were the middle-managers most susceptible to pressure for productivity, I arranged a series of meetings for December 15, 1969. At these meetings, with the assistant chief for field operations and the commander of the patrol division sitting in, I called in the district commanders, one by one, and informed each of them (1) that I knew that vast improvements in the criminal justice system were necessary to achieve ideal control over crime problems in the city, and that I would continue to support and press for those changes that were needed, but (2) that I was convinced that given the resources available to the department, it was reasonable to assume that something could be done to not only stop the constant increase in crime, but also to bring about a decrease, and (3) that each district commander was to develop plans, institute programs, and exercise the leadership to reduce crime within his territory within the immediately following months or the commander would be moved to some other position in the department and another inspector would be given an opportunity to try. At the same time, it was made explicitly clear to each district commander that he was authorized to complain about any lack of support he perceived from staff units of the department, that he should feel free to comment on any problems he encountered, and that such comments were not only welcomed but encouraged, but that no comment or complaint by him would be accepted as an excuse for failure to reduce crime.

There was a decrease in crime in December, 1969, which marked the beginning of a downward trend which would continue for at least three years. (Crime did not decline in all districts at first, however. Two inspectors were transferred from their commands and two others later retired while under pressure to produce results or be transferred.)

On January 17, 1970, the personal commitment of the President to crime reduction in the District of Columbia was translated into direct instructions from the White House to the city government to develop a list of whatever programs were necessary to reduce both the number of serious crimes in the District of Columbia and also the fear of crime within the city. These instructions were issued in a context making it clear that unless significant improvements were achieved, all city government officials responsible for law enforcement should expect to be replaced. The result was immediate development of several emergency supplemental budget requests, including an increase in the police force to 5100 officers, development of financing for a police helicopter program, and development of a major narcotics treatment program, based primarily on methadone maintenance, but with the assumption that users would eventually be shifted to abstinence programs.

By late summer of 1970, numerous changes and new programs had been instituted to strengthen District of Columbia law enforcement. The police force, by working men on overtime pending full recruitment of additional officers, had been operating with a force equivalent to 5100 police officers. The United States Attorney, the primary prosecutor for the District of Columbia, had increased by one-half the size of his criminal prosecution staff, had doubled their clerical assistance, and had instituted formal training programs to insure that newly hired prosecutor attorneys reached full effectiveness as rapidly as possible. The narcotics treatment administration had been organized in the spring, and treatment of a substantial number of users was under way by the early summer. A massive street lighting program, utilizing recently developed sodium-vapor lamps, had brightened the downtown business and government office area and was being extended to those residential areas where crime rates were high. The President's anticrime legislation, the District of Columbia Court Reform and Criminal Procedure Act, approved July 29, 1970, would later add indispensable ingredients to long-term solutions of crime.

For practical purposes it was fortunate for the city that many things were happening, almost simultaneously, to reduce crime. For theoretical study of criminology, however, it is unfortunate that so many diverse factors were interacting that it will be forever impractical to determine how much effect each factor had in the overall crime reduction.

The statistical graph in the appendix shows crime reaching its peak in November, 1969, and places the beginning of the decline at December, 1969, immediately following the assigning of responsibility to police district commanders. This could lead to the tempting conclusion that police effort and increased police manpower alone might have solved a substantial part of the problem. But improved police performance results not only from assigning responsibility to district inspectors, but also from strengthening of police morale by the fact that other improvements in the criminal justice system were being urged by the President and provided by the Congress; it became clear to everyone, including the police, that support for law enforcement was the unequivocal policy of both the President and the Congress.

As crime trends continued downward, President Nixon made frequent opportunities to express his appreciation for the work done by the Metropolitan Police Department, to make it clear that he supported the police officers in their efforts, and to make it clear that reduction of crime was a continuing priority of his administration.

The first of these events was a personal visit by the President to police headquarters on October 15, 1970; for that occasion the President personally directed that as many street patrol officers as practical be brought to headquarters to meet him. In September, 1971, the President addressed letters to each of the police district commanders thanking them personally and their men for their efforts in crime reduction. On April 19, 1972, President Nixon directed that the senior officials of the department, together with the recipients of the Annual Awards for Merit and Valor be brought to the White House to meet the President. In sum, the President repeatedly made it clear by his words and actions that he considered the police department primarily responsible for the achieved reductions in crime, and by inference that he would also hold the police primarily accountable if crime should again get out of hand.

Although not germane to the subject of this chapter, it is worth parenthetical mention that President Nixon went to similar pains to show his support for police on a national scale, calling groups of police officials from around the country to the White House to hear their advice, meeting with representatives of National Police Organizations, taking personal interest in the problem of shootings of police officers, directing full federal assistance when requested — all in all making it clear that the policemen of America had the personal support of the White House. President Nixon did not take a snobbish view of police officers.

Not surprisingly, once it became publicly known that district commanders had been charged with specific responsibility for reducing crime within their districts, apprehension was expressed by members of the media and by other interested persons that the result would be a tampering with crime statistics by district commanders rather than by an actual reduction of offenses. These charges began almost immediately and were being repeated in one form or another some three years later; the charges likely will continue so long as crime trends do not shift upward.

The most interesting and perhaps the most honest appraisal of this concern, and for what actually happened, came from a long-time official of the Democratic party of the District. Two days after the newspapers had reported the substance of my second meeting with the district commanders, the Democratic official met briefly with me to say, "I want to see crime go down in the District of Columbia. I want to see crime go down in the District of Columbia even if the Republican Party gets credit for it. But I do not want to see President Nixon taking credit for crime reductions on the basis of phony statistics, and I know what you're doing; you are telling the district commanders to hide crime reports."

I responded by telling him that I had made it absolutely clear to the district commanders that the crime reductions had to be real reductions, not statistical changes based on hiding valid reports. I also argued that the revised reporting system implemented during reorganization of the department, the prohibition I had issued against any district maintaining a complaint book, together with the field inspections division which audited crime reports, would combine to make it unfeasible for district commanders to hide any substantial number of Crime Index offenses.

We two parted with my saying, "You keep your eye on what is happening, and after we have claimed crime reductions for a few months, let me know if you don't agree with our claims; if you don't, we then will see what can be done to convince you."

Six months later, during a meeting on another matter with the same individual, I inquired about our earlier conversation, saying, "We have been claiming crime reductions for six months now, and I haven't heard from you yet that you think we are cheating with the statistics. Do you believe us?" The response was, "Yes, I believe you; I can't swear to the accuracy of your statistics, but I have asked all around town and everyone agrees that the situation is much better."

This exchange probably typifies the general attitude toward crime reductions in the District over the period. Most observers had some question of whether the claimed reductions were precisely valid, but after a few months of reductions no one questioned that the overall situation in the city was considerably improved.

The fact is, of course, that the reported changes in crime were not precise measures. For one thing, the existence of complaint books in districts prior to the fall of 1969 meant that 1969 data were not precisely comparable with subsequent years; additionally, there were substantial reasons to believe that there was significant accidental underreporting of crime during 1969 because of data processing problems as the reporting system was undergoing reorganization. For those reasons, the actual rate of change from 1969 to subsequent years may be greater than that actually shown. On the other hand, there is no question that making district commanders interested in their crime reports stimulated them and their subordinate officials to be careful that incidents reported as Crime Index offenses were actually crimes. In a department where a majority of the patrol officers, who are the primary writers of crime reports, are in their first year or two of service, a lot of incidents, particularly things such as vandalism, may erroneously be reported as crimes such as burglary, unless there is conscientious review of reports by the field officials.

In response to the continued questioning of the crime data, the President in 1972 directed that an audit be made of the Metropolitan Police Department crime reporting system to assure that the reported decreases of crime were statistically valid. This report confirmed not only that the trend had been downward, but noted that improvements in the reporting system during fiscal years 1971 and 1972 had offset some of the decreases, so that the actual decline was slightly greater than had been reported by the department.

Whatever else might be said, perhaps the best defense of the District of Columbia reports of crime reductions lies in the fact that the police department operates a system open to constant scrutiny of the media, permitting members of the media to ride in police vehicles almost at will, allowing them personal access to the crime reporting files, and maintaining a stated and a reinforced policy that members of the force may talk to the press about any matters which would not interfere with some criminal investigation. Given this open press policy, given that there was great political significance and, therefore, great public interest in the crime data, and given that the Metropolitan Police Department, just like any other large department, had a few disgruntled employees and former employees who were willing to talk to the press on all kinds of matters, it is inconceivable that the department could have hidden enough crime reports to achieve the halving of Index offenses from 1969 through 1972 without the media having been able to unequivocally prove that fact.

The lesson of the District of Columbia experience is clear: given a large enough police force, and given a force with clear signals that crime reduction is the priority mission, significant reductions in crime can be achieved.

The question is often asked, "What does a district commander do differently, when he is instructed specifically to reduce crime, that he did not do before?" The real difference is that, if his instructions are made clear to him and are reinforced by positive incentives, he comes to work each morning concerned more with crime reduction than with anything else, and he impresses that concern on his subordinates.

An organization probably can respond effectively to no more than two or three *significant* problems at one time. Police departments are engaged in a diversity of activities at all times, of course, and handle many of these with varying degrees of success. But at any given time, some one thing is going to be deemed much more important than the others. During the 1930's, traffic enforcement and traffic accident prevention had a high priority; in the 1940's, criminal investigation seemed to be the major objective; during the 1950's, emphasis shifted to youth-related operations; during the early 1960's, interest concentrated on planning and computerization; in the later 1960's, the emphasis was clearly on disorder control and community relations; the pattern for the 1970's unquestionably will be emphasis on crime control.

Once crime control became a priority of the Metropolitan Police Department, interest in crime reduction could be found among officials, and among patrolmen as well. By 1972, members of promotional rating boards commented that young patrolmen coming before them were able not only to describe crime patterns on their beats, but were able to relate with accuracy what the crime problems were throughout the districts to which they were assigned.

There is no question that once an administrator can devise a statistical measure for an objective, obtain adequate resources, and motivate his organization to achieve, seemingly impossible improvements can be accomplished.

One very important question is left unanswered by the Washington experience. The remedy for crime was comparatively expensive in police manpower and money; the per capita cost of police service for Washington is the largest of any city in the nation. Could the reduction have been achieved at lower cost?

The answer to this is unclear. For one thing, the Washington police force was for nearly two decades among the largest per capita in the nation (for many years exceeded only by Boston). In the middle 1950's even when reported crime in the city was steadily declining, the department obtained a substantial increase in police personnel (to 2,500 men in 1956). Throughout the twelve years of crime increases, the police force was large in comparison with other cities; in 1966, before the sharpest upturn in crime, Washington had the largest per capita police force of any major city in America.

The conclusion is inescapable that much of the crime increases grew out of adverse rhetoric, both within and outside the department, which subdued motivation of the police to prevent crime. This rhetoric was combined with an actual, serious lack of support from the prosecutor's office and the poorly organized court systems of Washington. It might have been possible to achieve gradual crime reductions, without increased police manpower, by policy changes, court reorganization, and narcotics treatment programs.

Crime reductions might have been obtained without the high cost of additional police, but the improvement certainly would have been more gradual. Although substantially increased police presence is a more costly remedy for crime than is court reorganization or court expansion, increased police presence can be obtained much more rapidly and its effects will be perceptible much more quickly. And quick action was what was needed. The clear policy of the federal administration was to create a rapid improvement in law enforcement in the Federal City. The deliberate policy of the President was to have an expanded, strengthened, and supported police force.

The one answer found in the Washington experience is that crime can be reduced by making crime reduction the *first* priority of the government and by making whatever investment is needed in resources.

The Washington community had made it clear that it wanted crime reductions. Mail from across the nation showed that Americans wanted a capital city which they could visit with pride and safety. President Nixon translated those desires into a priority objective. A combination of increased police force, improved courts, increased prosecutorial staff, narcotics treatment programs, improved street lighting, legislative action, and community support achieved the goal.

It seems a shame that such an effective crime fighter turned out to be engaged in crime himself.

4

Common Sense—
The Key to Handling
Civil Disturbances

DURING THE 1940's and 1950's, when all America was applying its efforts first to the winning of World War II and later to a stabilization of its economy and society to a prewar and, hopefully, to a pre-Depression level, a variety of forces tended to keep significant civil disturbances out of the American scene. Those demonstrations which did occur, such as the pickets against the death penalty in the Rosenberg spy case, and the disruptions growing out of integration of schools and other public facilities in the 1950's, while they posed some political problems, tended to be very localized in nature and, even though those demonstrations involved issues of major concern, the disturbances were assumed by most Americans to be temporary phenomena and not matters to generate continuing fear.

The experiences of the 1940's and 1950's certainly did not prepare Americans for life in the 1960's. The new decade found a generation of Americans who knew little or nothing of the civil disturbances of earlier American history — of the great labor strikes in the decades around and immediately following the turn of the century, of the race riots, of the bonus marchers, of the religious disorders of the 1800's and of the early twentieth century. The new decade found a generation of Americans who would learn that reading in a history book a single sentence or a half-paragraph reference to a civil disorder is not nearly so instructive as living through one. Into the 1960's the nation came, little suspecting that many Americans were soon to undergo a paranoia of impending revolution akin to that experienced by their grandfathers during the labor upheavals of the first quarter of the century.

The consequence of this lulling during the war and postwar decades was that neither the American public nor its agencies of social control were conditioned by either experience or training to cope adequately with massive civil disturbances.

It is useful, in discussing control of civil disturbances, to begin with some definition of what kinds of event might be considered to constitute a civil disturbance. Hereunder is a listing which both benefits and suffers from its inconclusiveness. It benefits because it would be difficult to conceive of anything one might call a civil disturbance which is not included on the list; it suffers from the fact that the listing is so broad that many things are included which some persons would argue are not civil disturbances.

With the understanding that some modifications will be offered later to improve its meaning, the following listing is offered for consideration:

1. Spontaneous urban rioting ignited either by festering social conditions or by some significant accident or incident and characterized by such acts as property damage, window smashing, looting, arson, and sometimes attacks on individuals
2. Large-scale (or perhaps small-scale) demonstrations aimed at influencing social, governmental, or institutional action, and including such phenomena as massing of large groups to demonstrate solidarity, peaceful picketing by small or large groups, peaceful civil disobedience, and either intentional or unintentional nonpeaceful civil disobedience with damage to property and/or injury to persons
3. Disorders on or related to campuses and other school properties (This category usually is simply a special category of the kinds of demonstrations referred to in category 2.)
4. Sporadic (or frequent) stoning of firemen, policemen, or passersby by youth in some specific neighborhood

5. Disorders deriving from such events as hotly contested athletic games or extra-stimulating musical attractions such as rock concerts
6. Jail or prison disorders
7. Bombings and bomb threats
8. Massive disasters, either natural or man-made

Most persons would agree with the foregoing listing, with perhaps some arguments against including peaceful, small-scale picketing among more clear-cut disturbances and against listing natural disasters with man-made events. But to complete the perspective of these events, and to round out the understanding of how they are handled, it is important to add to the listing, with underscored emphasis, another grouping of occasions which hardly anyone ever considers as disturbances (except when one of these events attracts a counter-group):

- Large traditional patriotic parades, fraternal gatherings, or conventions

The common denominator at all these things is that THEY DISTURB THE NORM. Each of these imposes on governmental forces an added dimension beyond their normal work load, and each imposes on the ordinary citizen and on the business and residential community a disruption of their everyday norm.

Perception of the Norm

The notion that any particular event disturbs some well-defined norm obviously bears scrutiny. To begin with, it is clear to all of us that what may be normal in one time and place may not be normal at another.

In late 1968, when most major American cities were buffeted between sharply escalating crime rates and almost constant, everyday mini or maxi urban disorders, some joker suggested that "things are so bad in the cities this year that it's hard to tell when the rioting ends and the normal crime begins." (Pause here and contemplate for for a moment how bleak the urban scene seemed in 1968 as contrasted with the promise of today — even with the problems we have today, and, if you are old enough to remember just those few years ago, you will sense an exemplification of the dulling effect the passage of time has on emotions and fears.) In 1968, the norm was something entirely different from the norm of, say 1960.

There are, however, examples of constant or frequently recurring abnormalities of operations other than the phenomenon of 1968. For example, several large American cities, principally New York City, San Francisco, and Washington, D.C., are the selected sites of so many parades and demonstrations that the smaller ones are accepted as common, everyday occurrences, usually handled by some special unit of the police department on a standard-operating-procedures basis, and are so frequent as not to be considered deviations from the norm at all.

The addition of traditional parades and conventions to a list of less popular events is deliberate, to demonstrate that what may be considered a deviation from the norm in one city may be a welcome continuation of the norm (or a welcome deviation from the norm) in another. Convention-oriented cities vigorously compete to attract these large gatherings which, if there were not facilities to accommodate them, would tax the resources of the community, and those cities welcome them even though their parades may seriously disrupt traffic and their merrymakers may slightly break the public peace.

A third example of the variable of the norm is the phenomenon of bomb threats, which demonstrate a marked variation in frequency. As with other civil disturbances, the intensity of reaction to a bomb threat varies with the frequency with which bomb threats are received. If a bomb threat is received only once each year, it is commonly cause for significant distress and likelihood of overreaction by the community; on the other hand, when bomb threats become daily or multi-daily occurrences, the community both becomes immunized to the threat and usually develops standard operating responses as well.

Yet another example is that of the exuberance of spectators during and immediately following popular athletic events or other occasions such as rock concerts. The mildest of these crowds often will produce more noise and disruption of traffic and other indicia of peace and quiet of the neighborhood than usually will be tolerated by a community. And the traffic for a major athletic event, attracting upwards of 50,000 automobiles, can produce more traffic congestion than many parades or demonstrations. But, within reasonable limits, the community has institutionalized this disruptive activity and will permit and even encourage it. (Clearly, however, the community grows intolerant when such disruption occasionally progresses to the point of damage to property or injury to persons.) Other examples easily come to mind. Campus rallies and demonstrations are not at all unusual, and so long as their purpose and their disruption are within certain unprescribed but perceived-by-all, standards, they are never considered to be objectionable by the community.

What all of this illustrates is a central aspect of civil disturbances. This is that a civil disturbance is any event which has the capacity, probability, or the actuality of disturbing what sociologists refer to as an "institutionalized norm," this being in any particular social system the "norm" which a large number of the members of the system accept, take seriously, and sanction. (It is useful to recognize that even natural disasters such as earthquakes can become acceptable under an "institutionalized norm." In some areas of California, minor earth tremors, which would strike fear in the heart of Easterners, are experienced without serious qualms. It is only when the tremors progress in intensity beyond what the construction has been designed to withstand that an earthquake is perceived as a disruptive force.)

This notion of the "institutionalized norm," and the perception of it by the community, and their tolerance of deviation from it are central to the issue of control of civil disturbances, as we shall see presently.

Classification of Civil Disturbances

If you accept all or even most of the preceding list of headings of categories of civil disturbances, you readily can imagine an almost infinite number of classifications of types of disturbances.

For practical purposes, however, the two important classification criteria are (a) the size or magnitude of the disturbance, and (b) the disruptive or destructive potential of the disturbance. (And, as a matter of practical politics, a third element which often comes into play is the intent or purpose of the event and the acceptability of that intent or purpose to the total community.)

The size or magnitude of those disturbances involving people as participants (as contrasted to natural disasters, and so on), ordinarily being expressed in terms of numbers of participants, ranges on a scale from a single picket to several hundred thousand. Clearly, for tactical considerations, neither the community nor its control forces look on the disturbance as being of a different class each time one participant is added or subtracted from the group. For tactical considerations, in judging such groups there are about five gradations, which are:

- A group greatly outnumbering control forces
- A group somewhat outnumbering control forces
- A group about equal to control forces
- A group somewhat fewer than control forces
- A group greatly fewer than control forces

Obviously, these are vastly oversimplified gradations, for even aside from the destructive and disruptive potential discussed hereunder, a whole range of factors other than pure numbers (for example, training, equipment, organization, experience on each side) will determine the capacity of one group to control or overwhelm the other, but in the final analysis it is likely to be the numeration by which method of control is determined.

The disruptive or destructive potential (or achievement) of the disturbance is the second major element of the classification. And this, of course, means: how much is this event going to disrupt the norm? How much is this event going to have potential for destruction of property or injury to persons? This potential is the second major consideration of the community and its control forces in assessing the way in which the disturbance will be handled. It is important here to recognize that the capacity or potential for disruption or destruction need not pertain to the entire group, but may be measured in terms of the capacity of some small portion of the group. Indeed, from the standpoint of tactical consideration, it is useful to recognize that the disruptive or destructive elements may not even be a part of the primary group at all, but may be unaccepted hangers-on or even counterdemonstrators. In any event, accurate assessment of the disruptive and destructive potential of the group will be important to how well the control forces perform their responsibilities.

Function of Control Forces

Query: What is the best way to handle the typical civil disturbance?

Answer: There is no "best" way to handle the typical disturbance, because there is no such thing as a "typical" disturbance.

Putting aside such superlatives as "best" or "only" as modifiers of ways for handling disturbances, a good rule of thumb is that the policy mission of control forces is: to keep or to reduce the disruption of the norm to an acceptable level.

As already noted, many events, including many socially acceptable events such as traditional parades, conventions, athletic events, and so forth, generate deviations from the everyday norm. Consequently, how control forces interpret the foregoing policy mission is obviously going to correlate to how they perceive the acceptable norm. What it ordinarily will boil down to is a rule of reasonableness; for example, a line of peacefully moving pickets, with intervening spaces, is almost invariably going to be permitted, while pickets blocking a doorway will ordinarily be proscribed; or 100 peaceful protesters ordinarily will be required to conduct their protests on the sidewalk, while 100,000 would logically be allowed to use roadways. These oversimplified examples are easy to accept, and few would argue with them. But in the real world, the issues become far more complex. Social and political acceptability of demonstrations and other events frequently are woven into the fabric of public perception of such events. Given that the mission of control forces is to reduce disruption to an acceptable norm, it is unsurprising that they perceive the acceptable norm in the light of public opinion and political rhetoric.

Another important factor weighing heavily on how public opinion will perceive a disturbance and on how control forces will handle it is that of continuity or repetitiveness. If an event either persists over a long period of time or is repeated with regularity, public reaction will require control forces either to adopt standard operating procedures to minimize the disruptive effect of the event or to take strong police action to end the event (or sometimes public opinion itself will cause the event to end). Public reaction to these factors of continuity or repetitiveness is sometimes, but not always, related to the initial social or political acceptability of the event. History reflects many examples of public reaction to continuing or repeating events.

A major athletic event, attracting many thousands of persons, can seriously disrupt traffic in the neighborhood of its stadium. If a city has a single or an infrequent such event, it is likely that traffic tie-ups of one or two hours will be tolerated, with few being upset more than temporarily by the fact. On the other hand, if the event is one occurring on a regular basis, the public will demand that police forces develop processes and procedures to insure smooth, efficient flow of traffic. Another example is the heavy snowfall; in climates where snowfalls are frequent, citizens insist that their governments provide equipment, manpower, organization, and processes to insure continuation of traffic during all snowfalls short of perhaps blizzards; on the other hand, in climates where snowfalls are infrequent, citizens will tolerate traffic tie-ups and shutdowns during even relatively light snows. Perhaps the best example of a major event recurring on a regular basis which citizens demand their government provide processes to handle is the traffic rush each weekday morning and evening in every major city.

The foregoing examples are apolitical events. History is replete, however, with events of political ramification which have been either assimilated into standard operating procedures or proscribed when they exhausted public tolerance. As examples, pickets against the Rosenberg executions in the early 1950's were present in the vicinity of the White House for many months. And the Quaker Action group, conducting its vigil against the Vietnam War, was in front of the

White House for more than a year. In Washington, D.C., and probably also in New York and San Francisco, there may be a demonstration or parade for one cause or another almost every day. None of the foregoing, however, is a particularly good example, as these events have rarely disrupted the norm even as much as a major athletic event.

Larger-scale political events, which significantly disrupt the norm, seldom will persist over an extended period of time without being proscribed both by public opinion and by boredom of their participants. Possibly two of the best examples of these kinds of events are the Bonus Army in 1932 and the Poor Peoples' Campaign in 1968. Each of these projects attracted to the city of Washington a large group of participants who, except for perhaps disturbing the esthetic senses of the community and engaging in some harassment of public officials, could generally be described as peaceful during the early and middle stages of their "campaign." Although some segments of the community objected to their presence in the city from the outset (and other segments, of course, were highly supportive from the outset), the consensus could best be described as one of toleration. It is almost certain that any strong governmental action against these groups in their initial stages would have been roundly condemned by the general population. But open-ended projects such as these suffer from a fatal flaw: neither public toleration nor participant interest and participant discipline can be sustained over an indefinite period of time. The initial public consensus of toleration is sure to shift to a view that the visitors are unwanted guests, if not intruders. (Before the end of the 1968 Poor Peoples' Campaign, local citizens who in its early stages had welcomed the project were in its later stages trying to gather money to hire buses in the hope that participants would take advantage of them and go home.)

While public toleration is diminishing, and exasperation is supplanting toleration, participant discipline is prone to dissolve. What before were peaceful demonstrations are liable to become increasingly disorderly, as the less interested participants go home and the more dedicated resolve to leave their mark. In the end, the project leadership, the project participants, the government, and the community probably all will be wishing that there were a way out of the project without dishonor, and by that point in time, fair but firm action by the control forces is likely to be welcomed by all. Several lessons are to be learned from the experience of long-term projects such as these, and from shorter-term similar projects which have succeeded better.

- Organizers of demonstrations should recognize that open-ended (and to lesser extent extended-period) projects are almost sure to become ineffective in the end.
- Government officials and their police forces need to recognize that the initial public support of such open-ended projects, and the initial organization and discipline of such projects, are likely to break down over the long run, and should accordingly be flexible in their approach so that they can vary their tactics as the factors of public sentiment and participant activities change.

Another illustration of the changing of public attitude toward continuing disturbance of the norm can be found in attitudes toward the urban riots during 1967 and 1968. In the early stages of those disorders there was widespread participation in the riots by ordinarily law-abiding citizens, there was secret if not open applauding of the rioters by an even wider group of ordinarily law-abiding citizens, and a great many Americans who would not fall into any of the foregoing categories were at least tolerant enough of the rioters to apologize for them on the basis that their actions were motivated by frustrations and by need for social change. However, after the major riots had burned out most of the small shops and a good deal of housing in the ghettos, and the inconvenience of those losses began to bear on ghetto residents, and as the mini disorders following the major riots continued to inconvenience the life-style and the economy of the cities, the tolerance of the outset was displaced by an overwhelming desire on the part of everyone to "knock it off" and return to the norm. (This is not all that happened to stop the riots, of course; for one thing, the logistics of circa 1967–1968 rioting depended on presence of shops convenient to ghetto areas, and once these were destroyed, widespread looting was impractical; for another, police and other governmental forces learned from experience how to cope with riots; still, the perceptible change in political attitudes, which almost certainly reflected public attitudes, undoubtedly had much to do with the diminishment of the riots.)

Returning to the thesis that the function of control forces is to restore the situation to a publicly perceived "norm," it is important to recognize that the norm may be publicly perceived as something different during a large-scale continuous demonstration than it is at other times, but also that the degree of disruption which will be an acceptable norm may be continuously shifting throughout a long-term demonstration. Control forces must be ready to adapt their tactics and their responses flexibly to meet these shifting criteria.

Another important factor in this environment of public attitudes constituting the norm is that the establishment of the norm can and likely will be set by the political leadership of the jurisdiction and the leadership, if any, of the disturbance. What those leaders predict is going to happen, their attitudes, the responses they call for from their subordinates are all going to weigh heavily on both how the norm is perceived and on what norm will be established and maintained. Presumably, since such leadership is either formally or informally selected on the basis of politics, their statements and actions will reflect the consensus of their constituencies; on the other hand, however, as political leaders are, after all, leaders, their statements and actions can obviously influence that consensus.

Given the hazy objective of maintaining or returning the situation to an ambiguous norm, compounded by the infinite combinations of types of demonstrations in terms of size, objectives, political acceptability, disorder and destruction potential, and locations, it is clear that there can be no "best" way of dealing with a disturbance situation. There are times for dispersing crowds with skirmish lines of policemen, there are times for dispersing crowds with tear gas, there are times for arresting leaders and agitators, there are times for making mass arrests, and there are times to be simply permissive as, for example, in deciding against dispersing a crowd from a park where they can do relatively little damage and then only to government property, when the dispersal would send them into a business or residential community where they may do great damage to private property.

The important thing both from a policy and tactical standpoint, is that there be selected an appropriate objective for the time, place, size of the confronting group, the adequacy of control resources, and the potential for immediate and long-range ramifications of the action.

Control of Confronting Elements

The history of demonstrations over the 1960's has clearly demonstrated the value both to the demonstrators and to the government of prenegotiated permits and ground rules and the value, both in negotiation of those matters and in operations on both sides during the demonstration, of establishing a clear liaison between the government and the sponsors or leaders of the demonstration.

It is an unfortunate fact of human nature that these negotiated permits and the related liaison often become political issues, on the side both of the government and of the demonstrators, in those demonstrations where the confrontation between the demonstrators and their target is the most critical and where potential for disorder is greatest — those demonstrations where permits and negotiations are most needed. In those cases, the cause of the demonstrators (regardless of what it is) is likely to be unpopular with a large proportion (if not a majority) of the nondemonstrating citizens. Their reaction is going to be one of aggravation in the first place, followed by downright anger if the demonstration evolves into disorder and property damage.

On the side of the demonstrators, leaders who are holding their group together by antigovernment rhetoric as much as anything else often are necessarily cautious about letting their followers know that they are negotiating on a good-faith basis with that same government. This dilemma of negotiators, of trying to maintain credibility with both sides, is a common one, however, and needs no further examination here than to recognize that it exists and that because of its presence in situations where there is potential for confrontation, it is especially important that the negotiators for both sides be carefully selected and be experienced in the art.

The advantages to the government of negotiated permits and ground rules are that they tend clearly to organize the demonstration so that everyone knows what streets or other areas will be used, so that the times of beginning and ending are clear, so that traffic control can be well planned and publicized in advance, so that marshals from the confrontation group may be obtained, organized, and trained, and so that limitations can be written into the ground rules against undesirable tactics which might otherwise be employed by all or segments of the demonstrators. The advantages to the demonstrators are equally numerous; the issuance of a governmental permit tends to legitimatize the demonstration, making it possible for the demonstrators to obtain a larger crowd, and to greatly increase the proportion of their crowd which is drawn from more mature and more responsible supporters (a factor also of advantage to the government); it gives them definite times, streets, and areas for assembly, and makes it possible for them to advertise widely without concern that the government may concentrate its resources at the advertised areas and force them into last minute changes of deployment, which are difficult to communicate to participants; it insures the provision of sanitary and health services for the demonstrators; and it lends some modicum of respectability to the demonstration, an important factor in any project hoping to influence public opinion significantly.

A prevailing major issue regarding the issuance of permits for demonstrations is the question of whether, and if so, how, to hold demonstration leadership financially responsible for property damages and other costs resulting from their event.

This question comes up before almost every major demonstration and is pressed after any demonstration during which there is related disorder and property damage.

The argument of proponents of financial bond is that sponsors of any event likely to result in damage to government or private property should be required to post an advance financial bond to provide appropriate reimbursement for any such damage. However, there are both constitutional and practical problems which foreclose its adoption except in a very limited sense, such as when there is a requirement that demonstrators pay for such things as special sanitary facilities, speakers' stands, or replacement of sod on lawn areas.

Constitutionally, it is untenable for the government to establish a bond or licensing requirement on any demonstration which proclaims itself as an assembly of people peaceably petitioning the government for a redress of grievances. Admittedly, some demonstrations in the past have not been so proclaimed, but it is a simple matter for any demonstration leadership to amend its rhetoric sufficiently to bring it within the ambit of the First Amendment. As a practical matter, however, the past history of demonstrations indicates that some demonstrations proclaimed as peaceable have ended with property damage, while some proclaimed as threatening have ended peaceably. A much greater practical difficulty in trying to bond demonstration leadership to pay for any damage done by their followers arises from the repeated experience that damage during demonstrations is almost invariably caused by a very small subgroup of individuals who it would be almost impossible to prove with certainty were adherents to the objectives of the permittee and not just passersby or even counterdemonstrators.

A sometimes successful approach to clearly unlawful assemblages or demonstrations has been the obtaining of court orders or injunctions to prohibit their beginning or to foreclose their continuance. Probably the first use of the injunction process to control potential disorders was in the Pullman strike in 1890. In the past decade, the most prevalent use of the injunction process has been in dealing with campus disorders.

The court order–injunction process gives the government some very definite psychological, public-image, and tactical advantages over a more direct dealing with the disorder by police forces. Psychologically, demonstrators who may be prepared to challenge authority of private institutions and of the executive branch of government ordinarily are much less willing to challenge the unique power of the courts to hold them in contempt. As a very practical matter, demonstrators who may be quite willing to risk or even demand arrest on charges such as disorderly conduct, trespassing, or even assaulting a police officer, usually in the hope that their attorneys can adequately defend before a court their offenses against executive and legislative authority, realize that their attorneys are going to be much more hard put to defend before a court any offenses against the judicial authority.

From a public-image viewpoint, the use of the court order–

injunction process enables the government to develop and (in the presentation to the court) to lay before the public a dispassionate discussion of the issues involved in the demonstration, with most, if not all, of the emotional street rhetoric deleted. Also, a finding by the court that the demonstrators should desist from their actions places the demonstrators rather than the government more clearly in the posture of aggressor if police action finally must be taken. As a tactical matter, the court order–injunction process makes it much easier for the government to discern between the violators of the law and nonviolators of the law in assembly situations, since ordinarily the court order will define what is permitted and what is prohibited more specifically and more clearly than generalized statutes and regulations. The disadvantage of the court order–injunction process is that, away from private property, or in very limited, specific areas of public property, courts are reluctant to issue orders prohibiting assemblies of persons alleging to be petitioning for redress of grievance. Further, it is often difficult to prove to a court, in advance of a demonstration, that the demonstrators are likely to engage in unlawful conduct, even though a few of their number may be claiming that they will, and by the time disorder actually begins, it ordinarily is too rapid and too fluid for effective response by a judicial process which is going to take at least several hours.

What can the police do to deal with a demonstration which has become disorderly or unlawful? There are even more answers to this question than there are combinations of types and sizes of demonstrations. One traditional response has been the use of skirmish lines of police officers shoulder to shoulder, which prevent crowds of demonstrators from reaching target areas, which press them away from the target areas, or which break the crowd into smaller groups on the assumption that with diminishment of the mob psychology the participants will simply disperse. A second approach has been the use of tear gas, in either limited and localized or unlimited, widespread quantities, a process intended primarily to disperse the crowd, again with the notion that dispersal will reduce or eliminate the mob psychology and thus end the disorder. A third approach has been to make arrests, either of the crowd leaders and principal activists, or mass arrests of large numbers or all of the participants. A fourth major method of disorder control is to declare a curfew, either an overall curfew controlling all or most of a city or a very limited curfew more in the nature of police lines around a small area such as some park or some small segment of the city where disorderly elements have been or are likely to assemble. (It is interesting that, notwithstanding all the research, planning, and expertise growing out of the experiences of the late 1960's, the principal methods of disorder control are still much the same as those in use fifty years ago. The contribution of science to the art of disorder control has been mostly the providing of better hardware, such as radio communications, automobiles and scooters for response personnel, and more potent tear gas, all of which have been beneficial, but in the final analysis merely enable police to do better what they have done all along.)

There are advantages, and countervailing disadvantages inherent to each of the four principal methods of police response to unlawful assemblies.

SKIRMISH LINES. Skirmish lines are useful if there is ample police manpower who are well trained, well organized and well disciplined, provided that the disorderly elements are not well trained, well organized and well disciplined and provided they are not too actively seeking to cause injury to police officers. Skirmish lines are particularly effective for clearing streets or other areas after a curfew has been proclaimed or after a police line has been established around the area, when there are relatively few individuals (not more than three or four times the number of police officers in the line) to be cleared from the area and sent on their way home. Skirmish lines are very effective for keeping a moderately disorderly group (perhaps even up to ten times the number of police in the line) away from some demonstration objective as, for example, an embassy, and are particularly effective in the quite frequent situations when the demonstrators really don't expect to reach the target objective but merely want to make a public showing of having tried to do so.

The chief difficulty with a skirmish line is that it places police officers in direct contact with demonstration elements. If the demonstrators are particularly militant, especially if they are intent on causing injury to police officers, this direct physical contact can be hazardous to the police officers and, unless the officers in the skirmish line are well trained, well organized, and well disciplined, it is difficult to maintain unity of the line and impersonal tempers under such adverse conditions.

TEAR GAS. Tear gas, in the wide variety of forms which were developed during the late 1960's, has proven itself extraordinarily useful for breaking up disorderly gatherings with a minimum hazard of injury either to the demonstrators or to the police. Tear gas has a significant advantage over either the skirmish line or mass arrests in that it can be utilized as a tactic with far fewer police officers, or with a much smaller ratio of police officers to demonstrators, than either of the other two tactics. A handful of police officers, even one or two, with an adequate supply of an appropriate form of tear gas can easily disperse several hundred disorderly individuals. And the wide variety of new dispensing methods developed in the past few years has made increasingly practical the use of tear gas in one form or another in almost any situation. Many of the original tactical problems with the use of tear gas, such as the need for proper wind direction and the problems inherent in use of wind-carried gas in residential areas where innocent bystanders (particularly women and children) might suffer from its effects, have been largely resolved by the development of a variety of forms of gas which facilitate effective, selective dispensing. Also, the former problem that, once use of tear gas was begun in a situation, it tended to be overused, has largely been resolved in most police departments by improved command and control techniques.

The greatest disadvantage of tear gas is that, although it is very effective in dispersing a crowd, experience has repeatedly shown that, unless it is used in great quantities, it is ineffectual in keeping crowds dispersed in situations of persistent disorder, especially involving youth. The simple fact is that being teargassed can be fun, especially for teen-agers and young adults. Time and again there have been situations where demonstrators have blocked streets or otherwise unlawfully assembled, have thrown stones at police officers or other control forces, have been dispersed by tear gas, and have come back within a few minutes, a few hours, or the next day to do the same thing over again and to be so dispersed again. Obviously what is happening in such situations is that the disorderlies are enjoying the pleasure of their disorderly or unlawful conduct, and are sitting around after their dispersal with tear gas, each trying to outdo the other with a "sea story" about how much he was gassed, much as police officers do in the locker rooms after they have been caught out in the same gas without their masks. Persons who have been tear-gassed a few times, and thus have learned that it only hurts for a little while, can easily see that on any scale of hedonistic calculus, teargassing is unlikely to deter, and even may encourage, some forms of unlawful or disorderly conduct. Therefore, while tear gas is useful in abating an immediate problem, it should not be viewed as a long-term deterrent tactic.

ARRESTS. Arrest and prosecution of persons engaged in disorderly or other unlawful conduct is the third common alternative for coping with civil disturbances. When the commander decides to make arrests, his choice lies between making a limited number of arrests of leadership of the dissident elements and perhaps a few principal troublemakers, or making mass arrests of all participants; ordinarily, his choice will be based on such factors as what the crowd is doing, what its objective seems to be, the capacity of control forces to make mass arrests at that particular time, and whether mass arrests are likely to restore things to the norm more effectively in the short run and in the long run than simple crowd dispersal. Given the wide range of variables in size, type, objective, and composition of groups which may engage in disorderly or unlawful conduct, it is impractical to say that any single method of dealing with them is universally the best. By 1970, the arrest and prosecution method had become widely accepted by most experienced police officials as a preferable one for dealing with most disorders. But it is important to recognize that this preference grew out of the types of disorders which occurred in 1970 and the preceding couple of years, to the composition of participants in those disorders, and to the political, social, and economic implications, at that particular time, of an arrest or conviction for engaging in a demonstration, as well as the experience cities had with the "trashing" response of demonstrators to the dispersal of disorderly groups.

In 1970, the typical demonstrator (if anything such as typical can be condensed from the wide range of demonstrators) was commonly a middle- to upper-class, college-age individual. By 1970 the social value of an arrest record for engaging in a demonstration, which had developed from the civil rights movement of the late 1950's and early 1960's, was greatly diminished; the nation had grown tired of disruptive demonstrations and street disorders; the United States Civil Service Commission in 1969 had adopted a policy that in hiring government employees it would look behind any arrest growing out of a campus or street disorder; additionally, the hot economy of the 1960's was beginning to cool and in the changed labor market competitors for jobs were less willing to have any single mark against them. But these conditions of 1970 which made mass arrests a very effective tool for dealing with disorders had not always prevailed, and indeed were not universally applicable in the 70's.

The Civil Rights Movement in the preceding two decades had transmuted an arrest for engaging in a demonstration from a stigma into a badge of honor. This philosophy carried over into the other social activist and antiwar movements of the 1960's. However, for a wide variety of reasons, this badge-of-honor concept was greatly diminished by 1970. Still, despite this diminishment, there were groups still willing to submit themselves to arrest as, for example, the Jewish Defense League demonstrators who submitted nearly 1,000 demonstrators to arrests in early 1970, and the Mayday demonstrators who deliberately submitted to some 6,000 arrests during the week before and after May 1, 1971 (this count includes only those arrests during which demonstrators deliberately placed themselves in situations where they were likely to be arrested, and excludes the 7,000 arrests made on May 3, 1971, where arrests were made in more fluid situations).

In addition to the fact that some demonstrators may simply want to be arrested, there are other very practical problems with the use of arrests for dealing with demonstrators. For one thing, if the demonstrators are not deliberately placing themselves in an unlawful position where they can be easily arrested and processed on a mass basis, it may be very difficult to apprehend each demonstrator in a situation where he is clearly in violation of the law and to process him in such a way that he can be prosecuted, on a rapid enough basis to serve the recommended policy objective of returning the situation to the norm. A spontaneous example of this kind of situation occurred during the 1968 Poor Peoples' Campaign when, after several hundred demonstrators had been arrested for deliberately blocking the entrances to the Department of Agriculture until each of them was arrested and taken away, a couple of hundred others decided that, rather than sitting in an entrance and waiting to be routinely processed, they would run into the rush-hour traffic and sit in the middle of the roadway; then, when the police arrest teams approached a group, as soon as one or two arrests were made, the remainder of the group would run to some other location farther down the block and sit again. Needless to say, this small scale preview of a "Mayday" situation was difficult to handle with the normal field arrest processing. The more spectacular example of this phenomenon is, of course, the carefully staged "Mayday" plan which was deliberately contrived to confound the normal field arrest processes.

It is one thing, as experienced Police Commanders have learned in dealing with repeated disorders, to adopt a policy of making arrests as a way of putting down and presumably preventing disorders, and it is quite another to make significant numbers of arrests in fluid situations where the disorder participants are not willingly submitting to arrest. It is very difficult in these fluid situations for arresting officers to make careful mental and written note of specifically what unlawful act each individual arrestee was engaged in, and the fluid situation disrupts the organization and command and control of arrest teams, a factor likely to result in production of fewer prosecutable cases and perhaps a loss of police discipline and restraint as well.

CURFEWS. An immensely effective tool in dealing with widespread disorder is the proclamation of a curfew, which in its strictest application can be tantamount to a civil version of martial law. The curfew enables police officers to almost arbitrarily arrest nearly any person found abroad on the streets. There are some very practical problems with the curfew, however, which militate against its general use in disorder control.

For one thing, the proclamation of a curfew requires the declaration of a state of emergency, which most jurisdictions are hesitant to do except in a very serious disorder. Further, in an urban environment, while the proclamation of a curfew does enable the government to quickly clear the street of disorderly elements and thus rapidly to put down the disorder, it simultaneously nearly totally shuts down the commercial and social life of the city. Given that civil disorders usually are confined to relatively limited areas of a city, the proclamation of a curfew may have the effect of disrupting the total city more than the disorder would have. Although a solution to this dilemma might be the proclamation of a curfew for only a part of the city, in most urban situations of today such action would have ethnic or racial overtones which would make it politically unfeasible. Too, in situations such as the preplanned "Mayday" events, the proclamation of a curfew would have had precisely the effect sought to be achieved by the demonstrators: the closing down of the nation's capital and of the federal government. It is for these reasons that, despite its effectiveness, the curfew is seldom used in disorder control except in the most serious urban disorders or in special areas such as a self-contained university campus, where the disadvantages of temporarily dispensing with normal functioning are not so severe.

A widely used technique somewhat analogous to the curfew is the establishment of a police line and exclusion of all persons from a relatively limited area. Many jurisdictions have municipal regulations authorizing the senior police commander at the scene of an emergency such as a fire, natural disaster, or disturbance, to establish police lines around a small area prescribed by him and to exclude all persons from it. Some disadvantages of this technique are that it requires a significant investment of police manpower to establish and maintain a reasonably clear line around the area, and it is a difficult technique to apply equitably in a residential area where residents need to come and go. It has the advantage, however, of being a technique which can be employed fairly rapidly, requiring little formal action for its implementation and even less for its relinquishing. The police line and the corollary exclusionary area has value not only for dispersing already disorderly elements but, within reasonable limits, can be useful for excluding potentially disorderly groups from favored areas of congregation.

Control of Police Elements

COMMAND AND CONTROL. As demonstrations and disorders of various kinds became prevalent during the 1960's, police agencies across the nation came to learn that special kinds of organization and control techniques were needed for dealing with them. Organizational concepts for dealing with such events vary from jurisdiction to jurisdiction, depending on such factors as how the police agencies ordinarily are organized, how often demonstrations or disorders occur or are likely to occur, and the potential magnitude of those which do occur. An examination of all varieties and nuances of organizational structure and command and control technique would take more space than would be useful here, but there are a few key techniques and significant points worth mentioning.

In what was the first of the really large demonstrations of contemporary times, the Rally for Jobs and Freedom in Washington in 1963, it became obvious to the government that some ad hoc changes were needed in the organization of the police agencies handling the event. From the outset, for purposes of the event all police agencies involved in the operation were placed under the command of a single police official. Secondly, the Metropolitan Police Department, by far the largest of the police agencies involved, was completely reorganized for purposes of the event, with a great deal of shifting of both line and staff officials from their everyday assignments to special command and staff posts involved directly with the event. Both of these practices have, in the shakedown of the 1960's, become so common that they are worth mentioning here only because their importance has elevated them to the status of principles.

The principles are:

1. That jurisdictions planning for civil disturbances or similar major events must, if more than one police agency is to be involved, develop a clear chain of command among the police agencies, with one official clearly designated as the commander, with ultimate authority and responsibility.

2. That in planning for major events, any large or medium-sized police agency must recognize that effective operation for a major special event will require some changes from its normal operation; staff units which will have limited, if any, ordinary responsibility for the event, should be given predesignated ad hoc responsibilities (as an example, a field inspection unit might be designated for handling prisoners in mass arrests) so that the personnel of the staff unit will be able to plan and train in advance for their special-event responsibilities rather than having the duties imposed on them at the last minute or at the peak of an emergency.

3. An organizational technique which has come into common use during the 1960's in those police agencies in large cities which have almost daily demonstrations is the establishment of special-events or tactical units which devote a major portion of time just to coordinating, escorting, and controlling small demonstrations and similar events. The advantages of such a unit are obvious; its officials become experienced in negotiating with demonstration leadership, men for the unit can be especially selected for their ability to deal calmly with demonstrations, and this ability can be reinforced by training and experience; the unit develops its own command and control techniques, and parades or other moving demonstrations which cross police precinct lines have the advantage of dealing with a single police unit rather than numerous police commanders.

4. Necessary for dealing with any major special event is the establishment of processes for coordinating not only all police agencies involved in the operation, but also other governmental and public service elements such as fire departments, health departments, sanitation departments, highway departments, public transportation agencies, and such public utilities as the local gas, electric, and telephone companies. Many of

these agencies tend to close down entirely or to operate with skeleton crews on nights and weekends (when many special events occur), making it very difficult, if not impossible, to obtain policy decisions or major commitments of their services on an emergency basis unless prearrangements have been made. To avoid this difficulty it is helpful to establish and regularly update in police communications centers, lists of officials of those agencies who can be contacted on an emergency basis; and for any major special event, an effort should be made to insure that at least one senior middle-management executive from each of those agencies is either on duty or absolutely readily available if needed; ideally, some responsible representative of the agency should be stationed either in police headquarters or on a direct tie line from police communications so that rapid response is facilitated.

Any significant special event will clearly demonstrate to the involved police agency the need for establishment of one or more special command posts for command and control of the agency during the event. Modern police agencies are usually organized to operate day-to-day with command and control disseminated through a staff function communications division. Ordinarily, these units are expected to handle not only the routine command and control, but usually are also expected to handle the command and control for any small, occasional special event which may arise. In most departments, however, such units are not furnished with either facilities, space, personnel, or equipment for effectively handling a major event or persistent, minor events. Most agencies, therefore, find it practical in planning for special events and emergencies, to establish some form of special command post for dealing with such occasions. This enables the departmental commander to establish processes for mapping and logging precisely what is going on in the demonstration, gives him a location for meeting with his staff and line commanders, and provides a system for disseminating his special event information and instructions with minimum disruption of the normal operations of the communications division which must (in addition to providing radio facilities for the event) continue its normal staff function of providing command and control over routine police operations in all areas of the jurisdiction. A department with only an occasional major special event will find that economy dictates its temporarily establishing this special command post in some conference room or other available office space, with little special expenditure other than installation of telephones and provision of special maps and chart boards. A department which experiences frequent special events of some magnitude will find it worthwhile to build and maintain a permanent command post for this purpose, and additionally often will find it worthwhile to purchase and equip one or more large trucks or buses for use as field command posts.

TRAINING POLICE FOR DISTURBANCE CONTROL. One of the very difficult tasks facing police agencies in the late 1960's when preparation for disorder control became imperative, was to devise and implement meaningful systems of training for the rank and file police officer in disorder control. The difficulty derived from the lack of any substantial experience in control of disorders, which made it very hard for police agencies even to devise firm policies and plans for dealing with disturbances, much less to devise training programs for implementing their policies and plans.

Prior to the initial outbreak of urban disorders in the middle 1960's, most disorder control training, if there was any at all, in a police agency, consisted almost wholly of drilling a relatively small riot squad in squad and platoon formations, supplemented by describing to the squad the types and uses of various chemical agents for riot control. Given the scarcity of substantial disorders in the preceding two decades, at that time it would have been illogical for police agencies to have done much more than that. When the urban disorders did begin to break out, and police agencies across America began to feel the need to develop contingency plans and programs against this new hazard, it became obvious that a great deal more training was needed in this area than had been available in the past. The federal government effort of that time in police training for disorder control was concentrated, of necessity, on acquainting upper and middle managers of police agencies with the national experience in various types of disorders, stressing to them the need for developing plans and programs for disorder control, and emphasizing the need for training all personnel in those plans and programs. Numerous seminars, of varying degrees of excellence, were conducted by several institutions, both with and without direct federal support.

It is one thing, however, to train top and middle managers in ways of developing policies and programs for disorder control, and quite another to train rank and file personnel in the implementing of those plans and programs. The former requires little more than the communicating and discussing of some principles, some past experiences, and some concepts and ideas; the latter requires not only communicating those things, but also instructing *and drilling* of large contingents of personnel in concepts, methods of operations, and procedures which are different from those ordinarily used.

First of all, for ordinary forms of disorder control, the police officer must be indoctrinated in the "squad team" concept, a direct contrast from the "individual officer" or "partner" concept which is drilled into him at the police academy and is reinforced by his day-to-day experience. Put simply, the police officer ordinarily is taught, from the time he graduates from police academy (if indeed not from the time he takes his oath of office) that as an officer of the law he is individually responsible for taking initiative and action in any situation or circumstance where his initiative or action is not clearly proscribed by law or departmental regulation. The gods of the police craft frown on the police officer who is hesitant to act or who calls the sergeant or dispatcher in a sticky situation to ask what should be done. Indeed, it has only been in the last decade that police agencies have developed sufficiently shortened spans of control and methods of communication to make it practical for street policemen readily to contact a supervisor in an emergency.

This individualistic craftsmanship, which is a necessity in day-to-day police operations, is anathema to effective command and control in disturbance situations, when the usual objective is to restrain individual actions of police officers, and to substitute organizational action, so that the command official rather than several hundred individual officers will be deciding when it is best to make arrests, when it is best to use gas, when it is best to hold back, or when it is best to charge forward. Effective substitution of the squad-team concept for the individual officer concept requires considerable training and a great deal of drilling for reinforcement.

Rank and file officers not only need training and drilling in that change of concept, they also need training and drilling in such special procedures as mass arrest techniques, tear gas nomenclature and uses, the special communications to be used by the department during major events, working with gas masks, the special police-community relations, and the unusual police-press problems in disturbance control, and in development of mental attitudes conducive to stability under such adverse conditions as verbal abuse or thrown objects from demonstrators.

It is much more easy to recognize the need for training police officers than it is to find time and resources to achieve it. A fact often overlooked by those who advocate more training of police officers, and who sometimes even offer to provide financing for program development or provision of instructors, is that the real expense of training large groups of men is not in the program development nor in provision of training staff, but is in the cost of salaries of the men attending the training. This is especially true of training such as that needed for disorder control. Here, the techniques to be taught will not be used on a day-to-day basis after the training (and indeed in many cases will be contrary to day-to-day experience); here, the techniques likely will not be used for some time, if at all; here, the training must include large blocks of time for drilling in the technique, so that a man not only knows how a mass arrest team is supposed to operate, but so that he has been through the process himself often enough that he is reasonably efficient when he is called upon to perform the task in the field, perhaps months later, without intervening experience.

Weighing the cost of such training for problems of uncertain potential against the need which all police agencies were feeling in the late 1960's for training to cope with problems occurring daily, it is unsurprising that the civil disorder training actually was very sparse, if not just on-the-job training when a real situation erupted. This fact, compounded by the inestimable value of experience, inevitably resulted in those departments facing the more frequent problems becoming the more proficient in the skills needed to cope with them.

COMMUNICATIONS. To the police commander dealing with the civil disturbance in the 1970's, with hundreds or even thousands of men spread throughout a city to concentrate on a single operation, it is an awesome thought that just forty years ago the command and control over the operation would have been done without any radio communication whatever. Today, it seems almost laughable that in the late 1920's many communication experts were saying that there were no practical police applications for the radio, until one realizes that not twenty years ago police communication experts were disparaging the value of the portable "footman" radio.

Even with the vast improvement of radio equipment, especially in the last ten years, there still can be significant communications problems in coordinating large numbers of police officers, especially when more than one police force is involved. To begin with, there is a problem because in most large cities the police radio channels are often saturated with normal day-to-day activity, the level of which is apt to become abnormal at critical points during a civil disturbance. Second, there is the problem that radio traffic for command and control of an emergency situation often necessarily lacks the discipline of day-to-day messages, because of the need for obtaining situation reports from the field in language lacking the conciseness of the better codified reports in repetitive radio traffic, and the fact that ad hoc organization of a department for dealing with disorder often requires more personalized radio traffic than the much better organized dispatching in day-to-day operations.

A significant problem may be encountered in trying to devise centralized command and control when several law enforcement agencies are cooperating on the same operation. A part of this difficulty comes from the fact that each agency is often using its own, separate radio channel. This creates situations where one unit in the field may need the support of another, and be unable to obtain it in a timely fashion simply because there is no ready way of communicating with them. Similarly, one unit may be totally unaware of a developing serious situation simply because the field situation reports are being discussed on the radio channels of some other department.

In a sense, however, the problem of communications between two separate police organizations addressing themselves to the same mission often is much more complex than simply a need for a common radio frequency. For one thing, the vernacular of the two departments may be sufficiently different to cause confusion in communications; almost certainly, in the ad hoc organizations for dealing with an emergency problem, even though there is prearranged agreement as to which senior official will be overall commander of that operation, there will be considerable confusion between agencies regarding how middle-managers rank among one another; obviously, the emergency decisions in the field at critical points in a special event are often made and communicated by the middle-managers rather than by the overall commander. (The problem is more complex than simply a deciding of which middle-manager outranks another, for actual field leadership often passes among middle-managers, not so much on which outranks the other as on which has the confidence of the other that he is able to assess situations correctly and properly pursue the objectives of the organization; this confidence among middle-managers is unlikely to exist between organizations which seldom have occasion to work together in ways that will acquaint the middle-managers with one another.)

Although difficult to overcome, these communications problems are not insurmountable. It is important that large departments, with heavy day-to-day radio traffic, make every reasonable effort to develop a plan for some separate radio channel for special events and emergencies. Desirably, of course, this should be a channel reserved exclusively for that purpose, but in those areas of the nation where frequencies are heavily crowded, it is likely to be necessary to devise some compromise solution, such as special-event shifting of day-to-day traffic from one channel to others so that at least the one channel is left open exclusively for the event. The problem of arranging coordination between various law enforcement elements engaged in a single operation requires carefully thought-out planning and attention. The technical problem of melding the several radio frequencies of the various police units into a single communications network is relatively easy to solve by simply establishing a joint communications center which has access to all frequencies and has responsibility for monitoring and dispatching between them. This command post technique could be even further strengthened by requiring the senior official from each agency to remain throughout the operation at a central command post, except that such officials often have other important things to do while emergencies are in progress, not the least of which is to be out in the field finding out firsthand what is going on, and leading their men.

At best, the simple bringing together at a communication center of the various radio frequencies will not begin to address the human problem of unclear lines of authority, unclear communication, and misplaced or nonexistent confidence between middle-managers who don't know one another. This not technical but human problem of communication is probably best resolved by the principal agency involved in the operation (usually, but not necessarily, the agency headed by the overall commander), assigning to the senior and major element commanders of the other units a competent middle-management official who has ability to assess and interpret situations for both the commander to whom he is assigned and for the commander of his own agency.

NEWS MEDIA RELATIONS. Inevitably, it is during demonstrations and disorders that relationships between the police and the news media are put to their greatest test. Whether relationships between a department and the news media are good or bad, there ordinarily will have evolved some form of accommodation and some forms of communications between the "regulars" covering the police beat and those police officials dealing in matters of daily interest to reporters.

However, those routine informal accommodations are unlikely to be effective during a major special event, demonstration, or disorder, when, for one thing, the number of reporters dealing with the police agency is certain to be increased manyfold, bringing into contact with the department large numbers of reporters who know little about the department and, often, little about the city government as a whole or the city itself; secondly, the ad hoc reorganization of the department for purposes of dealing with the special event, compounded by the fact that the special event brings into play new areas of interest for the media, reduces the effectiveness of the informal lines of communications between police beat regulars and the officials they have dealt with in the past on specialized subjects.

These factors make it imperative that the police agency establish or maintain a strong news media relations unit before, during, and immediately following the event. If the department does not ordinarily maintain a public information office, temporary establishment of one should be arranged in the temporary reorganization for the event; if the department has a permanent news media relations office, serious consideration should be given to strengthening it with additional personnel during the event.

It is not intended here to engage in a full discussion of the continuing importance of maintaining good relations between the police agency and the news media, nor to attempt here an enumeration of techniques for achieving such relationship. But it is worth noting here the fundamental principle that, especially during a disturbance or disorder, whatever individual office is handling relations with the news organizations must be one which has the confidence of the chief official of the police agency, and must be recognized throughout the agency as having that confidence.

In any major special event, the public information office will need sufficient resources to serve news media needs both at some headquarters location, where there will be numerous requests for organizational, policy, and statistical information, and at locations of critical activity in the field, where there will be some of the same kinds of requests for information, but where the more important function of the public information representative will be to act as a buffer between the news media and the operational personnel, assisting and shepherding the reporters and camera crews so that they can get good coverage of the event with a minimum interference to police operations. It is in this latter function of assisting in the field where the skill of the public information officer will be tested.

Inevitably, the attitude of the police toward the news media is going to be conditioned and reinforced both by the history of day-to-day police media relations of the department and, regardless of what policy statements may be made, by what the police officers in the ranks perceive is the attitude of the department leadership. If the rank and file believe that the department leadership wants cooperation with the news media, they will cooperate; if they believe that they want the contrary, they will be contrary.

Again without entering into a full discussion of the multifaceted problems of police-media relationships, it is germane to mention the special problems in that relationship which arose out of news coverage of both urban riots and other street and campus disorders during the middle and late sixties, when many citizens, both police and non-police, came to believe that news media coverage (especially television coverage) sometimes exacerbated and even generated disorders which would have died natural deaths without the coverage. These beliefs undoubtedly have some basis in fact, and today are shared by many responsible members of the news media itself. Because there continues to be a tendency, particularly in police circles, to comment negatively regarding this past activity of the media, and because people can still be heard blaming the news reporting for causing disorders, it is worth saying here something positive in their behalf.

The news media, just like the police and many other institutions, went through a great learning process in experiencing the demonstrations and disorders of the 1960's. The news media, just as the other institutions, had practically no reporters nor executives with any experience in how public news reports could affect actions and reactions of groups of people in turbulent times, for there had been no turbulent times in a generation; and television, which of all the news media is probably the greatest catalyst of public response to fast-breaking news developments, had not even existed during earlier periods of internal strife in American history, so no one could know of its potential impact. This inexperience, or lack of recent experience, was compounded by the inherent media responsibility to report to the public all news, good or bad, by the competition between the various media, between elements of each media, and between reporters in each element, and by the pressure of those complex forces working within a profession which has very ambivalent ethics, if it has ethics at all.

In defense of the news craft, however, it can be said that the public media, just like everyone else, learned well from its experiences and responded to the lesson. By late 1968, they had learned better to distinguish between community leaders and individuals who only claimed to be leaders; by late 1968, there was a conscious effort by the news media not to play up minor incidents to a point where perhaps news coverage alone might turn a minor event into a major disorder. Overall, given the fact that the public media, just like every other American institution, was forced in the 1960's to learn or re-learn about disorders in the school of experience, where the lessons are learned from one's own mistakes, it should not be held perma-nently accountable for its early errors. On balance, it probably made no more errors than the other institutions involved in the problem, and learned its lessons as well or better than the rest.

FLEXIBILITY IN FIELD TACTICS. Like all nonscientific activi-ties, especially those nonscientific activities which deal with control of human behavior, demonstration and disorder control is always going to involve some learning from new experiences. But even the new lessons learned are not immutable. After the early days of urban disorders, it was generally assumed that riot actions were going to be directed only against property and that innocent bystanders would not be injured, except perhaps incidentally and accidentally; but, while this assumption was found to be largely true, there were enough assaults on innocent parties to force police response on an assumption that innocent bystanders might be injured. Before and in the early days of the urban disorders, it was generally assumed that there was no value in police attempting to disperse a very large and disorderly crowd until they had assembled a relatively large force of police personnel to perform that function; however, experi-ence eventually showed that crowds of hundreds of individuals often could be dispersed by only a few police officers armed with nothing more than bullhorns and tear gas. In the early days of antiwar dis-orders, it was assumed that a desired method of dealing with a large, disorderly gathering was dispersal; however, the development of the technique of "trashing" by some elements of the antiwar movement made dispersal a sometimes nonpreferred tactic. Arrest and prosecu-tion of offenders has been generally accepted as a desired govern-ment tactic in response to unlawful activities; however, experience with both urban rioting and antiwar disorders has shown that, in fast-moving, fluid situations, arrests and prosecution may be highly desirable but very difficult to achieve.

All of this sums up to the fact that in disorder control, as in all activities dealing with human behavior, experience may prove to be a very bad teacher for, even though the opposing elements may not be well organized (and indeed may not be organized at all), their human response to any government tactic designed to frustrate their goal may be to forget their goal and to go about their legitimate business, but it also may be to simply try some way of circumventing the government tactic.

This phenomenon leads to what must be the tactical principle of disorder control: field tactics must be highly flexible, and field decisions must be made in the field.

5

New Processes for Improving Police Performance

A NOTION CURRENTLY IN VOGUE in criminal justice circles is that some alternative needs to be found to the clearly inefficient exclusionary rules now applied by courts to determine what evidence will be admitted into criminal trials and what evidence will be excluded. One concept which is suggested is that evidentiary problems might be better addressed by clear statutory or regulatory limits on police authority, reinforced by internal disciplinary machinery. Proponents of this concept speak in terms of "controlling police conduct as an alternative to the exclusionary rule."

There is a mild paranoia within the police craft regarding the frequent suggestion that it is the *police* who need to be restrained — with implication that the remainder of the criminal justice system is impeccable in its handling of evidence. The experienced police officer knows that the remainder of the system is far from perfect.

Unfortunately, continued experience with how the system functions can lead a police officer to the cynical perception that the remainder of the criminal justice process is motivated by much the same stimuli as the police: the Rule of Pragmatic Convenience!

The experienced police officer will often notice that the principal difference between the approach he takes toward a criminal and the approach taken by prosecutors, defense attorneys, and courts is that the latter group, members of the legal profession, pretend that their actions are governed by a code of ethics, while the police officer more readily will admit, at least to himself, that his actions are governed by pragmatism.

One clear example of the rule of pragmatic convenience as used by prosecutorial and judicial systems can be found in the situation in the District of Columbia where, until 1953, a police officer had no authority to arrest for a petit larceny, which is a misdemeanor, if committed out of his presence. In 1953, statutory authority was provided for such an arrest for misdemeanor larceny out of presence of the officer so long as there was probable cause for the officer to believe that the culprit still had in his possession the property taken in the larceny. But even before that statute was enacted, the practice of the courts in the District of Columbia was to convict persons arrested for petit larceny even though they were arrested illegally.

Everyone knew that this occurred. The prosecutors knew, the judges knew, the defense attorneys knew. Everyone knew it except police recruits, who in recruit school were taught a law of arrest which did not authorize misdemeanor arrests for offenses committed outside the presence of the officer.

Certainly, unless the arrestee happened to be an upper-class housewife who could afford some attorney other than the usual gaggle of courthouse hangers-on, her case would never get through the prosecutor papering process; but the ordinary case would be prosecuted just as though the arrest were absolutely legal.

The consequence of this state of affairs was that the police department taught its officers in recruit school the correct law of arrest. But with a few months' experience on the street, the officer learned that his recruit school instructions were incorrect, for misdemeanor larceny would be prosecuted, and convictions could be obtained, even though the arrests were improper.

If one were to ask a prosecutor at that time why the practice was carried on, he would call it "being practical," for the criminal justice system would not have worked well otherwise. The Rule of Pragmatic Convenience.

Another example of this "being practical" by the judicial system can be found in the *Federal Rules of Criminal Procedure* requirement that "an officer making an arrest . . . shall take the arrested person without unnecessary delay before . . . the officer empowered to commit persons charged with offenses. . . ." This is the language which led to the celebrated *Mallory* rule in the District of Columbia.

The wording is clear; the requirement is mandatory. The language has not changed in three decades; the rule was taught in the District of Columbia Police Recruit School in the 1940's. But the question is, "Does the rule mean what it says; has the rule ever meant what it says?"

In answer to those questions, it is clear that the rule has never meant, and does not now mean, that a judicial officer must be awakened in the middle of the night so that an arrested person can be presented to him "without unnecessary delay," unless an unusually important case is involved. The rule has never meant, and it does not now mean, that a person arrested at three o'clock on a Saturday afternoon in Washington, D.C., must be arraigned prior to the regular court session on Monday morning, again except in the unusual case likely to draw substantial public attention.

What is this ambivalent application of the rule called? By lawyers and judges, who do not want to be called to arraignments in the middle of the night or on the weekend, it is called "being practical." By police officers, who are accustomed to the notion that crime must be dealt with at all hours around the clock and on every day of the week, it is called "keeping regular office hours." The Rule of Pragmatic Convenience.

And before the *Mallory* rule was handed down in 1957, the clear, unambiguous language of the *Federal Rules of Criminal Procedure* meant even less than it does now. Then it did not mean that a prosecutor would not prosecute, nor that a court would not convict, nor that a United States Court of Appeals would not uphold an arrest and conviction of a rapist on a confession obtained during a seven-and-one-half-hour delay from arrest to presentment before the magistrate.

Police officers could read Rule 5(a) of the *Federal Rules of Criminal Procedure* and could comprehend its meaning. Additionally, they were taught in the police recruit school the Supreme Court pronouncements in the *McNabb* and *Upshaw* decisions. But the more important guidance which they quickly received after leaving school was an appreciation of what delays the prosecutor and the trial courts would tolerate, irrespective of the stringent language of the rule. "Being practical," the lawyers called it. The Rule of Pragmatic Convenience.

Yet, when the Supreme Court decided *Mallory*, the rule of the case quickly came to be accepted as a standard to "control police misconduct," even though there was no conduct of police officers in that case other than what had been regularly reviewed and upheld for years by the prosecutors and the courts. No one suggested that the prosecutor, the trial court, and the appeals court which heard the facts in *Mallory* during its progress to the Supreme Court — all of whom had far more opportunity for careful after-the-fact contemplation than did the arresting officer — were guilty of misconduct in affirming the actions by the police officer.

Exclusionary rules, then, come to be seen by police as rules of pragmatic convenience — rules applied with ambivalence by the bench and the bar — rules applied in practice so as not to seriously disrupt the tendency of the system toward mass-produced justice in unimportant cases involving poor people — rules applied so that judges and lawyers are conveniently spared the indignity of working nights and weekends, the times when most arrests are made.

There are other examples of the Rule of Pragmatic Convenience. One is the process which ends in what police officers jokingly call "not guilty by reason of continuance." This is the process whereby the defense attorney simply obtains as many continuances as he can, for as long periods as possible, in the hope that sooner or later a key prosecution witness will fail to show up for trial, whereupon the defense announces ready for trial, and obtains a dismissal when the prosecutor is forced to admit an unreadiness.

Such things happen frequently. A prime example of this ploy is the defense attorney practice of insisting that the chemist who made the analysis be made available for trial in a narcotics case; then, when the defense is finally forced to go to trial, if the chemist is there, the defense invariably agrees that putting the chemist on the stand to testify is unnecessary. In a system which handles hundreds of narcotics arrests each week, with narcotics trials proceeding in a variety of courts at the same time, the defense attorney has a good chance that sooner or later, in a series of continuances, the chemist will be unavailable; the judge, who is anxious to keep his calendar backlog moving, will then dismiss the case for lack of prosecution if the defense announces for trial and the prosecution is unable to produce the chemist.

All of the foregoing discussion of faults in other parts of the criminal justice system is certainly not to imply that police are blameless in the way they handle criminal cases. But police officers do not learn in recruit school how to abuse and manipulate the system. Young police officers come out of recruit school much as young lawyers come out of law school — dedicated to improvement of the community and impressed by the newly obtained knowledge of how the criminal justice system is *supposed* to operate.

It is after recruit school, in the school of experience, that police officers learn how the system really operates — and they learn these facts from prosecutors, from defense attorneys, from judges — or from experienced police officers who have already learned from those lawyers. Then, when the police officer puts this informally obtained knowledge into practice, if his cases are thrown out by the courts for exclusionary causes, his actions then are characterized as "police indiscretions" or "police misconduct."

How the process is often misconstrued is illustrated by a 1972 law-student research project examining feasibility of replacing the exclusionary rule by substitution of disciplinary action against police officers who make searches unlawfully. The student compiled a list of one hundred cases in which a motion to suppress evidence was granted by a judge, and asked the police department to tell him, for each of those cases, whether or not disciplinary action was taken against the officer.

Not surprisingly, disciplinary action had not been taken in any of the cases, nor should disciplinary action have been imposed, at least not against the police officer. No felony arrest is presented for arraignment or for trial until after a prosecutory attorney has fully reviewed the facts, including the evidentiary elements, and approved the case for prosecution. If disciplinary action is to be taken against a police officer for an unauthorized search, then it should be considered only in cases which the prosecution rejects.

After a case has been approved for arraignment by a prosecutor, then any disciplinary action to be taken because evidence is suppressed by the court should be against the prosecutor, not the police officer. The prosecutor invariably has far more time and far more facts available for deliberation, in the calm of his office, than the officer had available when he was forced to make a quick judgment in the confusion of the street.

To stress the logic of this principle to its extreme, if the police officer who questioned Andrew Mallory for seven and one-half hours in 1954 should have been fired from the police force, then the Solicitor General, who argued before the Supreme Court that the questioning was proper, should be disbarred.

There is prospect for improvement in the situation, however. Two important changes under way in law enforcement during recent years, supplemented by a third development still in its infancy, all show promise of vastly improving police performance in evidentiary matters. The changes may eventually eliminate errors at intake and reduce the number of compromises which have prevailed in the past in the prosecutors' office and in the courts.

The most important of these changes has been the advent of general counsels, or legal advisors, employed within large police departments. Police legal advisors were scarce at the time of the 1966 President's Commission on Law Enforcement and Administration of Justice, and those existing at that time usually had very limited roles within their departments.

One of the recommendations of that commission was that every medium- or large-sized police department should employ a skilled lawyer, full time, as its legal advisor, and that smaller departments should arrange for legal advice on a part-time basis.

With impetus from that recommendation, as well as special grant funding by the Law Enforcement Assistance Agency, the presence of police legal advisors has spread through many departments across the country, and a special section has been established within the International Association of Chiefs of Police to assist these officials in coordinating their efforts.

It is a paradox of law enforcement that some senior officials of various criminal justice systems around the country have been slow to endorse the police legal advisor concept and in many cases have actively fought against its adoption. Many prosecutors, many city attorneys, and even some police chiefs have resisted development of police legal advisor programs within their jurisdictions. Indeed, in the District of Columbia it took direct, forceful intervention from the White House staff to overcome the active opposition of the United States Attorney and the City Corporation Counsel and the passive resistance of the chief of police to the temporary hiring of the first legal advisor for the Metropolitan Police Department; a couple of years later, when permanent authorization for the position was being requested, the issue was again escalated to the White House staff level because of efforts by the City Corporation Counsel to have the position assigned to his office and then merely detailed to assist the police chief.

Both prosecuting attorneys and city attorneys will argue that their offices provide ample legal advice to the police — arguments which are seldom, if ever, factual. Certainly prosecutors or their assistants usually are available for advice to individual officers on a case-by-case basis, usually are willing to provide occasional lectures at the police academy, and sometimes if asked, will render formal advice on how the police should cope with some new law or court decision. But these are not the kinds of advice from which aggressive policy changes are fashioned. City attorneys, on the other hand, to the extent that they advise police departments at all on substantial law enforcement issues, usually advise the police only on how to avoid civil suits, a useful point of view but not the only one on which police policy should be formulated.

More than likely the real reason for the opposition from prosecutors and city attorneys to the police legal advisor concept is their knowledge that police departments, provided legal counsel of their own, will be better equipped to challenge the faults of the remainder of the criminal justice system. Such challenges will often be directed at faults within the offices of the prosecutors and the city attorneys. Furthermore, with legal counsel of their own, the police will be able to overcome the frequent response, when the police complain about some prosecutorial decision, that mere police officers cannot be expected to understand the full complexities of the criminal law.

The rationalization that it is police error rather than prosecutor and court policies which result in lost cases in the criminal justice system is frequently argued by prosecutors. For example, during District of Columbia hearings before the Senate Committee on Appropriations, the senior assistant United States Attorney for Criminal Prosecutions testified that the primary reason for so many felony arrests being reduced to misdemeanor charges by his office was that police patrol officers could not be expected to understand all the elements required to prove a crime, and consequently, that reviewing prosecutors had to reduce many police arrests to the lesser charges. Clearly, police officers do from time to time make erroneous charges, but the police error rate is insignificant in comparison to the number of charges reduced or dropped by prosecutors in most systems. At the time of that testimony in 1967, the major reason for reducing felonies to misdemeanors in the District of Columbia was that the judges of the United States District Court, which then had exclusive trial jurisdiction over felonies, flatly refused to take on any additional work load, and the United States Attorney was willing to accommodate them by wholesale reduction of felony charges to misdemeanor charges so that the trials then became the responsibility of the lower ranking Court of General Sessions.

Less easy to understand is why some police chiefs object to having their own, independent counsel. One possible reason is that the chief of police does not want to offend his prosecutor or city attorney, if one or both of them objects. Another reason may be that the police chief does not want to take on the added challenges and concomitant responsibility which having an aggressive counsel will impose on him; the symptoms of this latter condition, reluctance to use aggressive counsel, can also be found in some police departments where legal advisors are hired, but relegated to routine, bureaucratic roles.

Not surprisingly, the value of the legal advisor to a police department depends heavily on the caliber of attorney hired for the job. However, while the legal advisor program suffers in some cities where low salary scales are insufficient to attract experienced, sophisticated attorneys who can move about with confidence through the criminal justice system, everywhere that police legal advisors have been employed and used properly they have served to improve relationships between the police, the prosecutors, and the courts. History almost certainly will prove the advent of the police legal advisor concept to be a very important change for improvement of law enforcement.

A second major change of recent years, a change directly related to the employment of police legal advisors, is the increasing activity of police departments in making rules or setting standards for themselves.

This rule-making concept also relates to the work of the President's Commission on Law Enforcement and Administration of Justice, which recommended that police departments develop and enunciate policies giving their officers specific guidelines for common situations requiring exercise of police discretion.

Police departments have often been reluctant, for a variety of reasons, to publish as departmental orders clear guidelines in areas open to judgment of the officer on the street.

One example is in guidelines for use of deadly force. In practical police work, use of deadly force usually relates to firing of the service revolver. Until very recent times most police departments would merely publish the common-law guidelines on use of deadly force, which permit shooting a person fleeing arrest after commission of *any* felony. These broad guidelines were used, even though most police administrators know that many crimes which by statute are felonies are inappropriate for use of deadly force to apprehend a culprit who is almost certain to obtain a very light sentence from the court. Knowing these facts, police administrators would often frown at the notion of shooting at fleeing suspects in such cases, but seldom would issue direct orders prohibiting such shootings.

This reluctance to issue direct orders in matters of police discretion seems all the more strange when one considers the general tendency of police departments, especially large and medium-sized departments, to issue very explicit written instructions on almost every conceivable subject. Written orders are issued on what uniform to wear, how the hair is to be cut, how forms are to be filled out, even how one is to sign his own name in police correspondence — first name, middle initial, last name.

More so than most municipal agencies, police departments believe in spelling out in writing and in explicit detail how things are to be done. The reason for this tendency towards regimentation is that police departments have large groups of officers, particularly patrol officers, who operate as individual agents with minimum direct supervision, and with expectation that any one of them will be ready at any moment to deal with almost any emergency — be it traffic, criminal, injury, lost child, a littering violation, or myriad other events occurring on the beat or post of the patrol officer. These explicit instructions in how to perform a wide variety of tasks are necessary to operation of the police system.

It is a paradox that this tendency toward explicit instructions for housekeeping and procedural details has not heretofore been carried over into discretionary matters. It is illogical that a police department will instruct a police officer in great detail on how to aim his revolver and squeeze the trigger, but then only hint to him that there are some types of fleeing felons which the department would prefer that he not shoot. It is strange that a department will instruct a man in great detail in the mechanical aspects of driving a police vehicle in response to emergency calls, then only hint that he should be careful about rushing through city streets and intersections in a fashion unnecessarily likely to cause an accident. It is peculiar that a department will instruct a police officer explicitly in how to fill in the forms for an eyewitness identification, then hesitate at specifying the period of time after an offense has been committed during which on-the-street eyewitness identification will be permitted by department policy.

External and internal politics contribute to persistence of this contradiction. Police administrators are under very strong pressures to urge their men to pursue and apprehend criminals to the fullest extent *permissible* under the law. Too, as a matter of morale, police officers expect their superiors to urge them to full pursuit of criminals and to support their actions when they approach the brink of permissible conduct, and even sometimes when they go over the brink.

Some of these pressures on the police administrator are appropriate, some are inappropriate; some are logical, others are without logic; but — good or bad — these pressures are real, and the police administrator disregards them only at his peril.

The dilemma of the police administrator preparing to issue guidelines in discretionary areas is that guidelines issued by him must be more restrictive than the statutory and case law of the time. Inevitably, the police administrator who issues guidelines limiting an officer in discretionary areas must circumscribe the activities of the officer even more stringently than does the law.

The police administrator who does issue such guidelines is in a sense assuming a role traditionally assigned to the courts, the role of limiting the actions and perhaps the effectiveness of the police. This role of the courts, of course, is a very unpopular one in many quarters, particularly among law enforcement officials; thus, it is not surprising that a police administrator may be hesitant about taking it on unless he can see that by doing so he will receive some effective return to his primary objectives.

Another reason for the reluctance of the police administrator to publish to his men guidelines which are more restrictive than the actual law is the danger that the police officer, or the government which employs him, will be exposed to civil suit if the policeman takes some action which would be authorized under the law but which is prohibited by the guidelines; for example, there is a considerable danger of added exposure to civil suit if a police officer shoots a fleeing auto thief (a felon in many jurisdictions), permissible under the common law, if shooting at fleeing auto thieves is prohibited by guidelines issued by his own department.

The final reason for hesitance of police administrators to issue guidelines in discretionary areas has been simply the difficulty of constructing such guidelines, particularly with the limited legal advice which has been available to the police in the past. Such advice as was available tended to be from prosecutors who, for one thing, were usually too busy with their own problems to undertake the substantial task of guideline formulation for the police and who, for another thing, brought their advice to the police cast in terms advantageous to the prosecutor but not necessarily advantageous to the police.

The employment of police legal advisors for police departments shows promise of gradually overcoming all of these factors which historically have contributed to reluctance of police administrators to control the discretion vested in their men.

The police legal advisor bridges the traditional communications gap between the police and the prosecutors and the courts. Having an appreciation of both operational problems of the police and legalistic problems of the prosecutors and courts, he can assist the police administrator in pressing police objectives through the remainder of the criminal justice system. At the same time, the legal advisor is equipped by education and experience to clearly inform the police administrator and his subordinates on the problems of the prosecutor, couched in language and in contexts more palatable to the police.

Equipped with not only a knowledge of what the statutes and current case law provide, but also an appreciation of developing trends in court decisions which indicate what will be the case law of the future, the competent legal advisor is capable of constructing discretionary guidelines which, while they may be slightly more restrictive than existing law, can be fashioned to be less restrictive than anticipated future case law.

Ideally, of course, if reasonable guidelines controlling police discretion become the pattern across the nation, courts will be content to let the guidelines remain as the accepted standard of conduct rather than handing down increasingly restrictive rulings.

This desirable situation would have several benefits to law enforcement. First, as the guidelines are constructed with careful appreciation of the practical problems of the police, they are likely to be much more workable than broad rulings devised by judges in adversary hearings where, unfortunately, judges seldom enjoy the privilege of full, unbiased information. Second, being constructed with a view to application in all kinds of situations rather than on the case-by-case basis of most court decision, administrative guidelines are less likely to generate aberrant effects when transferred from one factual situation to another. Also, being administrative procedures rather than statutory law or case law, police guidelines can easily be amended if some unexpected effect does occur, thus overriding the serious fault of the exclusionary rule that, once the rule has been established as the law, there is no effective way to challenge it without making, prosecuting, and convicting on illegal arrests. Thirdly, as police departments begin to internalize as their own policies and orders, guidelines for protection of the accused in criminal cases, the basic objective of the exclusionary rules — protection against unreasonable searches and seizures — will be more nearly obtained, overcoming the principal fault of the present system that most abuses rarely come to the attention of the court but are screened out by the prosecutorial no-papering process.

There have been some very significant beginnings in the construction of police guidelines in discretionary matters. In recent years, many of the better police departments have adopted explicit guidelines to limit use of deadly force; in many departments, the common-law authority to shoot at *any* fleeing felon has been supplanted by department regulations which prohibit shooting at fleeing felons in offenses limited solely to crimes against property or other crimes not involving danger of injury or death to innocent victims.

Police departments also have increasingly adopted regulations circumscribing the way in which officers respond to emergency calls, requiring them to be much more cautious when exceeding the speed limit or when passing through red lights or other traffic signals, in order to reduce the danger of vehicular accidents, injuries, and death in these situations.

The foregoing are two examples of guidelines controlling police officer discretion in general operational matters. Examples of guidelines more directly related to the exclusionary rule processes are the Washington Metropolitan Police Department guidelines with respect to eyewitness identifications, issued to provide members of the force clear instructions for implementing the three Supreme Court decisions of 1967 on that subject, and the guidelines with respect to search of automobiles, issued to clarify the very complex case law with respect to those searches. These guidelines are printed in the appendix.

The eyewitness identification guidelines furnish an interesting case study of the problems encountered in guideline construction and in the advantages and disadvantages from the construction.

A very important question encountered during construction of these guidelines was: what is the maximum period of time following the offense that an eyewitness identification will be permitted without the formality of a lineup? The answer to this question was not to be found in the Supreme Court decisions; if the department established too short a period of time, it not only would impose an unnecessary work load on its officers, but also would risk losing cases which might be held valid by the courts; on the other hand, the question of the length of time to be allowed was central to the issue, and unless it were answered, the guidelines would be practically meaningless. The period of one hour was finally selected, admittedly somewhat arbitrarily. But the fact that the one-hour time period was arrived at arbitrarily is not so important as the fact that this discretion was exercised by the administration of the department, on an overall policy basis, rather than by individual police officers on a case-by-case basis.

The real promise of administrative guidelines, that they may have an effect on criminal justice far beyond simply the operations of the police department, is demonstrated by the reaction of the courts to the eyewitness identification order. In two separate cases (*U.S. v. Perry, U.S. v. Ash*), following issuance of the eyewitness identification order, the United States District Court of Appeals for the District of Columbia (which traditionally has been a very liberal court), refused to uphold challenges to the police lineup processes, basing their refusal principally on the fact that the department has through its administrative regulation insured a sense of fairness to the accused in the lineup processes. This response validates the notion that if police administrators move effectively into the control of discretion, demonstrating a commitment to essential fairness in the handling of criminal cases, the likely result is that continual tightening of the exclusionary rule processes will be abated.

On the other hand, however, the hazard that police administrative guidelines may go further than developing case law is also demonstrated by the eyewitness identification order. Since that order was issued, there have been some indications that the Supreme Court, which has become more conservative with appointments by President Nixon, may re-examine elements of the 1968 lineup rulings, which conceivably could leave the Metropolitan Police Department guidelines more restrictive than new case law.

Insofar as these particular guidelines are concerned, this would not be too drastic a development, as the department could very easily amend them to reflect any new decisions on the subject. But in theory, if there were widespread adoption of administrative guidelines by police agencies across the country on any subject, so that no cases of alleged abuse reached the courts for decision, it is conceivable that police practices might be more restrictive than would be permitted by the courts. This possibility, however, is more theoretical than probable.

The full impact of guideline issuance in police departments will result not so much from what is done in individual departments for themselves, but from comprehensive programs for development of guidelines suitable for implementation in departments across the nation.

Another example of how the police legal advisor can assist the department both in improving its own performance and in insuring that police officers are properly supported by the prosecutor can be found in the Case Review Section of the Metropolitan Police Department, which was established within the Office of the General Counsel to look explicitly at every criminal case (excluding only minor municipal violations) dropped by the prosecutor either by his not presenting the case to court or by nolle prosequi of a case initially presented.

The Case Review Section, staffed by a police lieutenant and two sergeants, reporting direct to the General Counsel, has several purposes. One of its functions is to assist the department in training police personnel to prepare their cases in a manner which will insure that they are suitable for proceeding to trial. As a matter of fact, the section was organized primarily for this single purpose, after a preliminary survey showed that many good arrests were being dropped by the prosecutor primarily because of poorly worded statements and reports prepared by inexperienced, nonverbal patrol officers.

This training process is accomplished both by bringing to the attention of the individual officer and his commanding officer those cases which are dropped by the prosecutor because of officer error, and also by lectures at training sessions by the Case Review Section personnel, who discuss the errors they have found in their review and ways in which these errors can be avoided. In bringing specific officer error cases to the attention of the officers and their supervisors, the department stresses that the objective is to train the officer, not discipline him, unless it is clear that the incident is one of intentional misconduct rather than error.

One might assume that the mere dropping of an arrest would be ample notification to the officer that he had made an error and that, by the experience of having the case dropped, he would automatically be "trained" not to repeat the error in future similar situations. This assumption is, of course, the foundation of the exclusionary rule; it is assumed that if officers see their cases rejected by the prosecutor or by the court, they will thereupon learn to comply with the rule.

But this assumption does not reckon with the realities of criminal justice systems where many cases are dropped by the prosecutor or rejected by the court for a wide variety of reasons not related to officer error. In this situation police officers become blasé about cases being dropped, and police training schools carefully instruct them not to take the dropping of a good arrest as a personal affront; thus only the more astute officers, who seldom make errors in the first place, are likely to perceive correctly when a case is dropped because of their own error. The Case Review Section personnel, however, usually are able to recognize instances of officer error, to bring specific instances to the attention of the individual officers, and to gather examples of persistent officer error for use in police training classes.

A second function of the Case Review Section is to enable the police department and the office of the prosecutor to evaluate enforcement policies carefully when it is found that some practice is resulting in consistent dropping of specific kinds of cases. An example of these kinds of cases is the intrafamily aggravated assaults.

In 1972, when the Case Review Section was established by the Metropolitan Police Department, it was discovered, not surprisingly, that a majority of the arrests dropped without prosecution derived from intrafamily aggravated assaults, more than three-quarters of which are dropped without presentation to the court.

Discovering these data, the police department undertook a very careful review of the cases which had been dropped to determine if there were some practical, better way to handle the problem; the final decision was that there is not. The police officer usually is faced with a situation where one spouse has been seriously and feloniously injured by the other. More often than not, the victim claims at the time a willingness to prosecute; whether or not the victim will prosecute, prudent judgment, for protection of both parties, almost always indicates that an arrest should be made so that the parties are separated until tempers are cooled. Yet, predictably, when the case is presented to the prosecutor for arraignment, the victim either will not show up at all for the hearing, or will appear and decline to prosecute, invoking marital immunity, leaving the prosecutor little choice other than to drop the charge, and at most, to refer the case to the family division of the court.

Ideally, of course, the police officer responding to one of these situations would be able to call a social service worker to the scene for intervention in the dispute and, hopefully, for alleviation of the problem without necessitating an arrest. But social service agencies rarely, if ever, are prepared to respond rapidly to crises of this sort, even during regular office hours, and typically are totally unavailable during nights and weekends, when most of these crises occur.

There has been some experimenting in a few departments with organization of family crisis intervention units, which are essentially designed to train and assign police officers to perform the role of social service workers. This is how police historically have gotten themselves involved in a wide range of nonpolice functions: filling the void left by inaction of the responsible governmental agencies. These family crisis units will undoubtedly succeed as demonstration projects, for demonstration projects seldom if ever are pronounced to be failures. But it is likely that when departments try to expand them sufficiently to deal with all of their family assaults, they will find that the number of family crisis intervention specialists needed to keep a sufficient number available for response to all the crises which occur will require more investment of manpower than they are willing to make (which is one of the reasons why the social service agencies do not provide such a response capability in the first place).

One possible alternative to family crisis intervention specialists is to train many or all patrolmen to deal with these crises through non-arrest counseling of the participants. In the past, this system was informally used by most police departments in America, and is still used today by some. But they don't call it family crisis intervention; instead, they express it as a policy of refusing to take a report and refusing to make an arrest in a family assault situation until after the individual assaulted has applied for a warrant. The difficulty with this policy is that not only does it tend to reduce police protection of lower socioeconomic classes, where most of the calls for police to intervene in these family crises occur, but it also exposes the parties in the dispute to greatly increased danger that one or the other of them will be even more seriously injured, or killed, after the police leave the premises. Prosecutor offices where decisions are made whether to go forward with or to drop family assault cases often have an informal "club" of assistant prosecutors who have dropped such a case or who have declined to issue a warrant at the request of a complaining spouse who later is murdered. It is highly undesirable for police departments to impose this responsibility upon all of its patrol officers, and it is likely that if they did so, they would greatly increase the number of such deaths by eliminating the period for cooling of tempers now furnished by making arrests.

A third purpose of the Case Review Section was, bluntly stated, to establish and maintain a pressure on the prosecutor to go to court with every case having any reasonable chance of success. This does not mean, at least in the District of Columbia in 1972, that the office of the prosecutor was less dedicated to law enforcement than was the police department. With court reorganization, and with strengthening of the Office of the United States Attorney under the Nixon administration, the clear policy of the prosecutor by 1972 was to engage in aggressive prosecution. But even with a policy of aggressive prosecution, there are some factors which encouraged the prosecutor to drop some arrests which, from the police point of view, should have gone forward to court. One of these factors is that, just as the police perceive their success from statistics of the number of crimes reported and of crime closure and arrest rates, the prosecutor measures his success with statistics of his conviction rate. But the prosecutor computes his conviction rate not on the basis of all arrests brought to him, but on the basis of all cases prosecuted by his office in the court. On its face, this basis of computing conviction rates is not at all unreasonable. The prosecutor certainly should not have his conviction rate skewed by improper arrests brought by the police which cannot be presented by him to the court. There really are not that many faulty cases brought in by the police, however; the fact is that most cases are dropped by the prosecutor, not because the arrest was faulty, but simply because there is insufficient trial or jury appeal (as in the case of possession of minor amounts of marijuana), or when the complainant does not want to prosecute (as in the case of family assault). Particularly in a large and busy court system, there is considerable incentive for the prosecutor to improve his conviction rate by dropping without prosecution some good cases which have only borderline possibility of conviction.

Some of this is certain to happen and is simply a practical solution to backlogged court calendars and excessive work load of a busy prosecutor's office. On the other hand, aggressive prosecution of most criminal cases is important, both to strengthen the effectiveness of police efforts and to maintain morale of officers making the arrests. This, a part of the reason for the Police Department Case Review Section, was to insure that the practice of dropping borderline cases was kept within reasonable bounds and did not revert to the excesses of the 1960's.

A final factor sometimes resulting in erroneous dropping of cases by the prosecutor is that many assistant prosecutors are very inexperienced young attorneys who, being inexperienced, often make errors of judgment when reviewing cases. Just as the police case review process makes police officers more careful in preparing their cases for presentation to the prosecutor, it also makes prosecutorial assistants more cautious in deciding whether or not to prosecute a given case, motivating them to consult their superiors in borderline situations.

The Case Review Section was begun early in 1972. At the time it was begun, 30 percent of the cases being presented to the United States Attorney were being dropped without prosecution. Six months later, prosecutorial dropping of charges was down to 23 percent, a rate which the department concluded was likely to prevail. More than one-half of those cases were family assault cases; if those cases were excluded, the rate of cases dropped by the prosecutor would be less than 10 percent.

One point of clarification needs to be made with regard to these data. The 23 percent rate for cases dropped refers to situations where every charge is dropped against the individual arrested; if the measure is taken of the total number of charges (as contrasted to arrestees) presented to and dropped by the prosecutor, the rate was computed to be 33 percent (the difference reflects primarily the process of plea-bargaining, where an individual charged with several crimes is prosecuted on only one or two of the offenses).

Both the police department and the office of the prosecutor had expected to find that faulty searches and seizures would be a significant reason for prosecutorial dropping of cases, but six months after establishment of the Case Review Section, it was found there were only fifteen cases out of fourteen hundred presented to the prosecutor where faulty search led to the decision not to prosecute. Even those were close cases, where review of the statements of facts indicated that the officer made the proper street decision, but where later review showed the question too close for taking to trial.

Thus, the work of the Metropolitan Police Department Case Review Section has demonstrated, once again, the great care which must be exercised in making assumptions on the basis of gross criminal justice system statistics. It is easy, when one sees a 23 percent dropping of cases by the prosecutor, to assume that such data reflect a high rate of police officer error or of prosecutor carelessness. However, when the data are broken down into various classes of crimes, and examination is made of individual offenses within the various classes, it is found that practically all of the cases dropped by the prosecutor involved legal and appropriate arrests by the police, but simply were not appropriate for prosecution either because of witness problems or because of presumed jury reaction.

On the other hand, it is important to remember that when the Case Review Section was established, nearly 30 percent of all cases were dropped by the prosecutor, and that the reduction from the 30 percent rate to the 23 percent rate undoubtedly reflects some significant improvements in the performance of both the police and the prosecutors.

To summarize, two major changes which have been taking place in police departments during recent years have been the advent of police legal advisors or general counsels added to the policymaking processes of police departments, and the recent trend, growing out of the advent of legal advisors, towards police rule-making in discretionary areas. And in at least one police department, these changes have been supplemented by a case review unit established specifically to improve police performance in preparation of cases for prosecution and, concomitantly, in improving police compliance with exclusionary processes.

There is a great temptation to argue that these changes will revolutionize the judicial process and eventually totally supplant the exclusionary rules in criminal prosecutions, but the promise of this occurrence seems unlikely. No matter how much police strengthen their own standards of fairness, there will be continual challenges to the way things are done and, in the long run, continual liberalization of court decisions as a result of those challenges.

Whatever the police do to improve their administrative rule-making, there always will be conflict between police objectives and objectives of some court decisions. An interesting example of the continuing problem occurred when the United States Court of Appeals for the District of Columbia held in *Robinson* (1972) that in taking a person into custody for a traffic charge, where no further evidence of the original offense charged is likely to be found, the police must confine their search of the person to simply a frisk for weapons. On the other hand, the District of Columbia Court of Appels, which is the senior local appeal court in the District of Columbia, held in *Simmons* (1973) that an officer is entitled to make a thorough search on any full custody arrest. As there is no effective way for an officer to be certain what he may find in a thorough search, and therefore no effective way for him to know whether the crime will be prosecuted as a local offense or as a federal offense (as in a case where he finds illegal narcotics), the department was forced to adopt a policy of instructing its men to follow the rulings of the District of Columbia Court of Appeals, a decision which might otherwise be stated as instructing police officers to disregard the ruling of the United States District Court of Appeals.

This state of affairs continued until the Supreme Court finally ruled against the United States Court of Appeals in *Robinson* in December 1973.

This experience, perhaps as much as anything, reinforces the need to recognize that police administrative rule-making is a far from simple matter.

6

Organizational Concepts

IT IS NOT PRACTICAL to discuss police organizational concepts without casting them in terms of the traditional principles. However, while this chapter is arranged under the headings of traditional organizational principles, it should be made clear at the outset that the purpose here is not so much to reinforce those principles as to discuss useful variations from them.

Ordinarily, when one sets out to establish or to review an organization, he takes into account the following considerations:

DEFINITION OF OBJECTIVES. A basic principle of management is that, to be successful over a long period of time, any organization must have its objectives well defined in both broad and precise terms.

CATEGORIZATION OF FUNCTIONS BY SIMILARITY, LOCATION, AND TIME. This process is the essence of the organization, for it is on this basis that organizational charts are drawn and units are assigned to do separate jobs under individual middle-management leadership.

SEPARATION OF LINE AND STAFF FUNCTIONS. This separation is almost automatically invoked during the categorization of

functions. It relates to separation of line functions (in police departments, usually referring to direct crime prevention, arrest and apprehension) from staff support functions (in police departments, usually
referring to such elements as communications, records, and personnel).

DETERMINING TO SPECIALIZE INSTEAD OF GENERALIZE.
This process also derives somewhat automatically during the categorization of functions. However, as will be discussed later, the process of specialization versus generalization has significant impact on
an organization, particularly on the police organization, and should
be subjected to careful, repeated consideration and review.

LIMITING SPAN OF CONTROL. Quite clearly, there are practical
limits to the number of subordinates whom a single supervisor can
effectively oversee. Although there are numerous exceptions based on
tasks being performed, locations of performance, and degree of skill
and proficiency of the supervisor and of the subordinates, it is generally assumed that a single supervisor can oversee effectively from
five to ten subordinates.

INSURING UNITY OF COMMAND. The principle of unity of command requires that every subordinate should be responsible to and
should receive orders from one and only one superior. Some authorities consider unity of command to be a basic and immutable tenet
of effective organization; however, as will be discussed, senior government executives (for example, chiefs of police) rarely enjoy the
privilege of having a single superior, and there are numerous other
examples extending down to middle and lower echelons of organizations where purposeful violations of unity of command are both useful and effective.

ASSIGNING AUTHORITY COMMENSURATE WITH RESPON-
SIBILITY. This principle holds that any subordinate assigned a responsibility to accomplish a task must be given conmmensurate
authority to perform that task; vice versa, the assignment of au-

thority to an individual imposes commensurate responsibility and accountability for the way that authority is exercised.

UTILIZING THE INFORMAL AS WELL AS FORMAL ORGANI-ZATION. Organizational purists, who believe that organizations always must be clearly defined in statements of objectives and in rectangles on organizational charts, argue that the informal organization should not be permitted to develop and, if it does develop, should be aggressively eliminated. However, executives who prefer results to purity of principle often recognize the informal organization as a useful and even a legitimate tool for accomplishing objectives.

The foregoing are organization concepts which have been well defined in numerous works on organizational theory and which should be carefully considered by the police executive. Once the executive has carefully considered these concepts and comprehends their purposes and meanings, he should not be reluctant to deviate from one or more of them in order to accomplish legitimate goals. The remainder of this chapter is devoted to discussion of how these principles often are applied in police organizations and to examination of some of the purposeful and accidental deviations which occur.

Definition of objectives of an organization is not a simple task. As has already been discussed in this book, it is particularly difficult to define the objectives of a typical police organization.

If one asks a police executive to state the objectives of his organization, he ordinarily will list prevention of crime, apprehension and prosecution of offenders, maintenance of public order, insuring smooth flow of vehicular traffic, and preventing vehicular traffic accidents.

The foregoing describe in broad terms the objectives of the usual general police agency, but the listing is not always effective if challenged for details in terms of listing headings or in terms of how each objective is achieved.

For example, while prevention of crime is often stated as an objective of the police organization, the police consider themselves and are considered by the public to be responsible for prevention of only certain kinds of crimes. They are rarely considered responsible for preventing or dealing with such crimes as income tax evasion, stock fraud manipulations, building code violations, or many other acts which are defined as criminal offenses in the business and technical world. The police are not ordinarily considered responsible for preventing some common-law crime; for example, the municipal police are not expected to engage in active prevention of such offenses as employee theft or shoplifting.

More complicated than the question of what kinds of crime the police will be responsible for preventing is the question of how the police department as a whole and how the subordinate elements of the police department will go about preventing crime. Patrol is the traditional method of prevention, supplemented in recent years by innovative tactical methods, such as canine patrols, casual-clothes units, helicopter patrols, and a variety of other systems which lead away from the generalist patrol officer of the past into specialization of functions and of police personnel.

An adjunct to prevention of crime is the development of measures of crime and the establishment of reporting systems which will produce statistical data and provide reports for prosecution of offenders, if apprehended. The paperwork incidental to these reporting systems creates a need for staff units for assimilation and storage of the data and also imposes a heavy work load on line personnel who must prepare and forward the reports which are presumed necessary.

Apprehension of offenders is considered an important objective by most police organizations because of the presumption that apprehension and effective prosecution of offenders will deter crime both by temporarily removing past offenders from the streets and by serving as an example to potential new offenders. However, as discussed elsewhere in this book, apprehension of offenders is more accurately classed as performance rather than as an objective.

Preservation of public order is a function which has come to have much greater priority in recent times, when disorder has been more prevalent, than was common during calmer years. The increased priority of this function demonstrates the flexibility with which definition of objectives must be viewed.

Maintenance of the flow of vehicular traffic and prevention of traffic accidents are functions which the police share with traffic engineers, and are functions of which many police administrators would be pleased to divest their organization. Significant proportions of police manpower and effort must be devoted to these functions, and during peak traffic periods, particularly during aberrational weather conditions, performance of these functions by the police may leave the city unserved in other areas of police responsibility. Additionally, traffic enforcement seldom improves the image of the police in the eyes of the public, particularly the middle-class public, which strongly supports most nontraffic police efforts.

But the traffic objectives of the government require wide-ranging patrol forces and substantial pools of manpower instantly available for emergencies, both characteristics of a police department which would be expensive to duplicate solely for traffic purposes. Additionally, police administrators often note the value of traffic enforcement in both prevention of other crime and in apprehension of offenders. Because of this observation, it has become common practice, especially with advent of computerized traffic and offender status systems, for police agencies to urge their patrol officers to make frequent courtesy traffic stops and spot checks as a method of apprehending not only automobile thieves but the entire range of criminal offenders.

Within the traffic function an interesting example occurred which shows how the police objective can become muddled and ill-defined, with a resulting waste of manpower and other resources. As a part of the objective of preventing traffic accidents, a subobjective developed of selective enforcement, that is, the apprehension of traffic offenders at times and places of high accident frequency. To implement the selective enforcement subobjective, a third-level objective of traffic accident investigation, reporting and analysis, was defined. During the 1930's and 1940's, the traffic accident investigation objective became highly developed, almost to the point of a pseudo-science; many departments established large units devoted exclusively to traffic accident investigation; many police officers devoted full careers to developing expertise as traffic accident investigators; and in some departments, where traffic accident investigators had the greatest influence, it was common practice to require police officers to make a report of every traffic accident coming to their knowledge.

It was not until the 1960's, when police departments began carefully to analyze utilization of resources in order to shift manpower to crime fighting, that city police agencies began questioning the value of reporting every bent fender coming to attention of the police. It was clear that some form of traffic accident reporting was necessary to keep traffic engineers and the police informed of changes in traffic hazards, but it was questionable that a report was needed from the police for every single accident in order to achieve that purpose. For one thing, in traffic-conscious jurisdictions it had become fairly standard practice to require drivers involved in traffic accidents to make reports on their own to the financial responsibility division of the state for any accident involving major property damage. Even though these reports were subject to the faults of error through inexpert preparation and through self-serving declarations of fault, they certainly were sufficient to obtain, without the costly investment of police manpower, generalized analyses of traffic accident patterns.

A secondary presumed function of traffic accident reports was to provide basis for prosecution of drivers charged with traffic offenses as a result of accidents. In most cases, however, where fault was clear enough for the officer to make a traffic charge, and where the accident involved only property damage not of a substantial amount, the charge was seldom defended at all or, if it were, was not defended vigorously enough to warrant extraordinarily careful preparation for the prosecution. In relatively minor traffic accidents, unless the offense is some very serious one such as drunken driving or reckless driving, there is substantial question whether it is worth the effort of the government formally to charge and prosecute the individual at fault, since the inconvenience of the accident and its effect on his insurance are themselves usually substantially greater deterrents to bad driving in his case than are the relatively minor fines usually imposed for traffic offenses. Arrests for moving violations not involving an accident are, however, another matter.

The third purpose of traffic accident reporting, and perhaps the one which most served to perpetuate it, was that it was highly useful to the automobile insurance industry which, by simply obtaining police traffic accident reports, was able to save substantial amounts which otherwise would have to be spent hiring more of its own investigators. This function, the providing of records for determination of civil liability, as contrasted to criminal liability, is one which the police have successfully avoided in all areas of their responsibility except in traffic accident investigation.

Observing the absence of logic to what they were doing, many departments during the 1960's changed their regulations to require police traffic accident reports only in cases of bodily injury or of very substantial property damage and, concomitantly, de-emphasized traffic accident investigation as a subobjective of their department.

There are some interesting similarities between the question of whether or not reports should be made, stored, and analyzed for minor traffic accidents, and whether or not reports should be made, stored, and analyzed for some types of crime, such as minor larcenies or intrafamily assaults. Because of nonreporting by the public, the police do not make reports for many very minor larcenies nor for most shoplifting offenses. It seems likely that future decades will find police agencies becoming far more sophisticated about the objectives of their crime reporting, as they are now becoming regarding traffic accident reporting, with the result that some offense reports will be simply omitted from reporting systems as superfluous and unnecessarily time-consuming exercises.

Categorization of functions by similarity, location, and time is accomplished in medium- and large-sized police agencies by first assigning the function to some unit or units of the department for performance and then determining how the function and its performance will be categorized for location and time.

Traditionally, prevention of crime is assumed to be the primary function of the general service police department, and patrol is assumed to be the fundamental unit for obtaining that objective. Most departments will, therefore, establish a patrol division as the basic and principal line unit of the department, containing most of its manpower. The other nearly indispensable line unit of the department will be the criminal investigation or detective division.

Formation of just these two line divisions, patrol and detective, complicates the definition of objectives, functions, and responsibilities of each. In most police departments the detective division investigates only certain kinds of crimes (for example, murder, rape, major robberies and major burglaries, check and fraud offenses), and the patrol division not only retains a joint responsibility for apprehension in those crimes, but also is left with responsibility for investigation of less major crimes, which of course are far more numerous. The consequence is that in almost every department there is an overlapping of responsibility between the patrol division and the detective division, and in most large departments this overlapping is recognized by the formal establishment of investigative units of detectives within the patrol division.

Another line unit found within most medium- or large-sized departments is the vice division. In some cases, the vice division will be a part of the detective division. But the special problems of vice enforcement (that is, gambling, narcotics, prostitution) persuade most police chiefs to establish a vice division as a special category reporting directly to the chief or through not more than one senior official. For this reason, vice enforcement typically will be separated from the ordinary detective division, although the establishment of a vice division usually does not altogether relieve the patrol division of the function.

To guard against the persistent potential for corruption of police by vice operators, the best practice is to make vice enforcement formally and clearly a direct responsibility of at least two separate divisions of the department (usually the vice division and the patrol division), which report to the chief of police through separate chains of command. For this reason, even though the vice division is performing a line function, it often will be found placed organizationally among staff units.

Many large departments also maintain a separate division as a line unit. As with detective and vice divisions, the traffic division does only a part of the job; the patrol division usually is expected to investigate traffic accidents, enforce traffic regulations, and keep traffic moving when personnel of the specialized division are unavailable.

Other divisions ordinarily construed to be line divisions are such units as youth, tactical, canine, helicopter divisions, and similar units which engage in what is presumed to be direct prevention of crime and apprehension of offenders, and all of which share their responsibility with the basic patrol division.

Categorization of these line functions by location and time varies, dependent primarily on size of the jurisdiction and of the department. In small and medium-sized cities, it is common to have little or no intermediate geographic organization of functions between the division level and the patrolman on the beat, except that a sergeant or lieutenant may be given sector control during his tour of duty. In larger cities, where geographic size is a greater consideration, it is common for the patrol division to be separated into police precincts (or districts, bailiwicks, and so on). Although the patrol division is frequently so divided, except in the very largest cities it is uncommon for the other divisions such as criminal investigations, vice, and traffic to be broken into geographic units, except to the extent to which they work directly within the patrol division geographic units.

The third division of functions, temporal, also tends to be dependent primarily on the method of operating the patrol division. Again, it is common for only the patrol division to have a highly structured, formal organization for continuity of supervision of functions during the night time. Frequently, the patrol division commander for the night shift will exercise some informal supervision over personnel from other divisions working during hours when their regular supervisors are off duty; another common arrangement is that the department will have a supervisory official nominally in charge of all elements of the department during the night tour duty, but who will concentrate his supervision on the patrol division except when some major occurrence brings his attention to personnel of other divisions working those hours.

Traditionalists in organizational theory sometimes stress importance of the *separation between line and staff functions,* emphasizing that it is the line units which perform the basic mission of the organization and the staff units which both support the line and the chief executive in his overseeing of the line.

Examples within police departments of clearly staff functions are such units as records divisions, personnel divisions, communications divisions, and inspections divisions. The records division exemplifies a unit which exists almost exclusively for the purpose of servicing the line function, by establishing, maintaining, and furnishing records needed for the primary objective of the department; ordinarily the records division will have practically no function except to service the line.

The personnel division varies in function from department to department. In small and medium-sized cities, and even in some very large cities, the important aspects of the personnel function, such as the hiring and firing of personnel and the development of important personnel policies, are performed by some central personnel agency of the jurisdiction, so that the personnel function left to the police department is little more than a record-keeping function which serves the line operation. However, in police departments to which are delegated full, or major, personnel responsibility and authority, the personnel division not only serves the record-keeping function, but also operates as a staff unit both to advise the chief of police on personnel matters and to insure implementation of his personnel policies throughout the line operations.

The police communications division is an example of a unit having "staff" authority to issue direct orders to line personnel in contradiction of the usual principle of unity of command. The communications division, in a sense, both serves the line and directs the line. The dispatcher has no command authority over the patrol officer, yet he has authority, within the communications guidelines of the department, to direct the line officer to undertake missions and to determine, on the basis of the reporting back by the patrolman, whether or not the mission has been properly accomplished. In the well-organized department, of course, radio communications are fully monitored by officials in the field who have implicit authority to override the dispatcher if, in their judgment, such action is necessary, but in practice this authority is seldom exercised.

The inspections division exemplifies those units which hardly service the line operation at all, but which act in a staff capacity to assist the chief administrator in his overseeing of the department. Inspections is probably the classic example of a purely staff function, which has no output nor "product" of its own other than its assisting of the overall operation of the department.

Notwithstanding these discussions of what is line and what is staff, the distinction is not all that clear in many departments, and the administrator often chooses to use a unit of the line to assist him in a staff capacity. For instance, the traffic division, a line unit, may also act as a staff unit, responsible for keeping the chief of police advised of departmental needs to insure proper traffic flow and traffic enforcement throughout the city and throughout the department.

Similarly, vice unit commanders and detective division commanders often are held responsible both for staff oversight of department-wide performance within the areas of their specialization and for line responsibility in the performance of their own personnel.

The distinction between staff and line is useful as a reminder to all employees of the basic purposes of the department and as a clarification of the sometimes complex relationships and lines of authority in middle-management levels.

Too frequently, however, that distinction is not clearly understood, even by some middle-managers. Staff personnel often delude themselves by thinking that their function, whatever it may be, is the primary objective of the department and that the line function and line personnel are there to serve their function. Sometimes this feeling of self-importance derives from the fact that the staff unit, such as the communications division in a major police department, is virtually indispensable to the operation; sometimes it derives from the fact, as in the case of a personnel division, that even its lower ranking employees come into more frequent contact with middle and senior executives of the department than do lower ranking patrol personnel; to some extent the self-importance derives from the simple fact that the staff unit is housed within a headquarters building or on the same floor as the executive offices of the department, so that its location implies importance.

Whatever the reason for the self-assumed importance, a common fault of a staff unit is that if given the opportunity, it will shift undesirable elements of its work load to line, operating units that the staff unit is supposed to be serving. For example, the complaint clerk in the dispatch center, instead of carefully explaining to a caller that the police do not perform some function (for example, a civil matter such as eviction of a roomer for nonpayment of rent), may elect to dispatch a patrol car to "see the complainant." Or the data processing division, to eliminate work for its coding clerks, may devise forms which impose on patrol officers in the field the responsibility for entering computer codes as they prepare the form. Or the records unit may press through procedures to decentralize to field units some records or to duplicate within field units some of its records in order to avoid having to respond to inquiries from the field.

To some extent, this shifting of staff work load to the field is necessary and, if done carefully and deliberately in accordance with policies of the chief administrator, it is entirely appropriate.

For example, the field patrolman may think of the dispatcher as having an easy job, away from the rigors of weather and the hazards of police work; but the fact is that in many cities the dispatcher is harassed, particularly during peak work load periods, by as much work as he can reasonably handle. Consequently, while there may be some periods of the day when the dispatcher has time to spare for engaging in courteous conversations with irate callers on nonpolice matters, during peak work load periods the dispatcher may be hard pressed just to answer all the calls and to insure prompt attention to those involving potential emergencies; at times such as these, the pressure on the dispatcher is to quickly terminate each call with assurance that a police patrolman will be dispatched, and to get on with answering the next call. But times such as these, when the dispatcher has the least opportunity for screening calls, are also the times when patrolmen are very busy and, therefore, are the times when screening of calls is most needed. Still, from the overall viewpoint of the department and the community, the predominant pressure on the dispatcher at that time must be to answer the next incoming call, for it may be a report of a very serious crime in progress, a fact which the police department cannot determine without having its phones answered; so the informal system evolves whereby the dispatcher does minimal screening during peak periods, except to give priority in dispatching to the more important calls.

The seemingly simple answer to this problem is to assign more personnel to the dispatcher function, but this may be an undesirable alternative; to insure ample personnel at peak dispatch periods would result in maintenance of an excessive number of unoccupied dispatcher personnel during low work load periods. From the viewpoint of the police chief, the better alternative unquestionably is to concentrate his resources for peak work loads in patrol functions, where at least theoretically the excess personnel will be reasonably well occupied during low work load periods in preventive patrol, if in nothing else.

Somewhat the same consideration, the fact that concentration of potentially surplus personnel in patrol is preferable to assignment of personnel resources to staff functions, may also persuade the administrator that it is better to have patrol personnel doing some incidental coding functions for a data processing unit than to assign additional personnel to the data processing division.

Determining to specialize instead of generalize should be undertaken with deliberate care. Three basic problems with specialized units are that they tend to develop an esprit de corps which implies that their personnel are better than ordinary police officers, that their limited specialty has more concentrated importance than the diffuse functions of the patrol division, seeming to imply that the specialized unit is more important than the basic patrol function, and sometimes by necessity, sometimes by preference, the specialized unit may contrive to transfer less desirable aspects of its work to the patrol function.

A fourth problem with specialized units, one of the most persistent problems in police administration and one which no large police department has yet adequately solved, is that specialized units have a tendency to draw off high-quality manpower from the patrol division. This results from several factors. First, specialized units such as planning units, field inspection units, internal affairs units, and training units perform functions which require logical-thinking, verbal personnel. Secondly, because the work performed by those units is often used by the chief of police and other senior officials of the department for decision making and affirmative actions, often in matters with high public visibility, there can be far less toleration of error by subordinate personnel than in the patrol division; paradoxically, both police agencies and the public they serve are generally more tolerant of an occasional erroneous arrest and even an erroneous shooting of a citizen than they are of sloppy administrative work by the department.

The need of staff units for quality personnel with verbal abilities is reinforced by the fact that the relatively small size of the staff unit (in proportion to operating functions such as the patrol division) makes it very difficult for the staff unit to absorb lower-quality personnel by finding or defining lower-priority assignments for them to perform.

This diversion of high-quality personnel from line units to specialized units has been alleviated in some departments by increased reliance on civilian personnel instead of police officers for administrative, technical, and clerical work. But for a variety of reasons, conversion of these assignments from police to civilian employees is not always an easy answer.

It is traditional in American police organizations to think of the police department as a generalist organization and as an organization of generalists. The police department often is called upon to fill the void left by nonperformance of other government agencies. For example, in many large cities the police department shares responsibility for enforcing licensing laws, zoning regulations, building regulations, fire regulations, and a variety of similar functions which are the specific responsibility of other municipal agencies which have their own field inspectors. Additionally, police officers are often expected to report such things as potholes in roadways, fallen trees, and health hazards. In many jurisdictions, the police have primary responsibility for removal of abandoned automobiles, which essentially is a sanitation function.

This sharing of responsibility with specialized agencies of government derives partly from the fact that the police department usually was among the first agencies formed by the local government, so that the police department naturally began as a generalist agency with responsibility for many functions, for which it often retained concurrent jurisdiction after a specialized agency took over primary responsibility. For example, when a jurisdiction adopts a licensing ordinance, even though some special office may be established to issue licenses, during the beginning years of the ordinance it likely will be considered more economical to use the police for license enforcement than to hire special license inspectors. What eventually will happen, however, is that as licenses and types of licenses become more numerous, and the problem more complex, either the police department will find it necessary to establish a special unit of license officers, or the city licensing office will press for establishment of its own corps of specialist license inspectors; in either event, the establishment of the specialist unit frequently will not absolve the general patrol officer from continuing to share responsibility in the licensing area.

A basic reason for this assigning of diverse functions to the police department is that the police department does in most jurisdictions have a relatively large pool of manpower on patrol. The patrol officers, seeming and in some cases actually, are not totally occupied (except in patrolling) during much of their work day. Also, in most urban jurisdictions the police patrol is so organized that some patrol officer can be expected to pass through just about every area of accessible public space at least weekly, if not daily. Consequently, government administrators see it as inexpensive (indeed, hardly expensive at all) to have the patrol officer on the beat responsible for reporting to the highway department such things as potholes in the roadway, or to the licensing department such things as new businesses opening; separate patrols for each of those purposes obviously would cost more.

Likewise, as police patrols are available around the clock, every day of the week, most government administrators consider it less expensive to make police responsible for barricading and placing warning lights on serious depressions or other hazards in roadways at night than to maintain highway department personnel on a twenty-four-hour basis for that purpose. Again, though, as with the example of licensing inspection, as the jurisdiction increases in size, traffic, and complexity, it is likely to be found necessary to establish, either in the police department or in some other government agency, specialist units to handle all or part of those problems.

For example, while the patrol officer in the quiet suburb or in a suburb-like residential section of a large city may have ample time during a tour of duty for listing potholes in the roadways or for placing barricades on highway hazards, his counterpart in busy sections of the central city is likely to be far too busy arresting felons and taking bleeding persons to the hospital to worry about such relatively insignificant matters; the consequence is that, unless some specialist personnel are assigned to those functions, the level of service in those matters will critically degenerate in the central city.

Parenthetically, it is germane to comment in this context that during the 1960's there were persistent complaints in many cities of inadequately unequal services to central core areas, voiced with the assumption that this inadequacy resulted from maldistribution of government resources. Although government resources probably were inappropriately distributed in some instances, in more cases the fact was and is that in central core areas there often are so many major human crises occurring each day that it is difficult for government employees dealing with those crises to shift psychological gears to also take care of the lesser service problems. In such circumstances, even a doubling of generalist personnel (sharing problems both for the crises and the service problems) may have little effect; the only recourse may be establishing of specialized units to deal with, of all things, the minor housekeeping problems.

The same factors which cause the general government at first to give generalized government functions to the police department and then gradually to sort out specialties for performance by other agencies similarly influence police departments, as the departments increase in size and the functions become more complex, to assign specialized personnel or specialized units to functions previously done by the patrol officer.

Specialization sometimes occurs within the police departments, as in any other organization, primarily by design of the administrators. But, because of the proportionally great number of generalists in any large police department, or in any large unit of the police department, it is also possible, much more easily than in most other organizations, for specialization to occur almost by accident. For example, if a generalist patrolman in a relatively unbusy area develops a special interest in apprehending drunken drivers, or recovering stolen automobiles, or arranging removal of abandoned automobiles, he may find it possible, if he is an active officer, to devote sufficient effort to his special interest to become a virtual specialist. Indeed, if he happens to select for his special interest some matter of currently high priority to his unit commander, he may very well find himself assigned as a full-time specialist, working only on that one function.

Such accidental specialization is not necessarily contrary to the best interests of the organization; so long as it can be channeled toward appropriate priorities of the department, such utilization of special interests and abilities of individual employees is beneficial. The important thing, however, is for the department administrators, middle-managers, and especially the line supervisors to recognize that such accidental or self-motivated specialization can and does occur, and carefully to watch performance data of patrolmen to insure that any self-motivated specialization does reasonably reflect the policies and priorities of the department rather than those of the individual officer. Narcotics officers have been known to concentrate their efforts on marijuana offenders in cities where heroin traffic was the greater problem.

Policies and priorities of the department should be the factors which lead to specialization. Current problems of major significance often will force specialization. A decision to specialize ordinarily is based either on a perceived need for special training to accomplish the function or the need to organize to achieve better results or on both. The need for special training is found in such specialized functions as evidence technicians, canine handlers, youth officers, detectives, and in large departments, in riot and disorder control.

A very high proportion of the patrol officers in any large city police department have the intelligence and aptitude to meet the minimal requirements for any of these specialized functions, and most of the officers in very small departments are expected, in one way or another, to muddle through, at least partially, if necessary, any of these functions, with the exception only of the canine officer. But as a police department increases in size, and therefore has both sufficient work load in a specialty and a sufficient number of police officers to make possible the assignments of some as specialists, a point is eventually reached where it is seen as more economical, practical, and effective to train a relatively few men in each high-priority specialist function and to organize their assignments so that most of their time, energy, and interest is spent on the specialty. Sometimes the specialists are concentrated in headquarters units, sometimes they are spread throughout the patrol division; sometimes the specialists are assigned full-time to their functions, sometimes they perform it only on an as needed basis.

However the specialization is organized, the department benefits by limiting the specialized training to a relatively few officers instead of its entire patrol force, and the formal training is reinforced by concentrating on the specialists instead of diffusing throughout the patrol division the experience to be obtained from those incidents which occur involving the specialty.

The second reason for specialization is to achieve results in matters of high priority. For example, in many departments it is common practice for each criminal warrant received by the department from the courts to be assigned to one of the patrol officers working the area of residence of the individual for whom the warrant is issued. The assumption is that the patrol officer sooner or later (depending on the seriousness of the charge for which the warrant is issued) will find it possible either to arrest the individual or to make sufficient inquiries in the neighborhood to determine his whereabouts. In small communities, or in communities with a stable population, where the patrol officer may be acquainted with most of the residents, this system works reasonably well. But in a large city, particularly in the center core of a large city, where thousands of highly mobile individuals may live on a patrol officer's beat, and also where there may be far more warrants for service than a busy patrol officer can reasonably be expected to handle, the department is likely to find it necessary to assign some specialists exclusively to warrant service.

There are numerous similar examples where specialization comes about, not because the specialty is a highly technical function which requires a great deal of training, but because in the large, busy, complex environment of a central city, if some function achieves high priority to the department or to the unit commander, and if there is a sufficient work load to justify it, specific individuals or units will be directed to specialize in its performance. This can occur with matters such as selective traffic enforcement, dealing with intoxicated persons on public space, family crisis intervention units, even the enforcement of garbage and rubbish regulations.

One of the principal disadvantages of specialization is similar to the disadvantages of having staff units. The specialist often loses interest in the primary goals of the department; for example, the officer assigned to selective traffic enforcement may argue that he is out there on the street preventing crime just like any other patrol officer, but it usually will be found that specialists seldom appear at the scene of any crime except a spectacular one. To some extent, of course, this loss of interest in the broader objectives of the department is appropriate, for one purpose of establishing the specialist unit is to concentrate a few personnel on the special problem rather than on the broad objectives of the department. But the department should tolerate this only with great care, and claims by specialists and specialist units that they are not only performing their specialty but also are engaging in general law enforcement should be accepted, when assigning resources, only if supported by substantial performance data.

Also to be recognized is that formation of a specialist unit within a department will often cause diminished interest among generalist personnel in the objectives of the specialty. The generalist, particularly if working in a high crime, high work load area, easily can develop an attitude that evidence preservation is the responsibility of the evidence technician, or that youth problems are the responsibility of the youth officer, if such specialties are established. This effect is likely to be even more pronounced if the specialty is assigned to some headquarters unit completely separated from day-to-day interchange with the patrol officers.

A striking example of this diminished interest — and even antagonism — toward a specialty occurred in some police departments in the 1960's when strong central community relations units were established. The community relations units related well to the public, but a by-product of their existence sometimes was that patrol officials felt absolved of responsibility to do community relations work. Thus, in many cases relations between the department and the public worsened, until administrators learned that the central unit should operate basically as a staff unit coordinating the community relations efforts of the patrol division rather than performing the substance of the function.

Some specialization is unavoidable in a large organization. But the disadvantages of specialization often outweigh the advantages, and the process should be avoided to the fullest extent possible. When specialization is determined to be necessary either to conserve training resources, to concentrate expertise, or to achieve important results, the specialists should, if practicable, be assigned as a part of the patrol division, where exchange and rapport between the specialists and the patrol officers will be enhanced rather than separated into a headquarters unit, where their isolation from the principal objective of the department is exacerbated.

The usually recommended range for span of control between subordinates and supervisor is between a five-to-one and a ten-to-one ratio. This range allows for variations in complexity of tasks being performed, geographical proximity or distance of the supervisor and his subordinates, and the amount of time actually available for supervisory interchange after allowing for other activities of the supervisor such as interchange with his own superior, public and private meetings, or technical or professional work which he must personally perform.

Few city police chiefs enjoy the luxury of unity of command above themselves. Instead, successful performance as a chief of police depends upon their finding some appropriate balance between the authority which appoints the chief (and to whom he ordinarily directly reports), the budget and legislative committees of the government of which he is a part, and various kinds of outside interests, which, appropriately or not, seek to influence police policies. The time-consuming complexity of the system through which he must interpret his own course of action is ample reason for the typical chief of police to keep the formal span of control between himself and his subordinates relatively low, even as low as four to one.

It was fairly common at one time in large police departments to find an executive officer reporting directly to the chief of police. But by the late 1960's, a more typical organization had the chief of police at the apex of a pyramid with from four to one-half dozen or more officials reporting directly to him, none of them through an executive officer.

The executive officer of the past reflected two influences. One was the tendency of many large cities, particularly eastern cities, to have a single politically appointed noncareer police commissioner giving policy guidance to a department operationally commanded by a career officer with a title such as superintendent. The "single commissioner" form of organization still exists, but more often than not, such commissioners are career police officials who act as operational rather than political heads of their departments.

The other influence derived from military organizational forms, which provide an executive officer to avoid any question of authority and responsibility in the events the unit commander is absent or is killed in action.

In an organization which has an executive officer, it can be assumed that unity of command, at least at the upper levels, will be almost nonexistent, for the active, operational head of a major police department would be certain to find too constraining a system of passing all of his instructions to the force and receiving all of his information through a single individual.

Most large departments have completely eliminated the executive officer position, substituting a level of several bureau heads reporting directly to the chief. In these organizations there typically is a bureau head for field operations, one for administration and technical services (sometimes with a separation of these into two bureaus), one for inspectional services, and one for planning and development. Ordinarily, but not necessarily, the head of the field operations bureau is considered to be senior officer present in absence of the chief.

These kinds of police organizations are designed with recognition that, although the field operations bureau contains the vast majority of the personnel of the department and is the bureau responsible for achieving the basic objectives of the department, a great proportion of the attention of the chief of police will necessarily be given to administrative and technical matters such as planning and development, data processing systems, budgeting, and personnel problems. However much the administrator may desire to emphasize the line functions, the ultimate public judgment of his performance will likely be based on his ability to deal with staff functions and staff problems.

How a senior executive should apportion his time among the various functions for which he is responsible is not susceptible to determination by formula. The apportionment will vary depending on what his past education and experience have been, on what are current priority problems, and on the competence of his subordinates in different areas.

The chief of police with experience in budgeting should spend less time in that area than one who has no such experience, while the chief of police with experience in criminal investigations should give less attention to that function than one without such experience.

Senior executives need always to guard against concentrating on the functions of their own expertise and experience, for such concentration will hinder the development of both themselves and their subordinates.

Changing priority of problems is perhaps an even more significant factor in apportionment of executive time and interest. If recruiting is a problem, then the chief will have to spend extra time insuring progress in recruitment; during the development of a data processing system, the chief will have to spend more personal time on that function than he will after the system is operating routinely.

A third variable in the need for special interest by the chief in a specific function will be the competence, training, and experience of his subordinates performing that function; as subordinates gain experience or as they are replaced by others either more or less competent, the interest of the chief executive should vary accordingly.

Administrators have a tendency to reorganize their departments so that functions of current high importance report directly to them. During the middle 1960's, when electronic data processing was being initiated into police departments, it was not uncommon for the data processing unit to report directly to the chief of police, but in recent years most ADP operations have been absorbed into technical services bureaus, a more appropriate location. In the heyday of police-community relations of the late 1960's, community relations divisions frequently reported directly to the chief of police, but most have since been placed lower in the organization.

There is merit to such reorganization, according to current priority, so long as it is kept within reasonable limits. It is a useful management tool in departments where reorganization is easily accomplished. In those departments where the table of organization is established by statute or by formal actions not easily changed by the chief of police, or in cases where the special interest of the chief of police would not appear to be necessary for more than a few weeks or months, then the same objectives can be achieved by simply violating unity of command and creating an informal chain of command direct from the chief of police to the official in command of the priority function.

The principle of unity of command holds that every person should report to one and only one superior. In formal military operations, the principle is often observed much like a commandment. In police departments, it commonly is observed as much in the breach as in the compliance.

Some values of unity of command are obvious; unity of command avoids confusion of conflicting orders and insures proper assignment of responsibility for actions taken. More subtle values are that unity of command enhances power of a superior over subordinates by permitting the superior to interpret broad rules into specific orders with minimum argument from his subordinates who, not having had direct commands from upper echelons, must assume that their superior knows facts which they do not; further, unity of command insulates upper echelons of the organization from unpleasant and sometimes time-consuming encounters with lower-echelon subordinates, and also insures that each link in the chain of command is kept apprised of pertinent happenings.

Exceptions to the principle of unity of command are frequent, particularly in the upper hierarchy of an organization. One exception is in the case of orders issued by staff personnel in the name of their principal. Perhaps the best example of this is the process discussed earlier whereby the police radio dispatcher "orders" patrol officers to respond to various calls for police service; another example is the direction of line units by the "implied orders" from the administrative assistant (or sometimes even the secretary) of a senior executive.

In a large, busy police department, unity of command is frequently breached even at the lowest levels of the organization. When an emergency occurs, it is common for the senior official in rank to take command of all police personnel at the scene, whether or not they are from his division, and he often will issue orders direct to various patrol officers at the scene, bypassing any intervening ranks of officials who may be present. Such violations of unity of command engender hazards, but the process is unavoidable in coping with randomly occurring, rapidly changing emergency situations in a large city.

This lack of respect for unity of command in active street operations is a natural outgrowth of the around-the-clock, seven-days-each-week police service, which makes it difficult to insure that a patrol officer will always have the same supervisor available at every emergency. Such deviation from formality is compounded by the general concept within police service that every police officer should be capable of handling any emergency situation occurring in his presence; ergo, the senior police official at the scene should utilize any available resources to cope with whatever emergency comes to his attention. With rare exception, this system works quite well, and it is this process which enables the police to respond very rapidly to emergency situations. It is only at the very immense or the complicated event, such as a riot or a shootout with a barricaded criminal, that disunity of emergency command may be a serious problem. In those events so many police officers are involved in the action that failure to establish a semiformal ad hoc organization for the mission and a concomitant unity of command may render the operation dangerously ineffective.

The patterns for observance of unity of command in large organizations vary from somewhat strict adherence to the principle at the lower echelons, where unsophisticated employees need the guidance, stability, and reassurance of having one and only one boss, to increasingly less rigorous observance at the middle- and senior-management levels, where division and bureau heads are expected to have the sophistication to deal with conflicting objectives, pressures, and instructions. As already noted, it is a rare chief of police who in actual practice has one and only one source of influence above him; there may be a single official with power to appoint and remove him, but in most cities he will be judged in effectiveness on how well he is able to balance a variety of constituent pressures.

The chief of police must carefully insulate his subordinates from the various political and administrative influences which press on him, and in that sense should preserve the principle of unity of command between his superiors and his subordinates; that is to say, the chief of police should seek to make it clear to his subordinates and to outsiders that command of the police department is his responsibility and that efforts to influence police operations must pass through him. Maintaining such exclusive control over the department and keeping outside influences properly channeled is often the most difficult organizational challenge facing a police chief.

While it is virtually indispensable for the chief of police to safeguard unity of command between outside influences and his department, the chief may find it useful within the department to violate selectively the chain of command, at his own option, between himself and middle-managers. When community relations is particularly important; during budget season, when the budget unit is important; during the early years of the tenure of a chief of police, when the personnel function is likely to be important; at some other time, when a newly formed division (for example, data processing) may be important — at times such as these the chief of police may want to take close control of a particularly important function.

There is an inclination at such times for the chief to reorganize the staff units so that the currently important division reports directly to him rather than through a bureau head. But a useful alternative is for the chief of police to leave the function of interest in its organizational phase and simply to violate the chain of command to the extent necessary for him to maintain close control. This process gives the chief executive the advantage of insuring that communications between himself and the division head are clear, that there is no misunderstanding of his intentions when directives are issued, and that there is no misunderstanding by him of reports from the division. Ordinarily, in this kind of situation it is implied or perhaps expressed that the division commander will keep his bureau head informed both of directives from the chief and of reports to the chief. The advantage of this process is that the chief is able to lend importance to the work of the particular division at crucial times, and is able to assure proper direction and understanding on important matters, but at the same time the chief is spared from dealing with routine, day-to-day problems of the division which the division director should continue to take up with the bureau head when appropriate; for example, if the division head is absent on vacation or because of illness, the chief of police can easily revert to having all of his contact with the division through the bureau head and thus avoid having to deal personally with employees of the division below the policy level.

The chief of police must be careful to insure that he assigns adequate *authority commensurate with the responsibility* he imposes on his subordinates. Conversely, he should hold his employees accountable for their exercise of the authority delegated to them.

Authority to make decisions should be clearly stated in the organization orders of the department. More important, it should also be reinforced by the day-to-day attitude of the chief of police, who must take care to encourage initiative, both by encouraging new ideas and methods and by realizing that innovation is never achieved without errors occurring.

Even though assigned authority and responsibility are set forth in clearly written departmental organization orders, unless the chief and his staff follow a stilted, ritualistic form of administration, it is probable that the informal organization will be more important than the formal, especially in the staff units. Indeed, the informal processes are likely to achieve more innovation and accomplishment than the formal.

Some managers make careful efforts to eliminate development or continuance of an informal organization. Aversion for the informal organization derives from the knowledge that it leads to development of cliques and blurs lines of authority and of accountability. (The informal organization often is nothing more than a coalition of cliques.)

Still, many managers recognize that organizations are of people, not of blocks and lines on a chart. Some men who rise to directorship of divisions or bureaus work out well, others do not. This occurs for a variety of reasons; men are selected for promotion on the basis of performance at a lower level and sometimes are inadequate at the higher level, having reached the level of incompetence described in *The Peter Principle;* some middle-managers are highly qualified to form or reform an organizational unit, but are marginally suited by aptitude and temperament to direct the unit over the years after the performance has become routinized; more commonly, an individual reaches the maximum rank level he can reasonably hope to achieve in his career and gradually loses interest and becomes a marginal performer.

Marginal performers at middle- and executive-management levels are difficult to deal with in any organization, and this is especially so in a civil service organization. A popular development (actually a revival of an old concept) during the 1960's was the establishing of "exempt" positions for officials at the division and bureau levels of police departments, the idea being that such officials would be totally exempt from civil service and would serve at the pleasure of the chief of police.

This is an appealing concept in theory, but it has not been demonstrated to be all that workable in practice. The problem is that marginal performers at the middle-management and senior-management level are very difficult to expel, even if the chief has unconditional authority to fire them or to reduce them in rank. Civil service protection or not, adverse actions against personnel at that level are certain to have coverage by the public media, and the chief of police is going to have to make some showing of cause if his action is challenged. Cause is usually hard to demonstrate, for officials who reach the middle-management level are mostly intelligent, reasonably hardworking persons who, though their overall performance may be unsatisfactory to the chief, are likely to be able to list a record of reasonable and sometimes exceptional effort.

The unsatisfactory middle-manager often as not is an earnest, hardworking team player. When told he is failing in management, he very likely will be able to produce an impressive history of recommendations he has made for improvements, and of requests he has made for more resources; his annual reports and his budget reports may be faultless; the implication is that it is the larger organizations, not his segment, and his superiors, not he, which have failed. The basic problem of such a manager often is that he knows and uses the rituals of the formal organization, but has never learned that most achievements are obtained by manipulation of the informal process.

The ultimate consequence is that authority to remove or demote persons from exempt positions is rarely used. More often, ineffective managers are laterally shunted to functions having lower current priority.

A promising concept for management selection and retention has been proposed for top careerists at the management level in the federal government. This system would provide for employment of managers on renewable contracts of about three years' duration. Under this system, the manager would be assured sufficient tenure to overcome inertia in the organizational function or to achieve reorganized performance before judgment were made of his competence. But retention after expiration of his contract, instead of depending on adverse action for his removal, would require an affirmative action for his continuance. This type of tenure, similar to the terms of office for which many police chiefs are presently appointed, would seem to be an ideal arrangement for police department middle- and top-managers as well.

Not having really effective options for removing marginal performers, the alternative of the executive is to rely on the informal organization to keep the institution operating in spite of the ineffective links in the formal hierarchy. This may be achieved simply by the violations of the chain of command referred to above. Or the top executive may purposely transfer power among subordinates simply by making it clear that the advice of one is sought and accepted more often than that of others.

By carefully selecting what officials he will see on a regular basis, the executive contributes significantly to the lines of the informal organization; indeed, the chief can consciously design an informal organization through this process if he desires to do so (or can do so unconsciously if he is not aware of the dynamics involved); it is a truism that those subordinates who regularly see the chief will, whatever their authority in the formal organization, achieve importance, status, and authority within the informal hierarchy.

Whatever else he does, the chief of police must recognize that the principles of organization need to be recognized and understood, but that the office of the chief of police and the department of police may operate as effectively on the basis of the personalities involved as on the formal principles of organization.

There is nothing wrong with violating the principles of organization so long as you know what the principles are and understand that you are violating them.

7

Police Personnel Issues

How a police chief apportions his personal effort among the diverse functions of management obviously will vary with the individual chief and how he perceives his responsibilities, with the size of the department and how it is organized, and with the issues of the time. But whatever his personal preferences, whatever the style of his department, whatever are the current issues, a large part of the time of the chief executive will be spent on matters dealing with personnel administration.

In an organization such as a police department, where 90 percent or more of the budget goes for employee salaries and benefits, the personnel function is a principal tool of management. It is within the personnel function that standards and quality of personnel are established and maintained, discipline and morale of the force are produced, and salaries, benefits and working conditions of employees, as well as management prerogatives in dealing with employees, are established. And personnel administration within a police department is not solely an internal matter of no interest to the public. Community concerns for such matters as quality of personnel, equal employment opportunities, behavior and discipline of police officers, and adequacy of salaries and working conditions keep police personnel policies before the public.

Because of this importance of the personnel function to the performance and image of the force, the personnel director of any medium or large police department should be a senior middle-manager, responsible either directly to the chief or to one of his top assistants. Ideally, the personnel director should be a professional personnel administrator, with broad education and experience in personnel administration; alternatively, care should be taken that the craft of personnel administration is well represented in the education and experience of employees within the personnel division. That ideal seldom is achieved; in many large police departments, and in most medium and small police departments, the personnel function has neither status commensurate with its importance nor expertise among its employees to justify appropriate status.

This lack of status in police personnel divisions results primarily from the fact that state and local government systems often centralize the more important personnel functions in a central staff agency responsible directly to the head of the government. Such matters as setting standards for employment, devising entrance examinations, negotiating labor contracts, developing salary and benefit systems, and disposing of employee appeals and disciplinary matters are dealt with at a level higher than the operating departments. In such systems, the personnel division of an operating agency such as the police department is relegated to functions such as preparing the paperwork for employment of individuals pronounced suitable by the central office, processing disciplinary appeals to the upper level, keeping time and attendance and pay records under pay systems devised by the central office, and performing similar nonpolicymaking administrative and clerical functions. When major issues arise, such as development of salary scales, negotiation of working conditions for police officers, and enforcement of discipline, the chief of police finds himself dealing, not with his own personnel director, but with personnel experts from a central office who may, but then again may not, be motivated by the same objectives as the chief of police.

The logic of this central office system holds up quite well in application to most government employees. Excepting policemen and firemen, teachers, sanitation workers, and perhaps a few other similar specialties, the salaries, benefits, and working conditions usually are standardized for the employees within each government system; consequently, department heads such as the chief accounting officer or the director of the welfare department are unlikely to have a continuing vital interest (other than personal) in personnel systems, for their personnel problems and policies are submerged in the larger system.

This system has caused persistent difficulty for chiefs of police during recent decades as salaries and benefits for government employees have consistently improved. The usual pattern is for the general government employees to be the first to obtain higher salaries and better working conditions (cynics think this is because the central personnel experts are included among the general government employees). These improvements are then followed by demands of police officers, firemen, teachers, and other specialist employees for commensurate increases in their salaries and benefits.

Frequently, however, by the time these large, identifiable groups of specialist employees demand what seems to them equitable treatment, the government system is encountering financial problems resulting from the cost of the improvements for the general employees and has insufficient revenues to provide equal treatment to all of the specialty employees. The consequence is a lot of negotiating from the government system in trying to reduce the cost of prospective benefits and a great deal of aggravation among the specialty employees who are demanding a full measure of what has already been given the general employees.

A common result is allowance of the benefits originally sought, frequently financed by enactment of a special tax increase publicly identified as an increase to finance a pay raise for policemen and firemen. Casual observers of revenue-raising publicity by local governments might well wonder whether there are any clerical and administrative employees in the system and, if there are, why it is that they never need revenue for a pay raise.

It is for this reason that employee groups such as policemen and firemen and teachers are periodically in the limelight over demands for increased salaries or improved benefits. And it is for this reason that department heads in those systems, such as the chief of police, periodically find themselves in the dilemma of having to support contradictory objectives.

On the one hand, as the leader of his department, the chief of police usually knows that his personnel deserve salary and benefit increases comparable to those of other government employees; the need for maintaining high morale among current employees and for attracting high-quality future employees are persuasive reasons for him to support the demands of his subordinates. On the other hand, as a part of the management team of the government system, he is committed to assist the head of government in his overall dealing with problems and formulating of policies; even though it is unfair to require rank and file police officers to bear the burden of insufficient revenues, the chief of police has a strong responsibility to support the government administration. The dilemma is likely to be exacerbated if the chief must rely for personnel expertise on a central personnel office not necessarily responsive to the needs of the police department.

This problem of having to deal with a staff agency not necessarily responsive to police objectives can be troublesome to the chief not only in setting of salaries and benefits, but in all aspects of personnel administration. Two alternative methods of dealing with the problem are: assimilation of the police personnel into the general personnel system, or development of a strong personnel function within the police department so that the chief of police will have sufficient authority and responsibility, with commensurate staff expertise, to deal with the police personnel problems.

The first of these alternatives, assimilation of police into the general personnel system, has occurred in some smaller jurisdictions (apparently with benefit to the police personnel), but seems unlikely to become a significant trend in large jurisdictions. Total assimilation involves placing police under the standard classification and salary scales for the general government, and giving them the same working conditions and benefits as general government employees. Although this is not impossible to achieve, it is difficult, both because the preserving of police generalization makes equitable classification with "civilian" occupations difficult, and because the physical and psychological demands of police work require a more favorable retirement system than is needed for the general employee.

What this says, of course, is that on balance — in the long run — police salaries and benefits are probably as good as or better than they would be under the general government system. The difficulty with police salaries and benefits usually develops, not in the long run, but in the short runs. In most jurisdictions the police eventually have obtained the same benefits as other employees — a five-day work week, pay for overtime work, compensation for court attendance, increased salaries, and so forth. The difficulty has been and is, as indicated earlier, that the benefits for police almost invariably come later than those for the general government (though often they are retroactive), and the intervening period is marked by anxiety and agitation.

These problems of short-run straggling of benefits could be avoided by partial assimilation of police into the general system, with every pay raise or new personnel benefit for the general government including a guarantee of commensurate treatment for other employees, such as the police, who are in specialty personnel groups. This arrangement, by forcing the government system to recognize and plan for the *total* cost of new salaries and benefits before enacting them for about *one-half* of its employees, would go far to preclude the serious morale problems and personnel strife which often occur during prolonged negotiations with the specialty groups.

If the police are not to be totally assimilated into the general personnel group, an assimilation including not only salaries and benefits but also disciplinary systems, selection systems, and promotional systems, the chief of police should try to strengthen administrative control over personnel matters by developing a strong personnel division staffed with at least partly professional experts. It is unquestionably true that in most governmental systems the chief of police can rely on the central personnel office for advice and assistance with his problems. But, just as busy prosecuting attorneys cannot devote substantial time to developing policy guidelines and procedures for the police, busy central personnel experts seldom can devote substantial time to developing specific police personnel policies and procedures. Consequently, for much the same reasons as he needs a general counsel or legal advisor, the police chief needs a professional personnel director or personnel advisor on his staff.

Properly recognized, the personnel function has an impact on almost every aspect of police operations, including a great deal more than merely the obtaining and administering of salaries and benefits for personnel. In succeeding chapters, four specific major aspects of personnel administration are discussed in varying depth; these four are recruiting and employment processes and standards, career processes for police officers, use of civilians, and training systems. Left unaddressed are such important aspects of personnel administration as unionization of police, setting of police salaries and benefits, and disciplinary processes, all of which are increasingly important issues of concern to every chief of police.

Personnel policies will develop within any organization, with or without guidance from the chief executive. It is crucial to the development of an effective police force that the chief of police recognize this fact and accordingly make personnel decisions with a consideration for the long-term policy as much as the case-by-case persuasions.

The personnel function is far too important to be relegated to the status of a clerical operation.

8

Recruiting and Employment
Processes and Standards

ASK A TYPICAL YOUNG POLICE OFFICIAL why he became a police officer. More than likely he will tell you a story of how police work was a childhood dream, or of motivation to serve his community and fellow man. For some reason it is considered nearly an act of disloyalty to the craft for a police officer to say publicly that he took the job for any other than highly motivated altruistic reasons; likewise, many police officers will argue that only persons with such motivations should be employed by police departments.

Indeed, during the early 1960's, at the beginning of concerted drives to get greater numbers of blacks on police forces, some senior police officials argued (along with a lot of other illogical ideas) that blacks generally could not be good police officers because they had no police officer forebears from whom they could have inherited the motivating traits of police work.

Undoubtedly, there are some police officers who entered the craft in response to a childhood dream, there certainly are some who became police officers almost as an act of heritage, following in the footsteps of their fathers and grandfathers, and there probably are a few who took the job primarily out of desire to help their fellow man. But if one were to hazard a generalization about so large and diverse a group as police officers, the generalization would have to be that an overwhelming majority took the job because it was a better job than they had before and was as good or better than other immediate prospects.

Notice should be taken that the foregoing paragraphs have discussed "becoming a police officer," and "taking a job," and "entering the craft." Care has been taken not to employ the euphemism "profession."

One of the unfortunate outgrowths of attempted universal high school education and of greatly increased college attendance in America has been development of a sort of snobbery which holds that an occupation is of low caste if it can be performed by dint of hard work and perseverance, without four years of college education. The development of euphemisms in the job market was spectacular and sometimes laughable; salesmen became "manufacturers' representatives," undertakers became "funeral directors," janitors became "building engineers," and trash collectors became "sanitarians." Police officers became "professionals."

Actually, one can debate whether or not police officers accurately can be called professionals, reusing the protest of H. L. Mencken, when news reporters first began to fashion themselves as professionals, that a true professional cannot be an employee of an organization which exercises control over his work, as is the case with most news reporters and all police officers, but instead must be an independent agent with full freedom to deliver his services in such (professional) manner as he sees fit, direct to the consumer, as is the case with most doctors, dentists, or prostitutes. This protest, of course, belies such commonly accepted terms as "professional soldier" and to some extent even the dictionary use of the term "professional teacher."

In a way it is unfortunate that so many police officers, as well as persons in other occupations, clamor to be called professionals, with some unspoken notion that being a professional is more dignified than being a workman, while at the same time they lament the general decline in quality of workmanship in their society. But the greater misfortune, in the case of police work and in some other occupations, is that this "professionalization" has developed ramifications which may go far beyond mere nicety of expression.

By the early 1950's, when the desire of police to be called professional began to develop in earnest, most of the large police departments in American had conducted formal recruit training programs for only a couple of decades; while those training programs generally were better than the training given most government employees, the content certainly was not adequate for so complex a task as police work. But a much more important deficiency at that time was that many medium-sized and small police departments in America had no formal training programs at all.

Then, when police officers began to fashion themselves as "professionals," careful thinkers were quick to point out that the term implied requirement of some specialized body of knowledge. At that time, no specialized body of knowledge about police work existed. There were a few books on police administration, which at best is more art than science and is hardly a specialized body of knowledge, and numerous books on criminology, which is far more closely associated with sociology than with police work. But, spurred by the desire to be called professional, and assisted by universities which saw professionalization of police as a desirable social goal, police officers and police departments pressed for development of college education programs in police administration and police science.

Except for grumbling by some older police officers who did not want to be troubled by going back to school, and hesitance by some police officials who suspected that educational programs would distract police officers from crime fighting, the movement was applauded by all quarters. Emphasis on police education by the President's Commission on Law Enforcement and Administration of Justice (1967) and financing by the Law Enforcement Assistance Administration resulted in dramatic increase in courses for police officers. Committees and commissions regularly reaffirm the President's Commission recommendation that before the next generation every police officer should be a college graduate.

It may very well be that all this emphasis on professionalization and on education of police officers will ultimately be beneficial to police service. The day may come when only college graduates will be permitted to serve as police officers. It is more likely, however, that such a goal will never be achieved; the police service would be far better served by recognition of what it actually is: a dignified occupation which can be adequately performed by many high school graduates, a craft which historically has served a useful social service as a step up the socioeconomic ladder for its employees.

Police recruiting patterns are usually tied directly to two discrete phenomena, the labor market and the public perception of police.

During the Depression years, police departments had no difficulty whatever in obtaining recruits; usually they had hundreds if not thousands of applicants for each vacancy; in many large cities, a high proportion of appointees during the Depression period were college graduates.

During the post–World War II years, however, the situation was dramatically changed. Employment in the general economy was high, there was a shortage of youngsters of police recruit age coming into the labor market, reflecting the reduced birth rate during the Depression; at the same time, city police departments were expanding in size as their cities grew and their problems became more complex. By the middle 1960's, it was common for West Coast cities to send recruiting teams to the East Coast in search of applicants.

A second phenomenon, public perception of the police, can be as important as the job market in police recruitment. A department involved in a highly publicized corruption scandal, for example, often finds it difficult for a year or two thereafter to attract recruits. During the last half of the 1960's, when police were the target of rhetoric and agitation from both black urban disorders and from white anti-war demonstrations, and when support for the police by government leaders seemed at its nadir, departments were having such great difficulty in obtaining recruits that suggestions were made not only that police officers be universally exempted from the draft, but that police service be formally established as an alternative to military service for a draftee.

This situation did not change until about 1970, when a combination of growing intolerance for crime by the general population and of clear and unequivocal support for the police by national and local politicians revived the attractiveness of police work as an occupation. Almost as if someone had thrown a switch, the danger, hazards, the exposure to elements, the night hours, and the heavy work load of police work, all seen as undesirable aspects of the job in the 1960's, were suddenly seen as challenges; police departments around the country were suddenly, almost magically, filled; the only recruiting problems were in meeting court-imposed minority recruiting requirements.

Keeping police department rolls filled involves not only recruitment of new officers but retention of current ones. Because police salary and benefit systems usually give heavy emphasis to the pension program, turnover in a police department tends to occur primarily among individuals in their first few years of police service; in most police departments, after a man has been with the department for five or six years, his investment in the pension program is too great for him to leave except for some substantial reason.

Police officials often decry the high resignation rate in the first few years of police service, and sometimes will go to extraordinary lengths to try to insure that each new appointee fully intends to make police work his lifetime career. This tendency to reject the noncareerist results in part from the mistaken notion that anyone not a "dedicated" police officer is undesirable police material, and in part from emphasis on the economic fact that a police officer who stays only a few months or years does not amortize the expense of his recruit training.

The substantial portion of the cost of recruit training is the salary paid the individual while in training. In most recruit training programs, the administrative and instructor costs are relatively minor when distributed across the total number of trainees. But during the 1960's new segments of police recruit training were added for each crisis which arose. Courses were added for community relations, for driver training, for control of demonstrations and disorders. By the end of the decade, many large city police recruit training programs were approaching six months in length, so that just the salary of the recruit added up to a substantial investment.

As most of the voluntary resignations of police officers occur in the first couple of years of service, after the recruit gets out on the street and finds that there are undesirable as well as desirable aspects to police work, a more economical process for recruit indoctrination would be to give only a few weeks of fundamental training at the outset, then to send the recruit out to do police work on the street for a probationary period of a year or so, followed by extensive training in a variety of specialized aspects of police work.

This system also would make it economically more feasible to use the probationary period as a clear extension of the selection process, so that the police department could make a far better judgment of the capacity and aptitude of the recruit than is possible from pre-employment background investigation of the typical youthful applicant, who has very little employment experience before being tried by the police department. This reduced investment in initial training also would make it feasible for the police department to encourage college graduates to experiment with police service as a part of their social development, with de-emphasis on lifetime commitment for those who clearly have other careers in mind.

The tendency of police departments to discourage noncareerists from applying is unfortunate, for the passing through police experience of persons eventually going into other fields would broaden the social outlook of police officers as well as produce a cadre of knowledgeable police sympathizers among all levels of society.

Recruitment of noncareerists for police work seems likely to remain an academic question, given the stress which police officials nationally have placed on careers, and despite the repeated recommendations for systems of lateral entry and transferral rights for pensions. And since the usual policy for the applicant to be a careerist is not and really cannot be formally stated, it is more likely to persist as a requirement than some of the formal standards which, being visible and clearly stated, can be more effectively attacked and changed.

Six standards worth discussing are those relating to education, physical requirements, character requirements, sexual discrimination, racial discrimination, and residence requirements. Also worthy of special mention, but discussed in Chapter 9 is the question of lateral entry into upper ranks of departments.

Educational Requirements

A fundamental issue to be decided by police administrators before the end of this century is whether or not a college education shall be required for every police officer in America. Both the 1967 Commission on Law Enforcement and Administration of Justice and the 1972 Commission on Law Enforcement Standards and Goals have recommended that college graduation should be required.

The notion that college education should be required for police officers has become popular only since World War II, and has had broad support only since the early 1960's.

Before World War II, the police patrol officer with a college degree was a rarity; typically, he had entered the police service during an economic depression and had done so because when he graduated from college he could find no other employment. Following that war, as college education became available to a wider range of the population, through financing of the GI Bill for veterans, and through such phenomena as the educational system of California, a gradually increasing number of college-educated men began entering police service. This trend was far more significant in West Coast cities than in more traditional eastern departments.

By the late 1950's the concept that college education was useful for a police officer had gained considerable currency, and educational programs in police administration, with classes arranged to accommodate the working schedule of police officers, could be found in many major metropolitan areas. Even so, the major effect toward education in police administration at that time was being done in the schools of California and at Michigan State University. The condition of law enforcement education during that era is illustrated by the fact that even into the middle 1960's the American University of Washington, D.C., experienced considerable difficulty in obtaining individuals with both educational qualifications and practical experience to teach courses in such subjects as Police Investigation and Police Administration.

Despite the increased emphasis on education, even into the middle 1960's many of America's largest cities still had no formal educational requirements for appointment to the police force. As examples, in both Washington, D.C., and Boston, civil service policies prohibited establishment of an educational requirement for appointment unless substitution of practical experience was permitted.

By the end of World War II, however, practices adopted by most school systems of America had made the high school diploma a relatively meaningless document. Responding to the social pressure for universal high school education, school systems retained in school and passed through and graduated many individuals who were either unable or unwilling to master scholastic work; conversely, recognizing that individuals who dropped out often were equally or better qualified scholastically than many others who remained and graduated, school systems began issuing certificates of equivalency on the basis of age, experience, and in some cases, testing.

The consequence of these policies was that by the mid-1950's, whether or not an applicant held a high school diploma had little to do with his mental or scholastic achievements. Within that context, it is safe to say that by the early 1960's almost all new appointees to American police departments were high school graduates or their equivalent, whatever that means.

By the middle 1960's, most large and medium police departments viewed high school education or its equivalent as a legitimate requirement for appointment to the police force. As noted earlier, there was increasing talk in police circles of requiring some college education prior to appointment, with a simultaneous interest in college educational programs for police officers already on the rolls. This predisposition toward more formal education for the police community came as a part of seeking "professional" status and perhaps was partially a reflection of the educational mania of the broader American community following the Russian leap into space with Sputnik — a consensus that the answer to all problems of America could be found in classrooms.

Even so, the notion that a college graduate would make a better police officer or that college education would improve a good police officer was not universally accepted in police circles. Veteran police officials had often observed than an unsophisticated individual, who was not academically oriented and who was troubled by scholastic work and scholastic tests, frequently was a very satisfactory and sometimes an outstanding street patrol officer or criminal investigator. Paradoxically, this conservative thinking eventually found support and quantitative verification from liberal quarters.

During the middle 1960's, most American police departments were experiencing serious recruiting difficulties. In an effort to open these job opportunities to individuals unable to pass the mental and educational qualifications, for the objectives both of increasing the number of job opportunities for inner-city blacks and of achieving a higher ratio of minority-group individuals among police officers, social planners began systematically to question whether the educational requirements and mental examinations for qualifying police officers were validly related to job requirements and actual police performance. Although the findings are too mixed for final conclusions, the studies of entrance examinations have given some indications that the mental tests and the educational requirements have high correlation to academic performance in police recruit schools, but significantly less correlation to effective performance as a police officer on the street.

Growing out of these findings were two major thrusts for change, both of which eventually failed. An effort was made to persuade civil service commissions and police departments to eliminate the educational requirements and to lower the mental test requirements either by test revision or by reduction of passing scores. Police officials vigorously opposed these proposals, arguing that it was a time to be upgrading rather than downgrading the mental and educational requirements for entrance into police work, in order to achieve "professionalism." An alternative thrust took the form of demonstration projects with the general format of trainee-status employment of groups of individuals who met physical and character requirements for employment as police officers, but who lacked the educational diploma or were marginally unable to pass the mental examination for appointment. As trainees, these individuals were required to perform part-time work and routine assignments within the police department and were enrolled as part-time students in remedial education classes, with the objective of enabling them to obtain high school equivalency certificates, if required, and to pass the mental examination for appointment to the police force. The proportion of trainees who eventually qualified for appointment as police officers was small, and such projects were discontinued both for that reason and because easier police recruitment by 1970 eliminated the vacancies which the projects were designed to fill.

Those ideas that mental and educational standards for police officers might be too high passed out of style. But the concepts, together with numerous equal-employment-opportunity suits, served to question high scholastically oriented standards as job requirements and tended to validate the perception of experienced police officials that scholastic ability and effectiveness as a police officer are not invariably correlated.

Many superior investigators and some outstanding performers in police administrative and technical functions score quite low or barely pass scholastically oriented examinations. Typically, these individuals lack the sophisticated verbal abilities which such tests measure best, but compensate for that shortcoming by understanding of human nature, by native abilities or persuasiveness, and by tenacity. One consequence of this is that some detectives who are most successful in closing cases lack the verbal abilities to prepare the prosecution reports resulting from their accomplishments; to offset this problem many detective units have one or more "detectives" who have good verbal abilities and who do more report writing than they do investigative work. Both of these kinds of detective are necessary to make a unit continually successful.

Those who insist on universal college education for police officers argue that college educated individuals can be obtained to perform equally as well the role now served by police officers with native intelligence and knowledge of their community but without high verbal skills. This argument disregards that much of the crime in America, at least much of the crime for which local police departments are responsible, has historically been committed by individuals from the lower socioeconomic strata of society, and that much of the success of the police officers and detectives with native abilities derives from the fact that they themselves came into police work from the upper-lower class or lower-middle class, and are able to operate freely and effectively within those strata.

The starkest example of this occurred during the 1960's, as the population of central cities shifted to ever higher proportions of blacks and other visually identifiable minority groups, while the police departments still were comprised primarily of whites. Police departments encountered considerable difficulty in recruiting black policemen, and those police departments which used verbal ability tests to select detectives found themselves with very low ratios of blacks among their investigators. When challenged about falling clearance rates, detective officials would complain about lack of cooperation from the black community, but when it was suggested that they should strive to get more black investigators, they would complain that this was impossible without lowering their "standards." In many communities, the result was almost ludicrous, for the white detectives going into all-black communities in "plain clothes" might just as well have been uniformed.

One of the problems of both the proposals for required college education and the existing verbal abilities tests is that these requirements tend to screen out a higher proportion of minorities than is desirable for police agencies which spend much of their effort serving and dealing with minority groups. A second, specific problem with the proposed college education requirement is that such a standard will close to lower socioeconomic groups the stepping-stone into the middle class which historically has been provided by employment as a police officer. This stepping-stone has had immeasurable social benefits over the history of the nation, and it should not be cast aside without good reason.

What are the reasons given by proponents of the college education requirement? Generally, they argue (a) that the great powers of discretion vested in police officers, including authority to deprive persons of their freedom and even to use deadly force, should be reserved to individuals with the sophistication of college education, (b) that the college education requirement is necessary to increase prestige of police work to that of a true profession, and (c) that police officers should be representative of the average of American society and that a college education requirement will be necessary to keep abreast of the increasing level of American education. Each of these premises deserves some discussion.

The notion that the ordinary patrolman in a large, well-organized police department must be vested with a high degree of discretion in order to perform his job is a myth. The fact is that in most departments the actions of beat patrolmen and of working detectives are quite closely constrained by either the law or by department policies and regulations. Certainly any voids in existing constraints can be better closed by immediate improvements in policymaking than by long-term increases in the educational level of police personnel. There is no reason for not having very clear and specific guidelines for such actions as use of deadly force or situations appropriate for arrest of individuals, and well-written guidelines should not require a college education for their understanding.

It may be arguable that a college education and a law degree are needed to qualify a person to construct valid guidelines on such subjects as eyewitness identifications or stop-and-frisk situations; even this argument is questionable. But there certainly is no reason why such guidelines should require a college education for their understanding.

The snobbish notion that requirement of a college education for employment as a police officer will increase the prestige of the police service is unfortunately true, but it is questionable whether this objective is worth either the financial or the social cost of its accomplishment. There needs to be serious questioning of the real value of requiring more education for any vocation than is actually needed. There are certainly numerous functions within the police service, such as traffic control, radio-dispatching functions, and many patrol and investigative functions, which not only do not require a college education but would be deadly boring to an imaginative college graduate if he found himself confined to such a function over a long period of time.

The point has to be recognized that, if college education is universally required for employment as a police officer, then *every* function performed by a police officer will be performed by a college graduate. Given that not everyone in police service can rise to higher ranks and responsibility, some of those college graduates will find themselves spending their entire careers in very routine, unchallenging assignments. The way to avoid this would be to redesign the employment patterns so that the less challenging functions were performed by some class of individuals other than police officers, but careful consideration of the high proportion of police time spent in routine patrol or in tedious, nondiscretionary investigative functions will show such a scheme to be impractical.

Police administrators would do their departments and the nation a service by preaching that conscientious, hard work at a craft is just as important as holding a degree and claiming to be a professional.

The nation needs to reassess its sense of what kinds of accomplishment deserve prestige!

The concept that police departments should be fairly representative of the broad spectrum of the community is appealing. But it is an error to assume that within a few years the average American will have a college degree. There are some suburban bedroom communities in America where almost every adult householder has a college degree, and in those communities there may be room for argument that each police officer should have a college education. But in much of America, and certainly in the large cities and in the industrial centers, far more Americans are engaged in crafts and trades than in professions, and college degrees are held by a relatively few adults. In fact, the median level of education in America in 1971 was only 12.2 years; almost half of all Americans were high school dropouts. In such communities, and these are communities that are served by the vast majority of police agencies of America, an argument that the police should be educationally equivalent to the average population is actually an argument against college requirements for police employment. One problem with the requirement of a college education for employment in large city departments is that such a requirement certainly will make more difficult the recruitment of blacks and other minorities who constitute a high proportion (and sometimes a majority) of the population.

Nothing here is intended to suggest that individuals with college degrees make poor police officers or that college studies will harm a good police officer. With very few exceptions, advanced education will broaden the perspectives and sharpen the judgment of almost any individual. The programs across America for encouraging police officers to attend college courses, tuition support for that purpose, and extra pay or promotional credits as educational incentives all are sensible undertakings. But the concepts that a college education should be a prerequisite for employment as a police officer, that only individuals with ability to assimilate college instructions should be employed as police officers, or that just employment which requires a college education can command respect and prestige in the community are all dangerous notions which should be discarded outright.

The minimum mental and educational requirements for police officers should be an ability to assimilate police training and to understand the policies and regulations of the department. Studies by the Washington Metropolitan Police Department indicate that the levels which *should* be achieved in about the tenth grade of a good school system are adequate for this purpose. Beyond this, police departments certainly should encourage interested college graduates to join their ranks and should encourage those within their ranks with college-level scholastic ability to obtain further education. But every large police department in America could achieve a great deal more improvement by developing and strengthening its in-service training programs than by establishing a college education as a minimum requirement for employment.

Physical Requirements

Virtually every police department requires that new appointees have general good health, good physical condition, and absence of any disabling disease or injury. This "general good health" requirement has never been subjected to any organized, consistent challenge. But during recent years the physical requirements pertaining to age and height (and to a lesser extent weight) have been increasingly questioned by sources both internal and external to police departments.

The span of ages qualifying an applicant for appointment to large police departments traditionally has ranged from minimums somewhere past the twenty-first birthday to maximums falling within the thirties. Both the minimum age and the maximum age for appointment varies from time to time and from city to city. In past years some cities have established minimums as high as twenty-five or twenty-six years of age, but by the middle 1960's, almost every large department in the country would accept new appointees who were only twenty-one years old. Such minimums have been based on the belief that mature judgment comes only after the twenty-first birthday and the historical legal concept that a person under twenty-one years of age is an infant and, therefore, not legally responsible for his actions.

The maximum age for appointment to police forces is set in most cities at somewhere around the thirtieth birthday, and ranges from there up to the middle thirties. The requirement of a maximum age for appointment as a police officer derives from several assumptions; first, that an individual who has not settled into a permanent career by his early thirties is likely to be an unsatisfactory employee for a permanent career organization such as a large city police department, secondly, that an individual who enters a police force in his middle thirties will too soon be unable to perform rigorous street police duties as he reaches his late forties and early fifties, and thirdly, because police pension systems are designed on the premise that police officers will serve twenty to thirty years of rigorous duty before they reach qualifications for retirement. In simple fact, the maximum age limits reflect the fact discussed earlier that police departments consider themselves as career employers and both discourage and, to the extent possible, disqualify noncareerists.

During the latter half of the 1960's, when police recruiting became especially difficult, departments began to question both their minimum and their maximum age requirements, especially the minimums. It became obvious to many police administrators that the twenty-one-year age minimum was purely arbitrary. Obviously, individuals mature at different ages, depending on their upbringing, their education, and their personality. Many youngsters are mature at seventeen or eighteen years of age, but many others do not mature until their late twenties.

To insure a high average level of maturity of its appointees, a police department would need its minimum at twenty-five or twenty-six years of age; with that minimum, immaturity of the individual would likely be reflected in his record of employment and conduct up to that time. But a minimum age in the middle twenties is totally impractical in an active and tight labor market; indeed, even with a minimum age of twenty-one years, many mature, ambitious youngsters are already employed in careers and are earning as much in crafts and trades as the beginning police salary before reaching the age of eligibility to become a police officer. To counteract this problem, several large police departments reduced the minimum age for appointment to twenty years of age, and in some cases to nineteen years of age.

Some argument has been made for also increasing the maximum age, but this proposition usually has been discarded on the basis that the change does not open a sufficiently large group of potential appointees to offset the disadvantages of higher age of appointment. The only large group of potential appointees to be reached by raising the maximum age for appointment past thirty years of age are persons retiring after twenty years' military service, and to reach this group would require a maximum age of about forty, which is much too high to assume a reasonable number of years of active, productive street police work before retirement.

Realistically, there is no reason why the minimum age for appointment as a police officer cannot be as young as eighteen, so long as close attention is given during the probationary period to weeding out immature individuals. However, a useful alternative to a minimum age of eighteen for appointment as a police officer can be provided by hiring police cadets, paid less than full police salaries and not having police arrest powers. Police cadets can be employed as young as sixteen years of age to serve in a cadet capacity until appointed as police officers upon reaching the twenty-first birthday.

The maximum age for appointment usually is a matter of less serious concern than the minimum age; from the standpoint of the police agency, a maximum age limit of about thirty years probably adequately serves the purpose of obtaining ample useful service before retirement.

Height and Weight

It is likely that no other single specific requirement for appointment as a police officer has been more often questioned than the minimum height requirement. Over the years individuals only an inch or a fraction of an inch below the minimum height requirement have tried repeatedly, but usually unsuccessfully, to find employment in large city police organizations. Frequently, these were military veterans who could point to honorable wartime battle service as evidence of their physical strength and agility and sometimes of their leadership ability, but to no avail. Others were holders of college degrees in police administration, whose practical lesson was that because they lacked height they were unable to obtain employment by any large police department except as a civilian administrative or technical employee.

Although height minimums were often questioned, those challenges came from individuals rather than from cohesive groups; therefore, police departments were able to preserve these standards with no more logical arguments than unverified assertions that a short police officer is more likely than a tall police officer to be physically attacked and to need deadly force to defend himself. During the last half of the 1960's, however, Spanish-surnamed minority groups began both to comprise significant elements of the population in several large cities and to actively seek employment opportunities equal to other Americans. This activism included demand for employment of Spanish-surnamed individuals as police officers, not only to increase the understanding between the police and the minority community, but also to make available to minority males the traditional stepping-stone of first-generation Americans into the middle class — through police work. But some Spanish groups tend to be shorter, on the average, than most other ethnic groups which comprise America, and the typical police department height minimum (usually sixty-eight inches and rarely below sixty-seven inches) excluded an inordinately high portion of their youth.

In response to demands for alleviation, some police departments tried to compensate for lack of height of Spanish-surnamed individuals by giving credit for ethnic characteristics, such as speaking the Spanish language. (The logic of this is unclear.) But most departments continued to discriminate against the ordinary white male if he failed to meet the arbitrarily established height standard.

The second cohesive challenge to the height minimum came from women's groups. As discussed later in this chapter, until the 1970's no large police department hired women for full-service police work; those policewomen who were employed were ordinarily restricted to work with juveniles or with women, or to administrative and technical assignments. When these hiring patterns for women prevailed, most departments had lower height minimums for female police officers than for male officers, presumably on the assumption that police-women were unlikely to be exposed to the dangerous situations in which policemen might find themselves. (They also often had higher educational requirements for policewomen.)

Once police departments began experimenting with use of police-women in all phases of police work, including patrol duties, they faced the question of whether it was logical to hire a full-service female officer without requiring her to meet the same height require-ment of a male police officer performing the same duties. But when police departments raised the minimum height for female police offi-cers to the sixty-seven-inch or sixty-eight-inch requirement for male police officers, women's groups vigorously complained that the height minimum was discriminatory against women, who on an average are shorter than men.

These challenges brought several police departments to carefully reexamine the rationale behind the height minimums; a lack of logic was found.

Proponents of the height minimums argued that taller persons are less likely than short persons to be physically attacked or to be in-jured or to need deadly force to defend themselves. But no statistical studies have validated this hypothesis, and effective study is imprac-tical so long as short persons are excluded from police employment.

A second argument of those that would exclude short persons from the police service is that taller men have an advantage in a crowd, being able to look over the heads of other individuals to see what is going on outside their proximity. A tall person well above average height clearly does have some advantage in a crowd control situation. But even with prevailing minimum heights, few police officers are sufficiently taller than average to easily see over the heads of a crowd. In any event, the ability to see over the heads of a crowd is an ad-vantage not needed nor used that often in day-to-day police work.

A third argument of defenders of minimum height requirements is that such standards assist departments in maintaining a uniformity of appearance among their personnel. To the extent that the uniform-ity of appearance is necessary or desirable, this argument is valid. But there is room for serious questioning of how far it is sensible to go in seeking uniformity of appearance in a police department.

It is unfortunate for American police work that uniformity of appearance has come to be accepted as so important, for such uniformity of appearance has contributed greatly to a misplaced stereotyping of police officers. Unfortunately, America has somehow come to visualize images so that, if a casual observation is made that "such and such police department is a really sharp looking group of men," the careless hearer will visualize a montage of tall, handsome, Anglo-Saxon males.

In a subtle, indirect way, it has been this notion of uniformity which has so long excluded from police work the blacks, the Spanish-surnamed, short persons, and women. In any event, uniformity of appearance is not all that important in police work. For investigative aspects of police work, uniformity of personal appearance can actually be a great disadvantage; it is because of the tendency to uniformity of appearance that most police officers and many criminals can recognize a policeman by sight.

Too, the miliary services of America, which place a great deal more stress on uniformity than do police departments, have found it possible to accommodate in their ranks individuals who cannot meet the minimum height requirements for most police departments. The standards for military officers usually range from sixty inches to seventy-eight inches (the Air Force will take officers at eighty inches). Some specialized units, such as the Military Police, prefer taller officers, but waivers of the desired minimum height for those special units are so common as to be a rule rather than an exception. Actually, taller men are more likely than shorter men to find themselves excluded from special assignment in the military, because of the difficulty of tall men operating within confined quarters of equipment such as tanks, aircraft, or submarines.

A final argument of proponents of closely controlled height standards is that significant individual deviations from the average height may be the result of glandular problems which should themselves form a basis for disqualifying the individual. The obvious response to this is that aberrational variations from height averages clearly should be cause for special medical examination to insure that there are no underlying problems, but the range of height among healthy Americans is far too broad for it to be sensible to insist that all police officers be at least average height and not much more or less.

The weight of newly appointed police officers, and for that matter of all police officers, should be reasonably proportionate to height. Standards for appointment should preclude appointment of individuals who are seriously underweight or who are even slightly overweight. Problems of weight, particularly overweight, plague police officers. Irregular dietary habits, which are a natural consequence of shift work, overtime, and court appearances, make it difficult for a police officer to keep his weight under control as he approaches middle age. Because of this, police departments need to be careful that new appointees to the force do not bring a ready-made weight problem with them, and are well-advised to require their personnel to adhere to reasonable weight standards throughout their careers.

In establishing weight standards, however, care must be taken not to adhere rigidly to outdated actuarial tables, many of which make no allowance for large-boned or well-muscled individuals. Weight tables which are prescribed by police departments should include some automatic latitude for these factors, as well as a system for administrative waiver of the prescribed weight when medical examination verifies that the overweight is bone or muscle rather than fat.

Height requirements for police probably should be abolished altogether, with weight requirements related to height, with administrative flexibility. If the height requirement is completely abolished, police departments will need to include as a part of the appointment process a required demonstration by the individual of ability to perform those standard, regularly occurring police tasks which require strength or size. For the ordinary patrol officer, these tasks are only three: capability to walk a full tour of duty with full police equipment, capability to drive a standard automobile without special equipment, and size of hand sufficient to handle the standard police firearm.

This proposal for abolishment of the height requirement does not take into account the characteristic of civil service boards to require specific, inflexible standards for government employment. If this requirement must be met, the alternative for the police department is to establish a minimum height, perhaps sixty inches, which is so low that challenge as being unreasonable is unlikely, yet is high enough to insure that appointees will meet the needs of the service as expressed above.

Character Requirements

It would seem that character requirements would be among the easiest to administer of the standards for admission to police forces. The fact is, however, that sensible character requirements are difficult to define, a problem to administer, and subject to illogical and sometimes emotional charges that they are either too lax or too stringent.

Character standards probably were easy to administer during the Depression years, when there were hundreds of applicants for every police vacancy and when standards for admission to police forces could be very stringent and rigid. Character standards of large police departments then usually prohibited any record of criminal conviction or any serious traffic record, and required excellent references from previous employers and from neighbors and acquaintances.

These very high character standards were carried forward by most departments into the 1950's and 1960's, even after recruiting had become much more difficult. But with a growing shortage of applicants, exceptions to the standards became common. For example, a juvenile charge of burglary for what had actually been a childhood prank was less likely to be considered a criminal record. Still, variations from mores of the past were slow and gradual; even until the late 1960's, the District of Columbia Police Department would automatically reject any applicant who admitted having fathered an illegitimate child, even though the applicant was responsibly making child-support payments. (As late as 1972, one large city department would reject any policewoman applicant who had given birth to an illegitimate child *if she still kept the child.*)

Efforts to bring increased numbers of minorities into police employment brought the first concentrated attention to the issue of character requirements. Higher arrest rates of blacks (and of other inner-city socioeconomic groups) made the unequivocal rejection of an applicant for any arrest record appear discriminatory. Similarly, higher illegitimacy rates of inner-city residents caused higher disqualification rates for minorities as a result of the "illegitimate child" policies. These policies seemed ludicrously Victorian, anyhow, in an era when high elected officials of the nation were involved in divorce actions and other activities which made it apparent that their not fathering illegitimate children was not because of abstinence.

Policies against employing an applicant who admitted a single experimental use of marijuana were clearly nonsensical when polls indicated that one-sixth of the youth of the nation had tried the drug at least once; instead of being rejected, the applicant who admitted experimenting probably should have been given extra credit for honesty.

But the critics of police character standards were not one-sided in favor of lessening the requirements. There were numerous voices within police agencies arguing that, notwithstanding shortage of police applicants and regardless of any logical argument for flexibility in some standards, requirements should not be changed in any way unless to make them more stringent. Superficial examination of these calls for "holding the line against lessened standards" could give an impression that they were racially motivated, but that conclusion may be unfair.

It is common for veteran members of a group to look upon freshmen as inferiors, not just in experience but in quality; police officers, just like soldiers, college students, and factory workers, have always thought that those who entered the service with them or before them were of higher quality on the average than those coming later, just as each immigrant group to America has disdained immigrant groups coming later. Thus, not all of the nonlogical arguments against "lowering of standards" for police should be dismissed as reflecting racial bias, for much of this was simply natural bias of older groups against younger groups. As a matter of fact, some of the most vocal opponents to any "lowering of standards" for police entrants were black police officers and middle-class black community leaders. Still, the potential of racial bias was clearly present in the fabric of such complaints. Every hiring of a black with an arrest record, even a juvenile charge on unsubstantiated circumstances, increased the potential for accusation of reverse discrimination, although most police departments could find among their ranks veteran white officers who years before had been hired with similar records. And every marginally satisfactory black hired and retained by a police department might be identified as a clear case of reverse discrimination, even though every large department in the country has numerous marginally satisfactory whites among their ranks.

There is no ready answer to the question of character standards. The commercially produced tests which purport to measure character and attitudes have never been shown valid and are considered worthless by many authorities. It was a vogue at one time to think that the solution was in psychiatric interview of every applicant, but experience has shown that psychiatric interview on a mass-production scale for police recruitment is a questionable use of professional time; it is doubtful that a psychiatrist in a short interview can spot potential for aberrational behavior any more effectively than can an experienced police recruiter or personnel interview specialist.

The current state of the art is that police departments have little recourse other than to adopt a general standard that police appointees be of "good character," to adopt some specific criteria, such as denying appointment for a felony conviction, and to recognize that for most factors involved in character measurement, the recruiters are simply going to have to consider the whole record of the individual rather than eliminating applicants on single incidents from their past history.

Sex Requirements

As this book is being written, many police departments are actively experimenting with the use of policewomen in full service police work, and some of the recalcitrant chiefs of police are being ordered by their city councils or other governing bodies to begin such experiments. A reasonable assumption is that by the time this book is in print, use of women in all phases of police work will be almost universally accepted. On the assumption that the question is becoming moot, what is presented in this subchapter is not further argument for unlimited use of women in police work, but a discussion of how the policy for full service use of policewomen came to be adopted in the Washington Metropolitan Police Department, and the problems which were encountered in its implementation.

The District of Columbia Police Department had employed policewomen beginning in 1919, but until the late 1960's had restricted them almost exclusively to working with women who were arrested and with juveniles. Policewomen were utilized by the sex squad, but their function there was more clerical (in taking statements from rape victims) than investigative; occasionally a policewoman might be utilized in an undercover capacity on vice work. Policewomen were eligible to take the promotional examinations for sergeant, lieutenant, and captain, but upon promotion they were restricted to supervisory positions in the Women's Bureau, where they supervised other women police officers.

During the 1960's, there was some activism in the District of Columbia government to broaden opportunities for women, an activism which produced various suggestions that the police department experiment with new assignments for policewomen. In response to these suggestions, I announced in 1969 that it would be my policy to experiment with employment of policewomen in various phases of police work. For this purpose, the authorization for policewomen was increased from fifty positions to one hundred positions in the four-thousand-man police force.

Initially, the policy change regarding policewomen was a matter of medium priority; the department was then struggling with a severe crime problem, with acute recruiting difficulties, with repeated major street disorders and demonstrations, and with legislative, budgetary, and other matters which diverted attention from the question of policewomen. Also, because the police department was moving forward in the matter, even gradually, the activists seeking opportunities for women diverted their attention to other city and private agencies.

The consequence was predictable; middle-managers of the department pressed forward halfheartedly, if at all. Two years later, when full implementation of the policy was undertaken, it was discovered that recruiters had failed to impress upon women applicants that they would be expected to perform full service police work; further, it was nearly two years before uniforms for policewomen were finally designed and purchased. (A subtle, yet striking example of the attitude of middle-managers toward the policy that policewomen would be utilized without discrimination was evident when the property division bought a different styled badge for them, engraved "Policewoman." I ordered them issued regular badges.)

During the first two years of the experiment, there was increased use of women in assignments outside traditional women and youth programs. Women were assigned as active investigators in several criminal investigations division squads, were used as dispatchers (over the strong objections of the director of communications), and were assigned in civilian clothes capacity to tactical force units operating on the street.

In early 1971, nearly two years after the policy of expanded use of women had been announced, I reviewed implementation and found that the program was not being actively pursued within the department. The matter then was given high priority, with my directing that by 1972 the officials of the department should plan on having uniformed policewomen working in patrol functions, being assigned indiscriminately.

Exemplifying the tendency of minutiae to become substance, more time was spent on selection of a proper uniform for policewomen than on any other aspect of the program. First, a suggestion was made that the uniform should be designed by the women themselves. The result of this effort was that after a few months of discussion, design, and production of samples, the policewomen came in with a proposal for a pretty uniform, in pastel colors, much like the kind an airline stewardess might wear. Whether this was a reflection of a desire by the women to have a feminine uniform, or their subtle attempt to sabotage the effort to use them on patrol work, is an unanswered question.

Obviously, a pastel dress was impractical for any woman who was going to be doing active police work, carrying a pistol, handcuffs, portable radio, and other equipment needed by a street police officer, and who would be climbing in and out of scout cars, walking through city alleys, and making arrests. In the end, it was left to me to make the unpopular decision that the uniform would be a standard military-cut skirt and blouse, designed as nearly as practical along the lines of the uniforms for policemen.

Numerous side issues arose over uniforms as the women actually began working the streets; it became evident that they would need belts of the Sam Browne type to carry the equipment of a patrol officer; and there was much controversy over whether or not they should have the option of wearing slacks in cold weather, until I made an affirmative decision.

To provide enough women for a concentrated experiment in use of policewomen in patrol work, the number of policewomen positions was increased from one hundred to two hundred, and I ordered that all policewomen who had been appointed under the changed policy since 1969 should be transferred to patrol duty and concentrated within two police districts. The purpose of this concentration was to make certain that the districts involved in the experiment would have such a high ratio of policewomen that they would be forced to use them in the total range of police service rather than subverting my policy by keeping the women in protected assignments.

It is unsurprising that, as the experiment moved forward, every mistake by a policewoman was used as an illustration for the argument that they could not perform regular patrol work. Invariably, though, when the officials of the experimental districts were pressed, they were forced to admit that some policewomen were in the "good to outstanding" category as police officers. Some policewomen are marginal performers as police officers, but some policemen also are marginal.

The ultimate consensus was that a random selection of one hundred women and one hundred men from American society would, because of cultural and physical factors, result in a higher proportion of police officer material among the men than among the women. But there is a high level of self-screening in police applications which results in most persons who are culturally or physically unsuited not applying. This self-screening factor is likely to result in there being as high a proportion of police officer material among women applicants as among men applicants, once women entering police service do so with knowledge that they are going to be exposed to the full range of police service.

Racial Discrimination

To this day, there are officials in police departments around the nation who argue that racial discrimination has never played a part in excluding blacks from the police forces of America. Veteran police officials in the Washington Metropolitan Police Department argued, even into the late 1960's, that there had never been any racial discrimination in the department. They argued this even though they knew that until the early 1950's, teletype messages calling for presidential details included the admonition "Send white officers only," and that until the late 1950's there were many beats and several precincts where only white officers were ever assigned. Into the middle 1960's, there were headquarters units of the department where no black officer had ever been assigned, and it finally fell to the mayor, in 1968, to order the integration of scout car crews.

Despite these evidences of discrimination, on the other hand the department had achieved over the years a gradually increasing proportion of blacks on the force, though by 1969, the force was still less than 30 percent black. (This compared to a 72 percent black population for the city; however, such comparisons do not take into account that the black population of a city often reflects very high ratios of very young and very old persons outside the age range of police recruiting.)

During the years 1969 through 1972, the department was able to achieve a substantial increase in the number of blacks, with an intake approaching 50 percent of all new appointees. By 1973, the total department had a ratio of 36 percent black officers, and the patrol division had a ratio of nearly 48 percent.

The success of the Washington Metropolitan Police Department in recruiting blacks can be attributed to two factors. For one thing, the department was engaged in a heavy recruiting campaign during that period, both to fill a large number of existing vacancies and to fill new positions authorized under the presidentially ordered anti-crime campaign. From July 1969 through December 1972, more than

2,000 appointments were made to the force. This high rate of appointments enabled the department to make a considerably better showing than police departments with recruiting confined only to filling vacancies resulting from turnover.

One factor which works against agencies trying to improve black recruiting is that while blacks often score passing grades on civil service examinations, their scores on average are not as high as those of whites. This results in many blacks being declared eligible, but being placed so far down in the register of eligibles that in an open register system they seldom are reached for appointment. High turnover or increased appointments vitiate this factor by forcing use of the lower elements of the register.

A second factor which assisted the Washington department in recruitment of blacks was that the department went out of its way to make it clear to blacks that they were welcome on the force. Special efforts were made to get the black community involved in the recruiting campaign, both to advise the department in ways of structuring the recruiting drives and to recommend specific black applicants to the department. Subsequent analyses never showed that the *direct* effects of such community input were particularly substantial, but the assumption is that the indirect benefits were significant; as one black police official put it, "The way to attract black applicants to a police department is to tell them that they are welcome in the department and to tell them in such a way that they will believe it." Involvement of the black community in police recruiting efforts, even though their involvement may not be directly productive, sends a clear signal to potential black applicants that the department is sincere in its efforts to recruit blacks.

There are substantial benefits to obtaining higher proportions of blacks in cities with large black populations, and even in areas without large numbers of blacks. In the black areas of large cities, the presence of a high proportion of black officers tends to soften the image of the police as a mercenary occupation force, composed of officers who live in middle-class suburbs and come into the central city ghetto only to earn their money by imposing middle-class standards on poor people.

The fact is, of course, that the black police officer is nearly as likely as the white to live in a middle-class suburb, and may be more strict in his enforcement of middle-class standards than the white officer. But ghetto residents, just like other groups, tend to base assumptions on perceptions related to skin color. Upon seeing a white officer, an inner-city black will automatically assume that the officer lives in the suburbs; upon seeing a black officer, there is room to wonder whether he lives in the suburbs, but the assumption that he does so is not automatic. The "occupation force" image is considerably softened when there is significant ratio of blacks among the patrol officers in all-black or nearly all-black residential areas.

There are similar advantages, although not quite as important, in the presence of black police officers in predominately white residential areas. For example, although the black police officer who makes a traffic spot check of a black individual in an all-white residential area does so for somewhat the same reason that a white police officer does, the perception of the individual checked is not quite the same as when, everywhere in the white neighborhood, all of the police officers seen by the black citizen are white men.

Outright quotas for ratios of blacks to whites among police agencies are clearly unreasonable. For one thing, sensible racial ratios are extraordinarily difficult to construct because the ratios of minority groups in the population of any given area are constantly changing. Also, because police departments tend to relatively low turnover of personnel, the racial or cultural composition of the city population is likely to change long before a similar ratio of persons among the police can be achieved. And given the usually low turnover in police department personnel, quota systems simply cannot be implemented short of outright reverse discrimination. The sensible policy instead of quotas is establishment of good-faith affirmative action programs constructed with recognition that integration of police forces cannot be left to pure chance.

The need for affirmative action programs is all the more important because of the fact that blacks, on an average, do not compete as well as whites on typical entrance examinations. During periods of a tight labor market, blacks are likely to be disproportionately eliminated by this civil service process. If the entrance examinations were related to actual performance on the job, the disproportionate elimination of blacks might be defensible, but the questions of entrance examination validations are too great for that defense to be used.

In a sense, what has happened during the twentieth century has been that efforts to eliminate the spoils system from police appointment processes have resulted in civil service constraints which confound the actual needs of police departments; some new selection system is needed which will give credit for cultural and natural abilities as well as for academic abilities.

Residence Requirements

During the decades following World War II, most large cities have eliminated the traditional requirement that an individual be an established resident of the jurisdiction in order to qualify for appointment to the police force. Although pre-employment residence requirements made some sense as a way of preserving police jobs for hometown entrants to the labor market, many authorities have argued that a pre-employment residence requirement is counterproductive to the concept of seeking the highest possible quality in individuals for police work. Pre-employment residence requirements certainly were impractical during the 1960's, when police recruiting teams were scouring the nation in efforts to fill their vacancies; for this reason such requirements were dropped by most cities.

During the late 1960's and early 1970's, pre-employment residence has been far less controversial a matter than post-employment residence. As America shifted increasingly toward a suburban mode of living, large cities saw many of their employees moving outside their jurisdictions into bedroom communities. This flight to the suburbs was accelerated by the racial and crime problems of the central cities during the late 1960's.

Although the question of nonresident employees should pertain to all departments of a city government, the public controversy in most cities had concentrated on the question of residence requirements for police officers. One reason for this has been the notion, which has some marginal validity, that requiring police officers to live within their jurisdiction will add measurably to public safety through increased police presence. A second factor has been the "occupation force" concept, referred to earlier, as racial compositions of cities have changed.

Except for the minimal value of increased police presence, there is no more justification for requiring a police officer to live within his jurisdiction than there is to require any other city employee to do so, and there certainly is less justification in the case of a police patrol officer than in the case of a middle-management administrator who has considerable influence on city policies.

As a matter of fact, the police officer has more personal incentive to live outside his jurisdiction than the ordinary city employee. In most cities, a police officer is considered to be at least theoretically responsible for taking action when any offense, even a misdemeanor, is committed within his presence; this is so whether he is on or off duty. Policies such as this make it impractical for a police officer to relax as an ordinary citizen until he has crossed the city line. Furthermore, given the usual level of salaries of the police patrol officer, he is attracted just as other employees are to the lower cost of housing in suburbs.

Still, there are valid reasons for a city to want its employees to live within its boundaries. For one thing, many central cities are faced with an eroding tax base which results in part from the movement of middle-class taxpaying citizens to the suburbs, leaving the city with a disproportionate ratio of the poor, the elderly, and others who pay few taxes and require many services.

Second, the city employee who lives within the city is almost certain to have a higher level of interest in the jurisdiction than one who lives elsewhere. A common lament of central city residents is that their school principal does not attend the PTA meeting because he is busy at the PTA of the suburban school his own children attend, or that a complaint to the police officer on the beat about crime conditions in the neighborhood brings a response implying "What do you expect, living in an area like this?"

Some cities are again requiring employees to live within their jurisdictional areas, usually imposing the requirement only on those appointed since the changed policy was adopted. Whether or not these systems can prevail in the long run probably will depend both on the nature of the city and its housing supply and on whether or not police recruiting again becomes as difficult as it was during the 1960's. Although there is a rationale for the desirability of urging city employees to be totally immersed in the life of the city they serve, there is substantial question whether this notion can prevail in a society where the emphasis increasingly is on recreational and other activities and where the employment of the individual is much less a focal point in his life than once was the case.

In the long run, the sensible policy for most jurisdictions seems likely to be one encompassing no concrete pre-employment or post-employment residence requirements, but including various forms of additional compensation and strong promotional preference as incentives for postemployment residence of police officers.

More than all else, it is important for government and community leaders to recognize that police officers are also people. Efforts to make them superhuman are ill advised.

9

Career Processes
for Police Officers

MOST AMERICAN POLICE DEPARTMENTS employ a rank structure fashioned partially along military lines. Typically, some form of civil service examination process is used in selecting persons for promotion.

The rank structure of a large or medium police department usually will progress from patrol officer to sergeant, lieutenant, captain, major, lieutenant colonel, and colonel (the chief or superintendent often holds the rank of colonel). A frequent variation is to substitute such titles as inspector, chief inspector, deputy chief, or assistant chief, for the positions above the rank of captain.

Some departments use the title "commissioner" for the chief of police. Until recent times a commissioner of police was usually a political appointee who made broad policies but left day-to-day operations of the police department to a career police official who reported direct to the commissioner. During the 1960's most "commissioner"-directed police departments were reorganized so that the commissioner has several high-level deputies reporting direct to him so that he has more operational as well as policy control of the department. Such commissioners still are sometimes selected from outside the departments they lead (as are increasing numbers of executive heads known as chief or by other titles), but by 1970 most police commissioners in "single-commissioner" departments were selected for administrative experience and ability rather than purely political considerations. (The terminology "single commissioner" is intended to exclude members of boards of police commissioners where such boards still exist.)

A few departments rely on a formal civil service examination process for selection of appointees to every uniformed supervisory position from the rank of sergeant through even the position of chief of police. But the more usual arrangement is to use a formal civil service process through the rank of captain, and to select promotees to positions above that level, without regard to civil service, from among incumbents in the rank of captain. Also, it is not unusual for promotion of detectives to be exempted from civil service and for there to be a separate career-ladder rank structure for detectives.

It is much easier to describe what is wrong with police career systems than to devise solutions. With apology for that fact, the following discussion is offered of what the problems are and why they exist.

A fundamental deficiency of police career systems derives from the reliance on military rank structures. An adverse by-product of this system is that many Americans consider the rank of patrol officer in a police department to be comparable with the rank of private in the army. This misconception is reinforced by some departments which call the patrol officer a "private" and by other departments which use either a "private first-class" or "corporal" rank for senior patrol officers. Even where the term "police officer" or "patrolman" denominates the basic rank, the ranking of supervisors as sergeants, lieutenants, and captains recasts the patrol officer as comparable to a military private.

These misconceptions are a more serious matter than euphemism. American society has a high level of awareness of military rank systems. Consequently, when an average citizen is confronted with disagreeable instructions from a patrol officer, the military rank structure causes the citizen to misconstrue the status of the patrol officer as that of lowest ranking member of a military organization, from whose decisions there is ready appeal to a sergeant or other superior, rather than that of a master craftsman whose judgments should be accepted except in the most unusual circumstances.

A second misconception regarding the patrol officer, induced by the military rank structure, is that the mis-analogy of the patrol officer to a private in the army misleads the public into thinking that there is something wrong with an individual who is satisfied to remain a patrol officer throughout his career. No careerist in the army remains a private, or for that matter a second lieutenant, until retirement; as a matter of fact, the "up or out" policies of the military prohibit an individual from remaining in those basic grades even if he should desire to do so.

On the other hand, though, no one thinks it strange if a master carpenter, or master bricklayer, or master plumber prefers the practice of his craft throughout his career instead of accepting promotion into the ranks of foreman or job superintendent. The same comparison holds true in more sophisticated occupations; nothing is thought strange about the newspaper reporter who does not want to become an editor, or the doctor who does not want to become a hospital administrator. In most occupations, it is entirely acceptable, both among practitioners and among outsiders, for an individual to spend his entire career at the craftsman or professional level. Within police work, practitioners readily understand that many individuals prefer remaining as excellent patrol officers rather than accepting promotion to supervisory ranks where different aptitudes, skills, and interests are required; however, because of the analogy to the military rank structure, outsiders, including even families and close friends of police officers, often think there is something wrong, which there certainly is not, with the individual who is happy to remain a "private" throughout his career.

Some small departments have experimented with discarding the military rank structure, together with insignia of rank, relying instead on the less formalized supervisor-subordinate relationships found in civilian crafts and professions. Although the less clearly identifiable rank structure may work in small departments, it may be difficult to institute in medium or large departments, where individual police officers are less likely to be personally acquainted with one another. When an emergency occurs in a large city, and several, or dozens, or even hundreds of officers respond to the scene, effective command and control requires that both the officials and the police officers present immediately recognize who has the authority and responsibility of command; a system of ranking, with easily identified insignia of rank, may be indispensable to this purpose. It is unfortunate, however, that the police of America did not avoid the use of terms such as sergeant, lieutenant, and captain, and devise some universal police system of ranking officers which would not be analogous to the military structure. The problem is a fundamental one which needs study for change.

A deficiency with police promotional systems comes from the necessity in large police departments to rely on written examinations to select individuals for promotion to the lower ranks of the supervisory structure. Construction of a written examination to select perhaps one hundred sergeants from among two thousand applicants is no easy task. For this kind of selection process, the examination must not only test applicants to determine which possess minimum knowledge needed for performance at the higher level, but also must be sufficiently difficult to insure a wide spread of test scores to serve as a "register" for determining the order in which successful applicants will be promoted, as vacancies occur.

A register-producing examination must be sufficiently difficult to make it unlikely that any examinee will achieve a perfect score. Because of this need, many police promotional examinations include numerous questions on obscure statutes and points of law which have little practical value in day-to-day police work. And others of these examinations resort to written questions intended to measure judgment. But to produce a usable register these kinds of judgmental questions need to have such close potential answers that correct response is likely to be little better than a guess.

The ultimate disadvantage of these kinds of written examinations is that they often force police aspirants for promotion to spend far more time memorizing seldom-used statutes and regulations than is useful either to the individual or to his department. A frequent criticism of these examinations is that they are more effective in selecting bookworms than in selecting leaders of men, but this criticism is only partially true, for it is common in large departments to find high-quality college graduates who are unable to score sufficiently high on written examinations to achieve promotion.

As a complement to the written examination, large departments commonly employ a performance rating system, or more correctly, a suitability-for-promotion rating system. These systems ordinarily employ numerical ratings, based principally on the judgments of the supervisors and administrative officials for whom the applicant works, of the potential suitability of the individual for promotion to the next higher rank. The intended purpose of these systems is to reduce the potential that a marginally satisfactory applicant will be promoted solely on basis of the written examination, and to enhance probability of promotion for the outstanding leader.

The suitability-for-promotion ratings are indispensable to an effective promotional system in a large department, but the system is not without its problems. It is very difficult to standardize the level of ratings between various units; some officials tend to assign much higher ratings, on the average, than others. To offset this tendency, it is possible for the department to require a prescribed average rating from each unit, but this works a disadvantage to the applicant in a small, specialist unit, which attracts and selects only better-than-average men. (On the other hand, as discussed later, the prescribed unit average has the effect of encouraging the better-than-average man to stay in a patrol unit where there are more rating points to be had rather than move to a specialty.)

A second difficulty with suitability-for-promotion ratings is that, particularly at the patrolman level, morale problems frequently arise when aspirants for promotion misconstrue the rating of suitability for promotion to be a rating for performance at their current level. It is abundantly clear, *to everyone except the hardworking aspirant,* that many individuals who are excellent performers as patrol officers have neither aptitude nor personality to become better than marginal supervisors.

It is also a common practice in police promotional systems to utilize an oral interview board, often of three or five individuals, to assess applicants either by assigning numerical ratings which become a part of the register developing process, or by listing in preference order for promotion those applicants who have successfully competed in the examination process.

Experienced observers of the oral interview process have noted that these boards are reasonably accurate, on an average, in assessing whether an individual has high potential or mediocre potential as a supervisor or administrator. But despite their accuracy *on the average,* it has also been noted that such boards fail often enough in their assessments to make the process questionable. Such a board frequently will misconstrue an articulate nonproducer to have high potential and some less verbal high-producer to have little potential. This hazard of mistaking articulateness for productivity is especially great when all or a majority of the board members are from outside the organization or from a level in the hierarchy where they have no prior knowledge of the individuals being interviewed.

Despite these failures of oral interview boards comprised principally of outsiders, some administrators feel that this process adds an element of fairness to rating procedures which might otherwise be skewed by personal biases of supervisors within the organization. On balance, however, a better way to deal with potential internal biases is to provide an appeals system which will insure opportunity to be heard at a higher level of the organization for an applicant who feels the initial rating is unfair.

The promotional process is an important part of the informal system which keeps an organization moving toward its objectives; not only is the promotion of each individual to the rank of sergeant a selection of a future eligible for promotion to middle management, but it is also an informal example to other patrol officers of the kind of individual they should aspire to be; difficult as the rating process is, it is too important a tool and responsibility of administration to be taken away from the managers of the agency and delegated to outsiders.

An unanswered question in career systems of large police departments is how to compensate specialists who perform necessary and sometimes exceptional services, but whose responsibility and authority are not appropriate for line rank commensurate with the salaries their duties justify. There are two broad categories of such specialists, which involve different problems and deserve separate discussion: one includes the technical specialists, the other consists of the detectives or investigators.

For a variety of reasons, in the usual medium-sized or large department there will be a number of police officers utilized in technical functions such as computer programming, handwriting analysis, operational planning, communications, fiscal affairs, and similar assignments not directly related to police work. Many individuals are selected for such assignments and are continued in them because they are exceptionally good men, intelligent, hardworking, and highly motivated (some others in these assignments, naturally, are mediocre). Some of these assignments are more complex and more difficult, in a different way, of course, than the job of a patrol officer, a sergeant, or perhaps even a lieutenant working in the field. Because of this higher level of complexity and difficulty, civilian personnel in such assignments would earn far higher salaries under a standard job classification system than do police officers within the police rank and salary structure.

For example, an expert handwriting analyst or a competent senior computer programmer, who may be a patrol officer or a sergeant within the police rank structure, might achieve a salary equivalent to that of a police captain or inspector in the civilian labor market — and could achieve that higher salary entirely on the basis of his technical skills without investing a great deal of off-duty time in study for police promotional examinations with questions irrelevant to his immediate assignment.

No simple, universal solution has been devised for this problem. Morale problems result among personnel of the line if there is extensive promotion to senior line rank of technical specialists who have little or no administrative authority or responsibility; these morale problems are exacerbated by systems which permit such specialists to obtain line rank without competing in the promotional examination process. Some police departments provide additional monetary compensation for police officers assigned to technical specialties, but this commonly is insufficient to bring the salaries of competent technical experts to an appropriate level. The most workable solution is a system whereby those who prefer to make a full career of their specialty can be converted to higher salaried civilian employment, working for the police department, while those who prefer to pursue a police career (either as a long-term career objective or in order to retain retirement and other benefits of a police officer) can make that choice even though it means they receive less pay in the short run.

The largest category of specialists, the detectives or investigators, presents a set of problems similar in some respects to but different in others from technical specialists.

The similarities center around the fact that some detectives or investigators become involved in and develop proficiencies for complex assignments which do not involve major command or administrative responsibilities, but on the basis of their complexity and difficulty would justify considerably higher salary than that of a patrol officer or a patrol sergeant. Also, the individual detective often concentrates on one or two types of crime; thus, just as for the technical specialist, the department-wide promotional examination with questions covering all aspects of police work and related statutes, regulations, and policies seems irrelevant. This lack of relevance makes study and preparation even more onerous than for the uniformed officer, who might expect to encounter the wider variety of situations, and also puts the detective at a disadvantage in competing on an examination with uniformed officers who have more recent and more frequent experience in the matters included in the examination.

The primary difference between the detective and technical specialist is that the duties performed by the detective are more commonly construed to be "police work" than are the duties ordinarily performed by the technical specialist. This is at best, however, a hazy distinction; what is "police work" as contrasted to "civilian duties" is not all that definite. There are a great many civilians, both in government agencies and in private industry, who perform investigative duties analogous to those of most detectives in large police departments. On the other hand, a technical assignment such as operational planning demands some police experience because it is essentially a carefully structured way of doing what the patrol sergeant and other patrol officials have always done — analyzing police problems and coordinating redirection of resources.

A second distinction between the detective and technical specialist is that, at least in some assignments, the detective cannot expect to work a standard eight-hour tour of duty and a regular five-day week. In most departments, it is considered important that serious crimes such as homicides, serious rape cases, and spectacular robberies be closed as quickly as possible; this emphasis on early closure of such

cases derives from both political considerations — the desire to reinforce public confidence in the department — and practical considerations — the fact that crimes are much harder to solve without immediate investment of significant effort in canvassing the area of the
incident, interviewing witnesses, and following through on initial
leads.

The pressures for rapid solution of major cases cause some detectives to perform inordinate amounts of uncompensated overtime.
However, an assumption that all detectives put in great amounts of
overtime would be an incorrect generalization. Detectives, just as
any other group when they talk of the demands of their job, tend
to emphasize the extremes; in most cities the probability is that about
10 percent of the detectives always or frequently work long uncompensated hours of overtime without respect to watching the clock,
that 80 percent of the detectives work regular hours but would like
everyone to think that all detectives work a great deal of uncompensated overtime, while the remaining 10 percent make no bones about
the fact that they work a forty-hour week and nothing more without
compensation.

All of this makes it difficult to construct a career system which will
properly compensate the detective and yet not overcompensate him
in relation to the uniformed force. A frequently used system is to
establish a separate structure of compensation and ranking for detectives, outside the civil service system used for promotion within the
uniformed ranks of the police department. Such systems have usually
contemplated that promotions within detective ranks would be based
on ability and potential as an investigator, rather than as a supervisor,
and have assumed that failure to perform adequately as an investigator would result in removal from the ranks of detectives and return
to the uniformed force. The concept is good, except that organizations seldom actually work that way; once promotions, particularly
for numerous positions at lower ranks, are removed from civil service,
various forms of favoritism, political interference, and overemphasis
on seniority develop. And the notion that mediocre performers will
very often be reduced in grade or fired is just not consistent with
what goes on in any organization, public or private.

An alternative is to provide a civil service examination system for selection of investigators to be promoted to supervisory ranks within the detective hierarchy. The difficulty with this process is that ambitious detectives aspiring to upper management of the police department find themselves disadvantaged when competing for promotion to higher ranks with uniformed officials having broader experience in supervision and administration.

A third possibility is to have no separate career structure for detectives. In this system, detectives, and all other specialists in the department, obtain advancement to higher ranks and grades only by competing in the civil service examination process for promotion within the department. This system contemplates that ranks above that of patrol officer are provided to fulfill supervisory and administrative functions, and that a well-qualified supervisor or administrator does not need experience in a specialty in order to supervise a specialized unit. This system also assures that benefit is to be gained for the department by inducing gradual but constant turnover in both operating and supervisory personnel of specialized units. Such turnover clearly is beneficial to career development of individuals involved, and deters development of any inbred specialist unit which perceives its own functions as the paramount objective of the department.

The police administrator inevitably encounters problems in selecting officials for specialized units. Because of the frequent public visibility of specialized units, and also because of the frequent interchange between supervisors of specialized units and the upper hierarchy of the department, there is a natural tendency to assign only better-than-average or outstanding officials to such units.

If allowed to occur unchecked, the concentration of high-quality officials in specialized units can result in serious lowering of the average level of competence of officials in the operational units of the department, particularly the patrol division.

A repeated lament of police administrators in general and of patrol commanders in particular is that specialized units draw off both numerically and qualitatively significant manpower from the patrol division.

Some highly capable and competent patrol officers are happy to remain in patrol division assignments throughout their careers, and some police officials have no desire to work anywhere in the patrol division. But these are the exceptions rather than the rule. In some departments there are many incentives for getting out of patrol division; specialized units offer better hours, more stable work assignments, the satisfaction of an individualistic job, and perhaps enhanced opportunity for promotion. For the ambitious police official, specialized assignments, particularly a series of specialized assignments, offer all of those advantages plus increased visibility to the hierarchy of the department for eventual promotion to middle-management positions.

In a deliberate effort to offset this tendency, the Washington Metropolitan Police Department established a requirement that promotional suitability ratings for each unit of the development be no higher, on an average, than a prestated maximum numerical rating. The purpose of this system was to give incentive for better than average patrol officers and better than average officials to remain in the patrol division. Higher ratings for competent aspirations in the patrol division were offset by very low ratings for marginally competent personnel who never are selected for special assignments and, therefore, are relegated to patrol. This concept was designed to reinforce the often stated but seldom implemented policy that the patrol division is the backbone of any police department.

Most American police agencies have a system of "exempt" ranks above a certain level in the hierarchy of the department. Usually, this means that positions above the level of captain, or in some cases lieutenant, are filled without regard to civil service examination processes. There are variations in the way this is done; in some cases the exempt ranks can be filled by promotions only from the highest civil service rank of the department, in other cases the exempt ranks can be filled from among any of the police officers in the department, or in still other cases the exempt positions can be filled either by police officers or by civilians without regard to prior service in the department.

It is not uncommon to find civilian employees working at relatively high-level administrative and technical posts within police agencies, and in many departments these duties vest the civilian officials with staff authority. However, it is uncommon to find line authority delegated to civilian employees within police agencies.

Probably the most significant effort made in recent history to integrate civilian officials literally into the line hierarchy of a major police agency was the work of O. W. Wilson with the Chicago Police Department. Wilson implemented a concept of "exempt" positions which provided that all positions above the rank of captain, including directors of staff units in headquarters, would be totally exempt from civil service, would be open to appointment of individuals from any rank in the police department or from outside the police department, and would have incumbents serving at the pleasure of the superintendent. Such a system assumes that the middle management of the department will be comprised of the best men available, both because the appointment process allows selection of highly competent individuals without regard to civil service examinations and other constraints and because the process permits easy removal of individuals who prove to be or become marginally effective.

This "exempt" rank system spread to other police departments, largely through the management survey of the International Association of Chiefs of Police, whose staff adopted the concept as basic policy. There are some minor variations in the concept. For example, in the St. Louis Police Department it had long been common to have civilian employees as directors of important staff units (for example, personnel division or planning division); however, while the Chicago format involved appointment of an "exempt" outsider to a position as a police official, the St. Louis format involved only appointment to a high-level directorship, but in a civilian capacity. Other examples of the same variation are Baltimore, which partially followed the Chicago format of appointments of civilians to police ranks, and Washington, D.C., which followed the St. Louis format of appointing high-level civilians to positions as bureau and division heads in the department, but as civilian employees.

The distinction may be nominal; rank and file police officers are likely to view any outsider appointed to a post within the police department to be "civilian," whether or not he is appointed to a police rank; the logic of this perception does nothing to lessen its effects. What is important is not so much whether exempt positions filled by outsiders carry with them actual police rank, but whether or not the chief executive of the department confers upon the incumbents implicit and explicit authority needed for them to function effectively.

Some form of exempt rank system is clearly necessary if a police executive is to develop an effective middle management within his department. But it is a mistake to think that civil service exemption of middle-management positions will absolutely assure appointment and retention of only well qualified individuals.

The police executive selecting a middle-manager from outside his department seldom has any absolute indicators to tell him whether an applicant is outstanding, marginal, or plainly incompetent. There are the self-serving biographical data supplied by the applicant, and there is the oral interview process which tells only whether or not the applicant is literate and articulate, which may or may not be important to the position. There are the comments from personal references and former employers listed by the applicant, but these rarely are useful. The middle-management applicant is unlikely to have been such a disciplinary problem as to get an adverse reference from former employers, who are likely to be charitable; current employers often give good references in order to rid themselves of marginal employees. This difficulty of appraising the potential of unknown outsiders is one of the reasons why police officers are used to fill jobs which more appropriately could be performed by civilian employees.

The system works somewhat better, but still imperfectly, for selection of middle-managers from among the ranks within the department. At least when selecting from among in-house candidates, the chief executive has some fairly reliable indicators of prior performance. But prior performance can be misleading, especially when the prior performance is in some supervisory line position and the selection is for a middle-management staff position, or even a middle-management line position.

Just as many individuals are excellent patrol officers but prove to be mediocre sergeants, some officials who are superior performers as sergeants and lieutenants (where the function is to implement the guidance and policies of middle management), are marginal as middle-managers in the line and incompetent as middle-managers in specialized staff units. The result is that the chief executive must rely on judgment to choose those officials believed likely to perform best as middle-managers and trust that the judgment will be correct at least a majority of the time.

But the selection process actually is more complicated than merely choosing the official judged likely to be the "best" performer, for the promotional system has functions other than simply finding the best appointee for positions. The promotional process also serves as a system of implied rewards for high performance at the lower level, and as an incentive to sustain good performance by moderately competent officials at lower levels.

Although there is a temptation to select only "best" men for promotion, the chief executive must ever bear in mind that an individual at a lower level who year in and year out is working hard at doing a better-than-average job may lose incentive and become a marginal performer if repeatedly passed for promotion. And in a system where only "best" men are promoted, those passed over will not be just a few individuals, but over a period of time may constitute three-quarters or more of the officials at the top civil service rank; comprising far too large a group of senior officials for the chief of police to disregard their morale. It may be pleasing and it may be comfortable for the chief to be surrounded by a group of "best" middle-managers, but if the person creates a morale backlash at the next level of supervisors, the chief will find it difficult to implement policy changes.

President Theodore Roosevelt resolved this problem in the military services by instituting the system whereby military officers passed over for promotion several times, or not achieving a specified rank by a stipulated age, are required to retire. Such a system has much to recommend it for police service, which, like the military service, is typically a closed personnel system with a reasonably good retirement system.

Without an "up or out" system, most police executives adopt a compromise policy of usually promoting "best" officials to exempt ranks but occasionally moving to that level some "above average" officials. Given the guesswork judgment inherent in personnel selections, this system is probably a reasonably effective management tool. The poorest system, of course, is that used by some administrators who are without courage to administer and therefore rely almost exclusively on seniority as a way of selecting for promotion to exempt ranks.

Although the general idea behind the "exempt" ranks is that incumbents of such positions serve at the pleasure of the chief executive, this concept is rarely invoked to eliminate incompetent or moderately competent managers.

The reason for infrequency of demotion from exempt positions is a simple one: incompetence or moderate competence of a middle-manager is very difficult to perceive, much less to describe. The top manager knows that something is wrong in a division; it is clear that performance needs to be improved. But the middle-manager called to account almost invariably can produce not only a list of improvements which have been accomplished, but also a list of recommendations for further improvements which were not implemented because of budget cuts, unavailability of resources, or documented lack of cooperation by other elements of the department.

The top manager may be left with a deep-seated intuition that more could and should have been done; if the middle-manager were a better salesman, the budget would not have been cut; a more persuasive middle-manager would have elicited cooperation from other units; a better middle-manager would have achieved more; but the top manager usually is unwilling to demote or to fire on instinctive reactions not susceptible to verbal expression or statistical display.

Fortunately, there are numerous alternatives for dealing with such a situation without either demoting or tolerating the moderate performer. The manager can transfer the incumbent laterally to some less critical position, or perhaps to an equally critical position better matching his particular talents.

Other options of the chief executive are to circumvent the moderate performer by reorganizing the unit with the incumbent reporting to some stronger middle-manager who will actually run the unit, or by appointing a deputy unit commander who will in practice report direct to the chief executive. Any of these kinds of action can work effectively. Practical manipulation of the bureaucracy can be nearly as effective a management tool as a good personnel system.

As with appointment to the rank of patrol officer, there is a fundamental question of what minimum requirements will be established for promotions to higher ranks within a police department. Police agencies ordinarily have a requirement for a period of service in the rank of patrol officers before promotion to the rank of sergeant, and further requirement of stipulated periods of service within each rank before promotion to next higher rank.

Except for promotions to "exempt" middle-management positions, the rationale for these experience requirements is reasonable so long as the time periods are not excessively long. A basic requirement of two or three years at the grade of patrol officer before promotion to a supervisory position, and a requirement of one year in grade for each rank thereafter should be sufficient to insure that the individual obtains a reasonable level of competence and can be properly evaluated in grade before each promotion. Unfortunately, some departments place too great emphasis on experience and require inordinate periods of service before each promotion, with the result that even outstanding individuals are prevented from attaining middle-management positions before middle age.

The college degree, noted in the previous chapter as increasingly proposed as a requirement for appointment as a patrol officer, is even more frequently a suggested requirement for promotion within police departments, particularly to ranks above the basic supervisory level. Although there certainly is more logic for requirement of a college education for managerial or administrative positions within a police agency than there is for the basic patrol officer function, there still are good arguments against using college education for an *absolute* prerequisite even for middle- and top-management positions.

One certain result of an unequivocal education requirement for promotion to middle ranks of the department will be an extraordinarily high level of interest among patrol officers in completing their educations and obtaining degrees. To some extent this is good; it can be hypothesized that no harm is done in urging police officers to further their educations. The fault of that hypothesis is that the furtherance of education can be overdone at the expense of other priorities of the police administrator. Concentration on obtaining a degree may detract from concentration on crime problems and crime reduction; there may be less willingness to work overtime or to make court appearances which interfere with studies; interest in knowledge and skills dealing directly with the policies and procedures of the department may diminish. Admittedly, these kinds of noneducational priorities are fulfilled by some patrol officers who are continuing their educations; on the other hand, they also frequently are not, particularly by police officers who place sufficiently high priority on obtaining the college degree to carry a very heavy educational work load. For this reason, if for no other, it is to the benefit of the police administrator to stimulate moderate, but not overwhelming, interest in educational achievements among his subordinates.

A second problem with an unequivocal educational requirement for promotion to higher rank is that some very competent individuals, who often prove to be highly effective in lower and middle line and staff supervisory positions, simply do not have the scholastic aptitudes to enable them to perform college work effectively and obtain college degrees. These are individuals who possess a combination of tenacity, innate managerial talent, personality, and sometimes charisma, which give them managerial effectiveness far exceeding that of some (but obviously not all) college graduates. A system of unequivocal requirement of college education for promotion to higher rank would rob the police service of some of its better administrators.

Far preferable to a flat requirement of a college degree for promotion is a system which gives some educational credit, possibly as an additional promotional rating, but which permits promotion to higher rank of individuals without the educational achievement, if they substitute either higher ratings of suitability based on performance or higher examination test scores. These kinds of system serve the purpose of encouraging police officers to continue their educations, while making allowance for those who substitute on-the-job performance for scholastic ability or for scholastic interest, or for both.

The final subject relating to police promotional systems is the question of lateral entry into police supervisory and middle-management ranks. During the middle 1960's, lateral entry was recommended by crime commissions and other authorities for the purpose both of rapidly moving blacks into supervisory and management police positions and for overcoming the inbreeding of concepts and policies caused by the closed promotional systems of most police departments. Actually, there are several facets to the question of lateral entry; the concept is different as applied to a small department than as applied to a large department; it is different as applied to supervisory line positions than as applied to middle-management staff positions.

A small police department, if it has only a few men with moderate levels of training, experience, and supervisory competence, may find lateral entry a useful way of obtaining an experienced and well-trained line lieutenant or captain from another police department. It is much less likely, however, that a medium-sized or large police department will find itself without ample candidates for line supervisory positions from among its patrol officers. And, given the fact that a large police department constitutes a bureaucracy unto itself, where the primary function of supervisory personnel is to enforce procedures, policies, and practices of the department, it is unlikely that a patrol officer or official from some other department can surpass the potential competence of the better patrol officer within house. As a practical matter, it is highly unlikely that any medium or large police department, except in very unusual circumstances, will be able to obtain better candidates through lateral entry than from within its own ranks when filling line positions beneath the middle managerial level.

Middle-management staff positions, however, are an entirely different thing. It is improbable that a medium or large department can improve the quality of its candidates for supervisory line positions by outside hiring; on the other hand, careful consideration should be given to the potential benefits of lateral entry into "exempt" staff positions.

The potential benefits of providing some lateral entry into middle-level staff positions go beyond the mere question of relative competence or qualifications of applicants within and outside the organization. Every organization can profit from occasional infusion of fresh ideas and outlooks which come from employment of middle-managers whose experience has been elsewhere, and a policy of making middle-management positions open to lateral entry reduces the tendency in a specialized unit for a favored subordinate to become an understudy heir apparent.

Conversely, lateral entry should not be overdone, for it is important to avoid stifling enthusiasm of subordinate personnel by giving an impression that promotion is foreclosed to them.

Career structures and promotional ladders of police departments need to blend carefully the objectives of providing high-quality supervisory and middle-management officials while also stimulating and sustaining high performance of subordinate personnel seeking promotion. To achieve this blend, it must be recognized that the term "high quality" does not necessarily mean the "best." Middle and upper levels or organizations, just like the lower levels, need to be composed of individuals with a variety of skills, experiences, aptitudes, and levels of intelligence, both to sustain the aspirations of subordinates for advancement and to keep the organization humanistic.

10

The Use of Civilians by Police Departments

POLICE ADMINISTRATORS are under continuous pressure to increase the use of civilian employees or, put another way, to reduce or avoid use of police officers in duties which could be more effectively or less expensively performed by civilians.

The term "civilian" as used in this chapter and in police work does not refer to the dictionary definition of "a person not in the military or naval service," but instead means a person who is not a "sworn" police officer. As a matter of fact, in some contexts, a soldier or sailor might be viewed by a police officer as a "civilian." Some police departments, however, avoid this semantical aberration by using the term "sworn" to designate police officers and "nonsworn" to designate nonpolice officer personnel; however, even this terminology is faulty, for all government employees usually are required to subscribe to an oath of office.

Actually, the distinction between "police" and "civilian" employees of a police department is less significant than one would imagine, considering the fervor with which the distinction is recognized and sustained by police officers.

The fundamental difference is that in most jurisdictions a police officer has a slightly greater power to make arrests than is vested by common law in ordinary citizens. Beyond the difference in power of arrest, the distinction between the two involves the factors of training and experience and of salaries and benefits.

Police training and experience, often used as justification for misplacing police officers in assignments better performed by civilians, are attributes easily transferable to civilians through intensive training programs, where and if these pertain to skills which are actually needed. More often than not, the police training and experience used to justify placing a police officer in a nonpolice assignment are less vital to the task than the broader training and experience which a properly selected civilian employee would bring to the position.

The differences in salaries and benefits for police officers are seldom a justification for retaining police personnel in nonpolice assignments; on the contrary, more expensive salaries and fringe benefits of police officers are the frequent basis of objections to use of police in nonpolice functions, particularly those functions susceptible to performance by low-salaried personnel.

Meager as the distinctions are between police and civilian, these are an important part of the sociology of the police craft. Almost instinctively, even in the most progressive police department, an employee is likely to be judged first on whether he is a police officer or a civilian and secondly on whether or not he is a competent employee. Police purchasing agents and planners note with amusement how purveyors of police equipment and of law enforcement consulting services go to great lengths to hire as representatives former police officers who, in not later than the third clause of introducing themselves to a police official, will refer to their own police background and experience. It is like ancient world masters of crafts carrying the secret words of their brotherhood from job to job and city to city with them. (Lest sociologists grasp these indicia of a closed brotherhood as further example of separation of police officers from ordinary folk, it should be noted without great elaboration that substantially similar attributes can be found among lawyers, physicians, and sociologists.)

There are three principal reasons which contribute to misassignment of police officers to nonpolice duties. The basic reason is the craft brotherhood among police officers. The second contributing process derives from civil service rules regarding hiring and disciplining of employees, rules which can be circumvented by misplacing police officers in jobs of a civilian type. Paradoxically, the third process often is the governmental budgetary procedure.

Police officers are more comfortable when dealing with other police officers, just as lawyers are more comfortable when dealing with other lawyers. Thus, even in such an ordinary function as searching an alphabetical card file in response to personal or telephoned inquiries from police officers, an experienced police officer is likely to be more efficient (if one disregards the cost) than a competent civilian file clerk. In relating information from the file to the caller, the police officer file clerk will usually be able to talk with a voice of experience and the vernacular of the police about the offenses or other matters listed, the areas of the city involved, the units of the department referred to, or similar matters which a civilian file clerk of limited experience in the police department may consider lifeless entries on the record. Except that it is often purchased at a very high cost in salaries and benefits, this kind of "bringing files to life" can be a valuable asset.

The importance of transfer of police training and street experience to administrative and clerical tasks increases when the tasks performed are more complicated chores such as taking and typing statements of witnesses, processing evidence and other property coming into custody of the police, or working with reports and records in police data processing. As the tasks become more complicated, of course, the cost difference between a police officer-clerk and a civilian clerk is reduced, but may still be substantial.

It would be a mistake to attribute solely to brotherhood among police officers the tendency or desire to misuse police training and experience in nonpolice duties. Police departments which employ civilians in middle-management and policy-making positions often find that those civilian managers are nearly as avid as are middle-management police officials in trying to obtain police officers to perform administrative and clerical chores within their areas of responsibility. Furthermore, most police departments find it necessary to keep constantly on guard against efforts by other agencies of the local government (for example, prosecutors' offices, licensing offices, inspections agencies) which try to obtain police officers for assignment to nonpolice duties within their agencies. A crucial need for police training and experience is the usually stated reason for such efforts to obtain misassignment of police officers, but the real reasons more often are related to civil service and budgeting processes.

Civil service rules regarding hiring and disciplining of employees are a major contributor to diversion of police officers to nonpolice assignments. An administrator who sets out to hire a clerk, such as for the property office handling evidence coming into custody of the police department, ordinarily must go to the civil service commission or board to obtain a list of eligibles. Hiring from such a list entails all of the classical problems of hiring from among unknowns, for there is slim probability of finding listed any applicant who is personally known to the administrator or to some person whose recommendation can be completely trusted. Even when a competent individual is obtained by this process, a considerable investment of time and effort will be required to acquaint the new employee with departmental procedures and regulations for handling evidence.

And, because such a clerical job is unlikely to pay more than about three-quarters the salary of a police patrol officer, the administrator realizes that by the time a competent new employee is well trained and is beginning to understand fully the processes of the office and of the department, he will be looking for another job with greater pay and greater responsibility. The problem of competent employees moving to other agencies for higher salary and responsibility is especially prevalent in those police departments where most or all of the supervisory and middle-management positions are filled by police officers. On the other hand, if the employee is marginally competent, or becomes a minor disciplinary problem, the manager faces an often overwhelming bureaucracy of civil service in trying either to discipline or to remove the employee, and is unlikely to effectively accomplish either, even if he tries. The manager may circumvent these aggravations by utilizing police officer personnel in assignments suitable for performance by civilians.

When a police officer is utilized in such an assignment, the administrator selects a new employee not from among a list of unknowns on a civil service register, but from among police officers known to him either from their having done day-to-day business with his office or through recommendations by other officials in the department. His chances of error in selection are thus greatly minimized, except that the wise administrator is always suspicious of a strong recommendation from the potential employee's current commanding officer, who may be trying to rid himself of an undesirable.

In addition to greatly improved chances of obtaining a satisfactory or better employee, the manager placing a police officer in an administrative or clerical task obtains an individual with training and experience in the overall police operations, with some sense of the processes of the new job to which he is assigned, with a comprehension of how the function fits into the overall departmental processes, and with acquaintanceship and empathy for the police officer clientele served by the operation. Furthermore, if judicious in selections, the manager will usually choose for lower-level jobs those senior, experienced police officers who are uninterested or unlikely to effectively compete in promotional examinations, thereby avoiding the turnover problem which results when ambitious personnel are placed in such jobs. Finally, a police officer who turns out to be marginally competent or a disciplinary problem can usually be removed from a special assignment, without going through bureaucratic civil service processes, simply by a lateral transfer back to the field, usually to the patrol division.

This whole selection and retention process comprises a secondary but significant problem with use of police officers in low-paying nonpolice duties; not only is there the financial waste of having police officers performing functions not commensurate with the cost of their salaries and benefits, but the whole process interacts to deprive line police operations, usually the patrol division, of some of the better, more experienced patrol officers. Marginal performers are rarely selected or retained for such special assignments.

The budgetary process which tends to subtly encourage diversion of police officers from street duties to nonpolice duties is the line item budget which specifies the exact number of positions of each kind allotted to the police department. Because government budget officers perceive, quite correctly, that careful control over number of positions is fundamental to executive control of finances, it is typical for even the most progressive forms of program type budgets to retain the feature of line-by-line itemization of positions authorized.

Because of this itemization of positions, substantial new functions cannot be absorbed nor new processes established by adding new positions, except for the very strongest justification, without waiting for the next budget cycle, when additional positions may be justified and obtained. Absorptions of new functions are especially difficult in an agency with measured and fixed production objectives, such as a tax assessor's office where a specified assessment schedule needs to be obtained, or a school system where a specific teacher-pupil ratio needs to be maintained, or a data processing operation with a carefully controlled work load.

But this kind of measured and fixed production does not pertain to a police department. The universally agreed major function of the police is to reduce or prevent crime, and no one has ever been able to measure on a comprehensive basis just what number of patrol officers is required for crime prevention. In every city there is some minimum number of patrol officers below which the department would be in serious trouble with its constituents; this level can never be precisely specified, but it will be perceived in performance such as response time to calls for police service. The citizens may tolerate upwardly spiraling crime rates, and blame them on other agencies, while a persistent failure or abnormal delay in responding to emergency calls is sure to be blamed on deficient police service.

But few police patrol forces operate at such a marginally low level of manpower that delay in responding to emergency calls will consistently reach the level of nontoleration by the public. Instead, most police patrol forces operate with sufficiently greater than a marginal number of patrol officers so that not only is emergency response usually prompt, but there is ample time remaining for such functions as random patrol, which is presumed to, and probably does, prevent crime through police presence.

It is from these random, nonproduction functions that vacancies in the patrol division, indeed vacancies in the entire police department, are absorbed. It is the existence of this nonproduction time which made it possible during the recruit difficulties of the 1960's for police departments to sustain operations even though they had vacancy rates running as high as 10 percent of their authorized strength (often translated into 25 percent vacancy in patrol division positions). And it is this nonproduction patrol time which makes it possible for a police department to take on a new function, or to establish a new process, or to absorb an increased work load by simply diverting manpower from the patrol division to any nonpolice duties required by the function, process, or work load.

Obviously, a 2,000-man patrol force can hardly relinquish 1,000 of its positions for nonpolice functions, but it can absorb a loss of 50 or 100 positions without an immediately noticeable adverse effect. And diversions of manpower seldom come even in that order of magnitude; in a police department with a 2,000-man patrol force, the diversions of police officers to nonpolice duties usually come as a chipping away of one or two or five or ten positions at a time. Ultimately, this results in buildup of a large number of police officers in nonpolice duties, with the positions lost from the patrol division often replaced by a budget request for additional manpower justified as needed to provide police patrol to combat increasing crime rates. Thus, the budgetary system which is designed to circumscribe establishment of new programs without budgetary review actually furnishes the incentive for misuse of police personnel in administrative programs and then is itself prostituted at the conclusion of the process.

It is one thing to describe the misuse of police personnel in clerical or technical positions which could be more appropriately filled by civilian employees with a cost saving of salaries and benefits. An entirely different matter, with a completely separate set of dynamics, is the question of use of police officials in supervisory, middle-management, or executive positions for which suitable civilian subject-matter experts may be available at approximately the same cost as the police officials.

These are positions in such functions as budgeting, personnel administration, training, records administration, or data processing. Activities such as these each involve relatively extensive bodies of knowledge not ordinarily obtained through line police work. However, these fields are mostly so nontechnical that it is possible for a competent middle-manager to do an adequate and perhaps even an outstanding job simply on the basis of general administrative skills and common sense. Experience has shown that even in as specialized a function as data processing, a strong manager without extensive technical knowledge often operates a more productive system than a technical expert who is misplaced in a managerial role.

For these middle-management, policy-influencing positions, where a civilian employee often will earn as much as or more than a police official, the question of whether to use a police official or a civilian is more subtle and more variable than in the lower-level positions where economic cost is a factor.

The difficulties of using civilians in these positions are much the same as those for lower-level employees. Recruitment of outsiders unknown to the appointing authority is a risky procedure. Disposing of a marginally satisfactory civilian employee through the disciplinary process is much more cumbersome than transfer to a less critical assignment of a marginally satisfactory police official. Unusually good civilian middle-managers are unlikely to stay very long with the agency, but will move on to better jobs elsewhere; a frequent accusation by police officials regarding civilian managers is that they have no "loyalty" to the department, but are always receptive to offers of better jobs elsewhere. (This complaint both reflects the notion that only careerists are assets to police departments and disregards the fact that most police department staffing systems furnish few promotional opportunities to keep competent civilian middle-managers with the police agency.)

Three added factors militate against use of civilian employees as middle-managers in a police agency. First, the use of civilians as middle-managers reduces the number of promotional opportunities for police officials. Complaints of this are more often heard if a position filled by a civilian is one which in the past has been filled by a police official and which involves nontechnical, commonsense functions. Internal objections to hiring of a civilian middle-manager are likely to be more vigorous if the position is as a director of training and the position formerly was filled by police officials, than if it is as a director of data processing, for which few police officials will consider themselves technically qualified.

Secondly, middle-managers are supervisors, and even in the staff operations for which civilian managers are likely to be hired, there invariably will be employed some police officer personnel. In many police departments, it is considered akin to heresy to have a police officer working under supervision of a "civilian." The extent to which this pervades police thinking is an amazing extension of the problems of use of military rank systems in police service; close observation of police department units headed by civilian managers sometimes will disclose a dual system of informal organizations, with one chain of command for civilian employees and another, with police official supervisors only, for police officer employees. However, it would be misleading to blame this dichotomy entirely on the police, for it is not at all unusual for a civilian who is hired as a middle-manager within a police department to request assignment of a police official as his deputy, to provide a strong supervisory position within the unit and to strengthen communications between that unit and the rest of the department.

A third element militating against use of civilian employees in middle-management staff positions is that service of police officials in such positions is important to career development within the department. Police departments, more than most agencies of government, have the characteristic of producing a high ratio of strong line managers. Grasping situations, making decisions, accepting responsibility, exercising authority, taking action — all of the qualities of a line manager — are drilled into a police officer from the day he enters the recruit academy; these attributes are reinforced by training and experience as a police official moves up the promotional ladder.

Fortunately, the police service also equips most of its police officials with rudimentary training in staff work. It is difficult in any medium-sized or large police department for an official to progress to the rank of lieutenant or captain without having or obtaining the verbal abilities for dealing with the public, for preparing position papers, and providing reports. Too, because promotional examinations often include detailed questions on internal operating procedures, the ambitious official is forced to learn not only the line operations, but the basic aspects of records, personnel, and training processes as well.

However, although police officials obtain knowledge of the basic procedures of staff functions, this limited exposure seldom conveys a full understanding of the policy issues and decisions which lead to the procedures. Thus, to round out the career development of police officials with potential for eventually reaching top management, there is great value in their serving a part of their middle-management careers as directors of staff divisions such as budgeting, and personnel.

Notwithstanding all of these advantages to use of police officials in middle-management staff directorships, there is a counterbalancing value to the police agency in having such positions filled from time to time by civilian directors. A police agency, more so than most agencies of government, has a tendency towards inbreeding, not only an inbreeding of outlook, but of policy and procedure. A police department which uses a succession of police officials as directors of any staff unit, without ever employing the services of civilian specialists in the planning and operation of the unit, runs the risk of continuing indefinitely some outmoded system, without ever realizing or considering new techniques and processes which are constantly being developed in other government agencies and in private industry.

The ideal process for keeping the various elements of a police agency continuously but gradually improved is to employ from time to time civilian managers for various staff units of the department. If such managers are selected on the basis of breadth of past experience and prior accomplishment, their presence in the police agency will bring expertise in their specialty, which should survive even after they are gone.

It is important, however, that it be made clear that civilian managers working within a police agency have fully as much authority over their subordinates and fully as much influence over agency policy as would a police official occupying the same position. If the civil service employment process permits, it is desirable that civilian middle-managers be given police official rank. (However, an untried but possibly better process would be to eliminate the police line rank from all incumbents in middle-management staff positions, including police official incumbents, so as to reinforce the organizational concept that staff authority is equally important although less formalized than line authority.)

All of this says that there can be no invariable answer as to whether any specific middle-management position should be occupied by a civilian or by a police official. A police department should strenuously avoid designating any particular position as a civilian slot or as a police slot, but instead should alternate between police and civilian managers in various staff units, with the incumbent of any unit at any given time depending on the current needs of that unit and currently available candidates.

In filling middle-management and senior-management positions of the department, the chief executive should disregard the provincial objection to civilians supervising police officers and ordinarily can disregard the relatively minor differences in salaries between police and civilian middle-managers. The long-term objective should be to strike a balance between the goal of career development of police officials by having them serve in various staff units and the goal of infusion of subject matter expertise and new ideas and tone of operation into the organization. This combined objective can best be met by deciding upon an approximate ratio (for example, 10 percent) of middle-management positions in the department which will be filled by civilian managers and by shifting that group of positions among the directorships of various staff units from time to time as vacancies occur, as problems arise, or as particularly appealing candidates appear. This system will avoid having any particular managerial post become classified in popular thinking as a "civilian" position, yet the established ratio will avoid potential morale problems when a formerly "police" position is filled by a civilian.

There is a third range of positions where police incumbents are frequently used where the salary differentials and the policy considerations are even less clear-cut than in the middle-management positions and in the lower-salaried clerical and technical positions. This third range includes technical posts involved in evidence gathering, radio dispatching, operational planning, and similar specialties which require techniques not ordinarily found outside law enforcement agencies but which, as the functions do not usually require an immediate power of arrest, do not require either that the incumbents be police officers. Whether positions such as these should be filled by police officers selected from within the agency or by civilian employees specially trained by the police agency for the function more often than not is resolved by using police officers. This resolution results as much as anything else from the fact that use of police in these positions avoids the civil service problems already alluded to in hiring and disposing of unsatisfactory civilian employees, compounded by the fact that because the salary differential is not great, there is little incentive for a department to make a special effort to replace police incumbents with civilian employees.

A final class of positions which tends to divert police officers from more important duties involves relatively routine assignments which require some intelligence and judgment, some training in police procedures and regulations, but no power of arrest. Typical of these are positions involved in parking enforcement, traffic control and direction, impounding of illegally parked automobiles, police motor pool assignments, and a variety of quasiclerical and custodial functions. These kinds of positions would be ideal for employment of civilian personnel, except that the level of responsibility involved will not justify enough salary to attract to the jobs qualified adults who will remain with the department long enough to amortize the cost of training needed for performance of the function.

Many police departments have learned that this class of positions is ideally suited to use of police cadets, who have all the mental and physical qualifications for employment as police officers but have not reached the minimum age for police appointment. Such cadets, ranging from seventeen through twenty-one years of age, are hired at lower salaries than police officers, so their pay is not excessively out of line for positions with a low level of responsibility. But, because the cadets are hired with the assumption that they will become full-service police officers upon obtaining minimum age for appointment, it is economically practical for the department to invest more time and expense in their training in police functions and procedures than is feasible for other lower-paid employees, who often move on to higher-paying positions in other departments and agencies as opportunities present themselves. The police cadet system has the further significant benefit of attracting to the police service highly qualified youngsters as soon as they complete high school; this often obtains highly qualified individuals who otherwise would enter crafts and trades after high school and then be hesitant to make the change to police service if they have reached a well-paying journeyman level by the time they attain minimum age for police appointment. A third benefit of the cadet system is that, low level though most cadet assignments are, they do provide valuable insight and experience in police service so that the cadet enters the regular police force with better-than-average conception of the functions of the department. A final advantage of the cadet service is that, because of the very young age at which cadets are hired, the cadet system will attract a higher proportion of local youngsters than is the case with recruitment for the regular police service. In the ideal situation, almost all appointees to the regular police force should come from the cadet process.

As can be seen, the dynamics which contribute to misassignments of police officers to nonpolice functions are complex. Police administrators find that it is no easy task to prevent or to eliminate such misuses of police manpower. The objectives should be to avoid such misassignments in low-skill jobs, simply as a matter of economy, and to achieve a reasonable balance between police officials and civilian managers in middle-management positions, as a way of mixing internal career development with fertilization of organizational progress through infusion of external experiences and viewpoints.

The principal fact for the police administrator to keep in mind is that the fundamental differences between a police officer and a civilian are slight. Unless the incumbent will be regularly required to make arrests, any job can just as well be performed by a properly trained civilian employee.

11

New Directions for Police Training Processes

DURING THE FIRST 150 YEARS after municipal police agencies were established in America, basic and advanced training of police officers was accomplished primarily through an apprenticeship system. The generation of police officers who retired from police service during the 1950's and 1960's came into the craft during a time when a rookie police officer received no formal training at all, but was simply given a gun and badge and sent out on the beat, in company with an older, more experienced officer, to learn by doing, as apprentice craftsmen historically have done.

In final effect an apprenticeship system cannot be discounted as a method for communicating skills from one generation of craftsmen to another, for basically it is a form of teaching by experience. And experience, after all, is an effective mode of instruction. But, although an apprenticeship system is effective, it is not very efficient, and in the police service it can be dangerous.

Apprenticeship teaching of police skills is inefficient first, because in such a broad ranging and complex occupation as police work, it takes the apprentice too long to gain a reasonably complete knowledge of the field; too many events occur only occasionally so that it may take years for the new employee to become a well-rounded journeyman, far too long to be practical where the beginner is paid at full or nearly full salary.

Second, learning from experience is essentially a process of learning by risking or by making mistakes. This is a process that can be expensive in many occupations, but it can be deadly in the police service, where persons sometimes die as a consequence of their own mistakes or those of others.

Third, teaching by experience in the police service is difficult because much of the experience of a police officer occurs in situations where he is without direct supervision. Many of the mistakes of a police officer may go undetected by superior officers; consequently, it is possible for the probationer to make repeated mistakes without ever knowing that they were errors and, therefore, without ever learning anything from the experience.

The logical process for overcoming the deficiencies in the apprenticeship system is not by casting aside the process of teaching by experience, but by improving on that process. This involves a gathering, sorting out, and codifying of experiences, including the mistakes, of those who have performed in the occupation over a period of time. These experiences are then organized into a formal course of instructions, with good and bad practices listed as such and explained. Ideally, during the course of the instructions, trainees are required to demonstrate a capacity to perform the various tasks required. This process of transmitting experience through formalized courses of training is simple in theory, persuasive in concept, but seldom followed in practice. It was not followed by police agencies when they established their recruit training programs in the 1920's and 1930's.

When police departments made the change from "teaching by experience" to "teaching by training," they made the error of confusing educational techniques with training techniques. The consequence of this confusion was that, instead of establishing "how to do it" training programs, they devised "academically" oriented programs. These academic training courses placed heavy emphasis on classroom lectures and discussions organized along subject-matter lines. There was very little "how to do it" in this arrangement. The curriculum usually was a listing of such subjects as: (a) the law of arrest; (b) the penal code of the jurisdiction; (c) the municipal ordinances of the jurisdiction; (d) the traffic regulations of the jurisdiction; (e) the police department internal regulations.

The only agenda items approaching "how to do it" in the typical police training program are firearms training and self-defense courses. Often, even these are not designed to really show a man "how to do it." For example, a police firearms training program often trains the officer to shoot at a fixed target under ideal range conditions, which are unlikely to occur in a field situation, and self-defense training courses seldom require sufficient repetition and retraining to insure that an officer can develop and retain a level of skill to be used with confidence in an emergency.

Since the police recruit training programs were set up some forty years ago, there have been no really fundamental changes in the design. Admittedly, there has been some progress made. As training has become a better organized skill, particularly in the government services during post World War II decades, there have been several improvements in training techniques. Methodological changes have been made, such as changing from straight lecture methods to increased student participation, and increased use of visual and technical aids. Further, there have been many additions of new subject matter to police training curricula in response to new issues and needs in the police service; these additions have included such subjects as police-community relations, automobile driver training, disorder control training, and in some cities, training in foreign languages.

During the postwar years, especially in the 1950's and 1960's, major emphasis has been placed on college education for police officers. Many police training programs now include some classes conducted under auspices of a university, so that college credits are awarded to graduates of the police recruit school. Further, police departments often sponsor programs for members of the force to attend college during off-duty hours with tuition paid either by the police department or under federal grant funding. But college education should not be confused with nor be considered a substitute for training!

Police recruit programs take longer to complete, approaching one-half year in some jurisdictions, and large numbers of police officers are now attending college. But first-line supervisors still lament that some police recruit school graduates cannot perform such basic tasks as making a traffic accident report, or handling a robbery, or a variety of other jobs without long periods of on-the-job training with a senior partner where they *learn from experience.*

These complaints certainly do not apply to all rookie police officers. A significant proportion of rookies come out of recruit school and, after a very short period of familiarization with their patrol unit and patrol area, are able to perform as well or better than their seniors. These are officers, usually scholastically oriented persons, who have the innate ability to synthesize "academic" training into usable "how to do it" skills. The problem arises with those individuals who do not have that ability, or perhaps more correctly, are not as strong in that ability. These are individuals who have a poor aptitude for translating written, or scholastic, instruction into practical applications. The exclusion of individuals such as these from the police service is one of the bases of the repeated recommendations that a college degree be a prerequisite for employment as a police officer; for an expected attribute of a college graduate is ability to synthesize and internalize diverse instructions into specific, useful, practical applications.

But there remains the fundamental question of whether or not a college education is actually needed to perform the police function and whether or not nonscholastically oriented individuals can perform effectively as police officers.

As noted in an earlier chapter, during the 1960's several studies were made to determine precisely what makes a good police officer, to determine whether the currently used testing processes are effective for selecting good police officers, and to determine whether those tests relate to actual police performance on the street. Sketchy and incomplete as those efforts are, there is ample evidence to cause careful thinkers to wonder whether or not scholastically oriented entrance examinations do always select the best applicants for the job. The crux of the findings to date seems to be that scholastically oriented entrance examinations correlate much more strongly to performance in police recruit training schools than to actual performance of police officers on the street. These correlations are not at all startling when one understands that the typical police recruit training curriculum is more closely related to scholastic skills than to street skills of a police officer.

In 1970, the Washington Metropolitan Police Department, operating under a grant from the Law Enforcement Assistance Agency, undertook an effort to strengthen its recruit training program. Not surprisingly, the initial contractual offerings were a variety of proposals for improving on the existing, academically oriented "subject matter" organized training program. Also not surprisingly, because of American mania for "whistles and bells" technology, some of the proposals suggested use of new techniques, such as computerized systems, to better teach recruit police officers such subjects as the law of arrest, the penal code, the municipal ordinances, the traffic regulations, and the police department internal regulations. With new technology, contractors promised that the department would be able to give more and faster training than ever before, in the same old subjects.

Review of those proposals and of what had been tried in city police departments around the nation made it obvious that what was needed was not technological improvement of the presentation of courses already being conducted, but instead a fundamental change in the kinds of courses given.

The repeated complaint of field officials was that recruits came out of training able to recite the law of arrest, but unable to apply it in a real situation; able to recite the traffic regulations, but unable to fill in a traffic accident report; knowing the elements of a robbery, but unable to broadcast quickly a lookout for one. It was obvious that the recruit training school was dispensing the proper knowledge, but was dispensing it in the wrong way.

The result of this enlightenment was a complete redesign of the recruit training program. The "subject matter" oriented curriculum was replaced by a "task oriented" system of training. For example, after being exposed to the subject matter training method, when a rookie police officer in the field received a radio dispatch to a robbery, it was necessary for the officer to recall (while actually in the process of the emergency response) specific bits of information from such broad subject areas as: human relations, use of firearms, the District of Columbia Code, communications, report writing, and crime scene preservation. Scholastically oriented officers, with high levels of understanding and retention of written instructions, could do this almost automatically immediately after graduation from police recruit school; but less scholastically oriented officers required various periods of in-service training before, if ever, they were able to fix in their mind the proper steps and the proper sequence of steps of actions to be performed in any given task.

The crux of the problem was that the department was instructing an officer in the recruit school in how to "perform" the District of Columbia Code, even though that broad subject from the training curriculum did not equate with any specific task to be performed on the street. The result was that the trainee was required to synthesize all of the subject parts, under the pressures of performing specific tasks in the field, often during the stress of emergency situations.

To relate training more closely to street situations, the training division staff undertook a determination of each task likely to be performed by a police officer on the street. This was done by first consulting with field officials to specify each task likely to be performed by a patrol officer. Various units of the department then were asked to assign from their ranks patrol officers whom the command officials considered to be highly effective and efficient performers. These patrol officers then met with the training staff in group sessions where each patrol officer task was carefully analyzed, separated into subtasks, and a listing was made of each action taken, in the proper sequence, for its effective performance.

Tasks, or rather groups of tasks, were then organized into training modules for presentation to the students through written instructions, oral instructions, visual aids, and *student performance*. The restructured training program was aimed at insuring that no recruit graduated from the recruit training academy without having demonstrated not only knowledge of basic laws and regulations, but an actual ability to perform the tasks included in the more than one hundred training modules deemed essential to demonstrate the basic skills of a patrol officer. Because much of the training format was changed from classroom instruction to individualized performance, the system also permitted a more able student (who indeed is likely to be scholastically oriented) to assimilate the training and reach required performance levels in about twelve weeks; the student who assimilates training more slowly may take as long as seventeen weeks (the same as the period of training under the academically oriented process) before reaching performance requirements. The important fact, however, is not the difference between the time taken by the slow learner and the fast learner in achieving graduation from recruit school, but the fact that both kinds of student will take with them to street service a demonstrated ability to perform the required tasks of the job.

It is reasonable to assume that the same kinds of task-oriented programs can be translated into training for advanced subjects such as police supervisory techniques and police investigative techniques, both of which received very little attention until the middle 1960's and neither of which has yet been fully addressed in a manner commensurate with its importance to the police service. Many departments still will promote an individual from patrol officer rank to supervisory rank with little or no attention to the need for training in his new duties and responsibilities. Quite a few police departments in America still insist that it takes two or three years of experience to produce a competent investigator, an insistence which reflects the fact that the only training they give to their investigators is through the apprenticeship process.

A fundamental by-product from the task-oriented training method may be a significant change in processes for selecting recruit police officers for appointment. As already noted several times in this book, there is reason for strong suspicion that present entrance examinations are much better for selecting candidates for academically oriented training courses than for practically oriented street police work. It is entirely possible that the task oriented training courses will go far in debunking the current fad for educational snobbery which suggests that every police officer needs a college degree. The careful analysis of police tasks needed to structure task-oriented training eventually may result in reconstruction of the basic processes for selecting police officers.

Nothing in the world is new!

During the 1930's police departments across America stopped handwriting their reports and began requiring that they be typewritten. During the 1950's some departments considered making typing skills a prerequisite for appointment, and others instituted typist training programs in their police recruit schools. By the 1960's, police departments had learned that most policemen are never going to be very good typists, and "progressive" police departments began using handwritten reports again.

During the 1930's, when police departments discovered that the criminal element was becoming mechanized, the police themselves moved into the new automobile technology. They rid themselves of bicycles and foot patrolmen. By the 1960's, "progressive" police departments were beginning to learn that motorization may have added some efficiency, but it detracted from effectiveness by removing police patrol officers from direct contact with the public they serve. Police departments again began to emphasize various forms of foot patrol and were again using bicycles and their modern counterparts — motor scooters.

In the 1930's, police departments stopped using the "learn by doing" method, and established academically oriented training programs. In subsequent decades, those academically oriented training programs were reinforced by programs for attendance at college by police officers. A plausible prediction is that by the end of the 1970's, "progressive" police departments will find themselves using a revitalization of the old "learn by doing" training system.

APPENDICES

Table of Appendices

APPENDIX A

Crime Classifications

The following are brief definitions of the crime classifications utilized in the national Uniform Crime Reporting program. Discussed in Chapter 1 in more detail are the first seven of these classifications, which comprise the Crime Index.

1. **Criminal homicide.** (a) Murder and nonnegligent manslaughter: all willful felonious homicides as distinguished from deaths caused by negligence. Excludes attempts to kill, assaults to kill, suicides, accidental deaths, or justifiable homicides. Justifiable homicides are limited to: (1) the killing of a person by a peace officer in line of duty; (2) the killing of a person in the act of committing a felony by a private citizen. (b) Manslaughter by negligence: any death which the police investigation establishes was primarily attributable to gross negligence of some individual other than the victim.

2. **Forcible rape.** Rape by force, assault to rape and attempted rape. Excludes statutory offenses (no force used — victim under age of consent).

3. **Robbery.** Stealing or taking anything of value from the care, custody, or control of a person by force or violence or by putting in fear, such as strong-arm robbery, stickups, armed robbery, assaults to rob, and attempts to rob.

4. **Aggravated assault.** Assault with intent to kill or for the purpose of inflicting severe bodily injury by shooting, cutting, stabbing, maiming, poisoning, scalding, or by the use of acids, explosives, or other means. Includes attempts. Excludes simple assault, assault and battery, fighting, etc.

5. **Burglary.** Breaking or entering — Burglary, housebreaking, safecracking, or any breaking or unlawful entry of a structure with the intent to commit a felony or a theft. Includes attempts.

6. **Larceny.** Theft (except auto theft) — (a) Fifty dollars and over in value; (b) under $50 in value. Thefts of bicycles, automobile accessories, shoplifting, pocket-picking, or any stealing of property or article of value which is not taken by force and violence or by fraud. Excludes embezzlement, "con" games, forgery, worthless checks, etc.

7. **Auto theft.** Stealing or driving away and abandoning a motor vehicle. Excludes taking for temporary use by those having lawful access to the vehicle.

8. **Other assaults.** Assaults and attempted assaults which are not of an aggravated nature.

9. **Arson.** Willful or malicious burning with or without intent to defraud. Includes attempts.

10. **Forgery and counterfeiting.** Making, altering, uttering or possessing, with intent to defraud, anything false which is made to appear true. Includes attempts.

11. **Fraud.** Fraudulent conversion and obtaining money or property by false pretenses. Includes bad checks except forgeries and counterfeiting.

12. **Embezzlement.** Misappropriation or misapplication of money or property entrusted to one's care, custody, or control.

13. **Stolen property; buying, receiving, possessing.** Buying, receiving, and possessing stolen property and attempts.

14. **Vandalism.** Willful or malicious destruction, injury, disfigurement, or defacement of property without consent of the owner or person having custody or control.

15. **Weapons; carrying, possessing, etc.** All violations of regulations or statutes controlling the carrying, using, possessing, furnishing, and manufacturing of deadly weapons or silencers. Includes attempts.

16. **Prostitution and commercialized vice.** Sex offenses of a commercialized nature and attempts, such as prostitution, keeping a bawdy house, procuring or transporting women for immoral purposes.

17. **Sex offenses** (except forcible rape, prostitution, and commercialized vice). Statutory rape, offenses against chastity, common decency, morals, and the like. Includes attempts.

18. **Narcotic drug laws.** Offenses relating to narcotic drugs, such as unlawful possession, sale, use, growing, manufacturing, and making of narcotic drugs.

19. **Gambling.** Promoting, permitting or engaging in gambling.

20. **Offenses against the family and children.** Nonsupport, neglect, desertion, or abuse of family and children.

21. **Driving under the influence.** Driving or operating any motor vehicle or common carrier while drunk or under the influence of liquor or narcotics.

22. **Liquor laws.** State or local liquor law violations, except "drunkenness" (class 23) and "driving under the influence" (class 21). Excludes Federal violations.

23. **Drunkenness.** Drunkenness or intoxication.

24. **Disorderly conduct.** Breach of the peace.

25. **Vagrancy.** Vagabondage, begging, loitering, etc.

26. **All other offenses.** All violations of state or local laws, except classes 1–25 and traffic.

27. **Suspicion.** Arrests for no specific offense and released without formal charges being placed.

28. **Curfew and loitering laws (juveniles).** Offenses relating to violation of local curfew or loitering ordinances where such laws exist.

29. **Runaway (juveniles).** Limited to juveniles taken into protective custody under provisions of local statutes as runaways.

APPENDIX B

Crime Index Offense Rates for the United States 1933-1972
(Rates per 100,000 population — from Uniform Crime Reports)

YEAR	COMBINED RATE 4 MAJOR VIOLENT CRIMES	CRIMINAL HOMICIDE	FORCIBLE RAPE	ROBBERY	AGGRAVATED ASSAULT
1933	153.6	7.6	3.7	93.9	48.4
1934	131.3	6.1	4.0	74.3	46.9
1935	116.7	7.0	4.4	61.1	44.2
1936	106.5	7.1	5.1	49.9	44.4
1937	107.9	7.0	5.3	53.3	42.3
1938	104.6	6.6	4.5	52.4	41.1
1939	103.0	6.6	5.3	48.5	42.6
1940	100.3	6.5	5.2	46.4	42.2
1941	98.0	6.5	5.3	42.8	43.4
1942	113.0	6.4	6.1	46.6	53.9
1943	108.8	5.5	7.4	44.6	5.13
1944	114.2	5.6	7.9	43.6	57.1
1945	131.5	5.9	8.9	54.2	62.5
1946	142.0	6.9	8.7	59.4	67.0
1947	139.8	6.2	8.5	55.8	69.3
1948	135.9	5.9	7.6	51.9	70.5
1949	138.0	5.3	7.2	54.8	70.7
1950	132.9	5.3	7.3	48.7	71.6
1951	127.7	5.1	7.5	46.8	68.3
1952	139.1	5.3	7.1	51.5	75.2
1953	145.2	5.1	7.3	54.9	77.9
1954	146.5	4.8	6.8	57.6	77.3
1955	136.6	4.7	8.0	48.2	75.1
1956	136.0	4.7	8.5	46.7	76.7
1957	140.7	4.6	8.4	49.6	78.1
1958	147.6	4.6	9.3	54.9	78.8
1959	146.8	4.8	9.3	51.2	81.5
1960	159.0	5.0	9.4	59.9	84.7
1961	156.4	4.7	9.2	58.1	84.4
1962	160.5	4.5	9.3	59.4	87.3
1963	166.2	4.5	9.2	61.5	91.0
1964	188.2	4.8	11.0	67.9	104.5
1965	197.8	5.1	11.9	71.3	109.5
1966	217.2	5.6	12.9	80.3	118.4
1967	249.9	6.1	13.7	102.1	128.0
1968	294.6	6.8	15.5	131.0	141.3
1969	324.5	7.2	18.1	147.4	151.8
1970	360.0	7.8	18.3	171.5	162.4
1971	392.7	8.5	20.3	187.1	176.8
1972	397.7	8.9	22.3	179.9	186.6

Note that these data reflect the Crime Index without larceny under $50.

YEAR	COMBINED RATE 3 MAJOR PROPERTY CRIMES	BURGLARY	LARCENY $50 AND OVER	AUTO THEFT
1933	631.3	328.3	57.9	245.1
1934	564.7	288.0	58.3	218.4
1935	487.6	242.3	58.6	186.7
1936	453.4	236.6	56.5	160.3
1937	463.2	247.0	55.4	160.8
1938	444.4	248.9	56.1	139.4
1939	443.4	258.6	54.1	130.7
1940	440.4	260.4	51.0	129.0
1941	440.0	246.1	57.4	136.5
1942	432.0	235.6	74.1	122.3
1943	463.5	239.8	87.2	136.5
1944	488.8	244.0	96.0	148.8
1945	580.9	287.2	116.2	177.5
1946	593.6	303.2	130.0	160.4
1947	559.6	297.6	135.8	126.2
1948	550.9	295.4	141.6	113.9
1949	554.3	314.8	131.8	107.7
1950	559.6	312.4	136.0	111.2
1951	582.3	303.2	153.0	126.1
1952	652.5	324.8	192.1	135.6
1953	680.6	345.7	194.5	140.4
1954	695.8	367.9	196.5	131.4
1955	670.2	342.5	192.2	135.5
1956	723.0	358.9	209.7	154.4
1957	791.2	395.4	229.1	166.7
1958	853.6	437.7	248.4	167.5
1959	849.5	431.1	250.3	168.1
1960	964.4	500.5	282.3	181.6
1961	981.8	510.6	288.9	182.3
1962	1030.8	526.4	308.4	196.0
1963	1125.8	566.9	344.0	214.9
1964	1251.7	623.8	382.6	245.3
1965	1314.2	651.0	408.8	254.4
1966	1449.5	708.3	456.8	284.4
1967	1671.7	811.5	529.2	331.0
1968	1940.2	915.1	636.0	389.1
1969	2137.7	965.6	749.3	431.8
1970	2380.6	1067.7	859.4	453.5
1971	2514.0	1148.3	909.2	456.5
1972	2431.8	1126.1	882.6	423.1

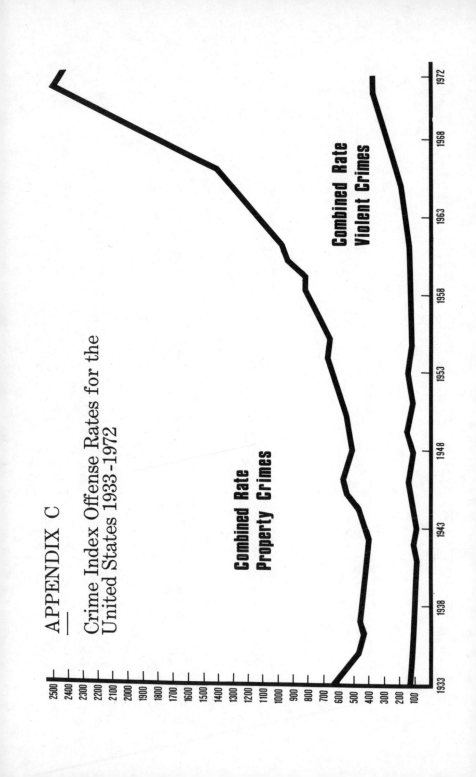

APPENDIX C

Crime Index Offense Rates for the
United States 1933-1972

Combined Rate
Property Crimes

Combined Rate
Violent Crimes

APPENDIX D

Crime in the District of Columbia

(Selected Years — 1958–1973)

JANUARY–DECEMBER — CALENDAR YEAR

OFFENSE	1958	1962	1966	1969	1970	1973
Homicide	79	91	144	287	221	271
Forcible Rape	65	82	134	776[a]	720	596
Robbery	709	1572	3703	12423	11816	7176
Aggravated Assault	2535	3005	3177	3621	4089	3591
Burglary	3642	5022	10267	22902	21740	11801
Larceny	7354	9202	14593	31972	32638	22901
Auto Theft	1899	2581	6565	11364	11110	4713
Totals	16283	21555	38583	83345	82334	51049

[a] Reporting procedure changed

Crime Index Offenses Reported in the
District of Columbia—by Month

CRIME INDEX OFFENSES

Murder
Rape
Robbery
Agg. Assault
Burglary
Larceny
Auto Theft

AVERAGE PER MONTH BASED ON
PAST TWELVE MONTHS

NUMBER OF MONTHLY OFFENSES

APPENDIX F

GOVERNMENT OF THE DISTRICT OF COLUMBIA
Metropolitan Police Department

December 1, 1971

GENERAL ORDER NO. 304-7
SUBJECT: Procedures for Obtaining Pretrial
Eyewitness Identification

The purpose of this order is to establish procedures to promote the reliability of eyewitness identification by eliminating suggestive behavior and, more generally, to increase effectiveness in bringing investigations to a successful conclusion. This order consists of the following parts:

PART I   Responsibilities and Procedures for Members of the Department

PART II Responsibilities and Procedures for Supervisory and Command Personnel

Part I

A. *Return of Suspect to the Scene of the Crime for Identification.*

1. If a suspect is arrested within 60 minutes of an alleged offense and within an area reasonably proximate to the scene of the crime, he shall be returned to the scene of the offense or the eyewitnesses shall be transported to the scene of the arrest for identification of the suspect.

2. Even if the suspect has a weapon or tools similar to that used in the commission of the alleged offense or proceeds similar to those taken in the alleged offense, police officers shall return the suspect to the scene for identification purposes. For example: There is a lookout for a robbery-holdup that has just occurred. One suspect was armed with a chrome-plated, .22 caliber pistol. Twenty minutes later and five blocks from the scene, an arrest is made of the holdup man who is found to be armed with a chrome-plated, .22 caliber pistol. He shall

be returned to the scene of the holdup or the witnesses shall be transported to the scene of the arrest for identification of the suspect.

3. When a suspect thought to have been injured while perpetrating a crime appears at a hospital or other place for treatment within 60 minutes of the offense, the eyewitnesses shall be taken to the hospital to make an identification. If an injured suspect appears for treatment later than 60 minutes after the offense and is not in critical condition, the eyewitnesses shall not be permitted to view the suspect, but may view the suspect's photograph as provided in Part I, paragraph G of this order.

B. *Critical Condition Viewings.*

If a suspect is admitted to a hospital in critical condition later than 60 minutes after the offense, eyewitnesses may be taken to the hospital to make an identification. In those cases where the victim of an assault is admitted to the hospital in critical condition, a suspect later arrested may be taken to the hospital for identification by the victim regardless of the time lapse between the offense and the arrest. For example: the victim of a robbery has been shot and is not expected to live. An arrest is made 2 hours later several miles from the scene of the shooting. The suspect may be taken to the bedside of the victim for identification *if* the victim is still in critical condition since the victim may die before a court-ordered lineup could be arranged.

C. *Viewing at Police Facilities.*

Regardless of the time of arrest, there shall be no identifications or lineups conducted *at police facilities* without the specific authorization of the United States Attorney's Office. For example: Officers investigating a Burglary I have broadcast a lookout and have requested the complainant to accompany them to the district station to view photographs of suspects suspected of other burglaries in the neighborhood. While at the station an arrest is made by another unit one-half hour after the offense was committed and only three blocks from the scene. There should be no identification made at the station. The complainant should be driven either to the scene of the arrest or to the scene of the burglary to make an identification.

D. *Presenting Suspect for Identification.*

1. When presenting a suspect to the eyewitness for identifica-

tion, police officers shall remain as neutral as possible consistent with their maintenance of custody and control over the suspect.

2. Police officers shall neither say nor do anything which will convey to the witness that the suspect has admitted his guilt, that property similar to that stolen has been recovered, that weapons similar to those used have been seized, or that the officer believes the suspect is guilty. For example: Do not tell the witness, "He's given us a full confession but we still want your identification." Do not display the proceeds of the crime by holding up the stolen wallet and saying, "He had your wallet but we haven't found your pocketbook yet."

3. When a suspect is returned to the scene of a crime for identification or when eyewitnesses are taken to the scene of the arrest, all witnesses shall view the suspect. To the extent practicable, each witness shall view the suspect independently, out of the immediate presence of the other witnesses. For example: There has been a holdup of a liquor store and the suspect was arrested a short distance away. When the suspect is transported back to the scene he should not be taken into the store area where the witnesses are gathered. Instead, each witness should be taken separately to the front of the store where the suspect is standing.

4. This order does not bar the accepted police procedure of transporting victims and eyewitnesses in police vehicles and cruising an area in which a crime has occurred in order to point out the perpetrator of the offense.

5. When an arrest is made of a subject which is based in part on the description of distinctive clothing, the arresting officer shall request the Identification Branch, Central Records Division, to take a color photograph of the prisoner. Transporting officers shall be alert to the possibility of prisoners exchanging clothing with other prisoners or discarding clothing prior to their being photographed at the Identification Branch. In appropriate cases, such clothing may also be seized as evidence in the case.

E. *Spontaneous Remarks.*

It is extremely important that the officer make written notes of any statements made by each witness viewing the suspect. In presenting a suspect to a victim or eyewitness, police officers shall be alert for spontaneous exclamations or excited utterances or other reactions by the witness since an officer can testify to these events in court and such testimony may enhance a subsequent in-court identification. These statements should be incorporated in the statement of facts of the case. For example: Upon viewing the suspect, the victim of a rape exclaims, "That's him. See the scar on his neck." This statement should be recorded verbatim on the statement of facts.

F. *PD Form 725 (Spot Check Card).*

Before any suspect is released for lack of witness identification, the circumstances of the incident, including the person's name and address, shall be recorded on the PD Form 725 to provide an official record for the department.

G. *Use of Photographs for Identification Purposes.*

1. The use of photographs for identification purposes prior to an arrest is permissible provided the suspect's photograph is grouped with at least eight other photographs of the same general description.

2. Adequate records of the photographs shown to each witness must be kept so that the exact group of photographs from which an identification was made can be presented in court at a later date to counteract any claim of undue suggestion and enhance the reliability of the in-court identification. This information shall be recorded in the statement of facts of the case.

3. Each witness shall view the photographs independently, out of the immediate presence of the other witnesses.

4. When an arrest is made following a photographic identification, the officer handling the case in court shall request an Assistant United States Attorney to obtain a court order to require the defendant to appear in a lineup.

H. *Court-Ordered Lineups.*

1. Officers are reminded that the court may issue two types of lineups:

    a. Wade Order — when a subject is involved in one particular offense at one location.

    b. Allen or Adams Order — when the subject is suspected of being involved in more than one particular offense and not necessarily at the same location but with similar modus operandi.

2. It is the officer's responsibility to make sure he obtains the proper order.

3. Officers bringing cases before the courts for presentation shall discuss all aspects of the case with the Assistant United States Attorney or Corporation Counsel concerning identification. It should be determined at the first appearance in court if a lineup is appropriate in the case. At this time, the names of all witnesses and complainants involved in the case shall be given to the court.

4. When a suspect arrested in one case is thought to be responsible for other unsolved crimes of a similar nature and involving the same modus operandi, the officer handling the unsolved criminal case shall request an Assistant United States Attorney to obtain a court order (Allen- or Adams-type order) to require this suspect to stand in a lineup to be viewed by witnesses in these unsolved criminal cases. The officer shall not permit the witnesses of the unsolved case to attempt to make an identification by attending the suspect's arraignment or preliminary hearing in court. Officers, when requesting the above-type orders (Allen or Adams), shall bring with them and present to the Assistant United States Attorney all names of witnesses in these cases and the time, date, and locations of offenses.

5. The officer handling the case shall execute a summons (PD Form 30) for each witness who will attend the lineup. The officer shall note on the summons his own name, the type of offense, the location of the offense, the date of the offense, the date and time of the lineup, and the location of the lineup. The witnesses shall be directed to bring the summons with them when attending the lineup. On the date of the lineup, the officer handling the case in court shall contact the detective sergeant in the Major Violators Branch, Lineup Section, prior to 1600 hours and provide him with all requested information concerning the case, including the names of witnesses who will appear and the names of the suspects which the witnesses are to view.

6. Court-ordered lineups will be held in the Criminal Investigations Division Lineup Room, Room 3106, located on the third floor of police headquarters. The officer handling the case in court shall be present and shall be responsible for having the witnesses present for all court-ordered lineups.

7. Lineups for adult Negro males are held every Monday, Wednesday, and Thursday evening. The officer handling the case in court shall report to the Lineup Room, Room 3106, by 1830 hours, at which time a PD Form 140 (Court Attendance Slip) will be executed. All witnesses shall be directed by summons to report to the Lineup Room by 1900 hours.

8. In those cases where a lineup is appropriate for a juvenile, the officer handling the case in court shall contact the Corporation Counsel's Office, Family Division, for an appropriate time and date. He shall also contact the Youth Division to arrange to have a member of that unit present during the lineup.

9. Lineups for all other suspects shall be specially scheduled through the Major Violators Branch, Lineup Section. The officer handling the case in court shall contact the Major Violators Branch, Lineup Section, to establish a date and time for such a lineup. The witness's summons shall reflect the time and date agreed upon. Special lineups will be conducted during the 0800 to 1600 hour tour of duty in the Criminal Investigations Division Lineup Room, Room 3106. Special lineups are for all white males, all females, and any other subject who because of an outstanding feature could not be placed in a regular lineup on Monday, Wednesday, or Thursday evenings. Some outstanding features would be excessive height, weight, age, or any feature which would tend to create a partial lineup.

10. The officer requesting this special lineup shall give all the pertinent information as to the subject to be viewed including name, sex, color, race, height, weight, and any outstanding feature this subject may have. This information enables the Lineup Section to create a fair and impartial lineup for this subject to stand in.

11. All information concerning lineups and special lineups can be obtained from the Major Violators Branch, Lineup Section, Metropolitan Police Headquarters.

12. Counsel for a suspect appearing in a lineup will not be given the names of the witnesses who will view the lineup in the case involving his client, nor will any prior description of the suspect given to the police be made available to him by police officers.

13. Witnesses shall view the lineup one at a time. If more than one witness to a particular crime is present, each shall view the

lineup separately and independently. Witnesses should not converse or otherwise communicate with the other witnesses after viewing the lineup until the last witness in the case has viewed the lineup.

I. *United States Attorney.*

The United States Attorney's Office shall be responsible for notifying the defendants, the defense counsel, and for having an Assistant United States Attorney present at all court-ordered lineups. Part II

A. *Notification of Defense Counsel.*

Counsel for a suspect appearing in a lineup shall be given the date, time, place and, nature of the offense prior to the beginning of the lineup by the detective sergeant of the Major Violators Branch, Lineup Section.

B. *Instructions Regarding Lineups.*

Prior to the beginning of the lineup, the detective sergeant in charge will instruct all witnesses, police officers, and defense counsels as to the procedure of the lineups and the responsibilities of all parties.

(signed)   *Jerry V. Wilson*
Chief of Police

APPENDIX G

GOVERNMENT OF THE DISTRICT OF COLUMBIA
Metropolitan Police Department

December 1, 1971

GENERAL ORDER No. 602–1

SUBJECT: Automobile Searches and Inventories

The purpose of this order is to establish the policy and procedures governing searches and inventories of vehicles. This order consists of the following part:

PART I Responsibilities and Procedures for Members of the
Department

Part I
A. *Searches.*

A search is an examination of a person, place or thing with a view toward discovery of weapons, contraband, instrumentalities of a crime, or evidence. It is to be distinguished from an inventory. A search of an automobile can be classified in one of the following categories:

Searches connected with an arrest.
Searches not connected with an arrest.

1. *Searches Connected With an Arrest.*
   a. *No Probable Cause to Believe Evidence Is in the Vehicle.*
      (1) *General Rule.*

If a full custody arrest is made of a subject in a motor vehicle and the officer does *not* have probable cause to believe that the vehicle contains fruits, instrumentalities, contraband, or evidence of the crime for which he has been arrested, only those areas which are within the immediate control of the defendant (the area from which the arrested person might gain possession of weapons or destructible evidence) at the time of his arrest may be searched incident to that arrest. The search shall be conducted in the presence of the defendant. (The scope, time and place of the search shall be governed by part I, paragraphs A1a(2) and A1a(3) of this order.)

Examples of searches with no probable cause are:

(a) *Carrying a Dangerous Weapon.* An officer making a routine traffic stop observes a pistol in the glove compartment which was opened by the driver as he reached for his automobile registration. The driver is arrested for carrying a dangerous weapon. Only those areas of the interior of the vehicle within the driver's immediate control at the time of his arrest should be searched because there is no probable cause to believe there is other evidence of the offense for which he was arrested in the vehicle.

(b) *Full Custody Traffic Arrest.* An officer arrests a driver of a vehicle for driving after revocation. Before he is transported to a district station, those areas of the vehicle within the immediate control of the defendant at the time of his arrest should be searched, However, areas beyond his immediate control should not be searched because there is no cause to believe that the vehicle contains fruits, instrumentalities, contraband, or evidence of the offense of driving after revocation.

(2) *Scope of the Search.*

The arresting officer may search all areas of the vehicle which are within the *immediate control* of the defendant at the time of his arrest, including those areas from which he might gain possession of a weapon or destructible evidence. If items discovered during his limited search give the officer probable cause to believe that fruits, instrumentalities, contraband, or other evidence of a crime is in the vehicle, then those areas of the vehicle which could physically contain such evidence shall be searched. An example of the scope of the search is:

An officer arrests a driver of a vehicle for driving after revocation. A search under the driver's seat, incident to the arrest, reveals a bottlecap cooker and syringe. The officer may now search the entire vehicle since there is probable cause to believe that other implements of a crime may be in areas of the vehicle beyond the immediate control of the defendant.

(3) *Time and Place of the Search.*

If a full custody arrest is made of a subject in or near a vehicle and the officer does not have probable cause to believe that fruits, instrumentalities, contraband, or evidence of the crime for which the arrest was made may be found in that vehicle, the limited search of that vehicle incident to the arrest shall be conducted at the time and place of the arrest within the immediate presence of the defendant.

(4) *Plain and Open View Rule.*

Nothing in this order should be construed to limit the authority of an officer to seize any item which he observes in plain and open view (including items observed in plain view at night by means of a flashlight) beyond the immediate control of a subject, if the officer has probable cause to believe that such item constitutes fruits, contraband, instrumentalities, or evidence of a crime.

(5) *Non-Custodial Arrests.*

Traffic violators who are asked to accompany an officer to a district station (e.g., non-resident traffic violators who commit moving violations) and are not placed under full custody arrest shall not be searched and their vehicles shall not be searched unless an officer reasonably suspects the violator to be armed, in which case the subject may be frisked for weapons.

b. *Probable Cause to Believe Evidence Is in Vehicle.*

(1) *General Rule.*

If a full custody arrest is made of a subject in a motor vehicle or of a subject in close proximity to a motor vehicle who has just departed from or is about to enter a vehicle, and the arresting officer has probable cause to believe that the vehicle contains either fruits (e.g., stolen goods), instrumentalities (e.g., tools used in a burglary), contraband (e.g., narcotics, sawed-off shotgun), or evidence (e.g., clothing worn by a robber) of the crime for which he was arrested, the vehicle shall be searched. (The scope, time and place of the search shall be governed by part I, paragraphs A1b(2) and A1b(3) of this order.) Examples of probable cause searches are:

(a) *Vehicle Used in Robbery.* An officer has observed a vehicle described in a lookout for a robbery holdup which occurred one hour earlier, in which two men wearing ski masks and carrying pistols obtained an undetermined amount of money. After arresting the two occupants of the vehicle, the entire vehicle should be searched at the scene of the arrest since the officer has probable cause to believe that the money obtained and the pistols and ski masks used in the robbery may be hidden in areas within and beyond the immediate control of the suspects.

(b) *Sales of Narcotics from Vehicle.* A plainclothes officer arrests a subject in or near a vehicle. He has had the subject under observation for the previous hour for the sale, from the vehicle, of narcotics to individuals who approached the vehicle. All areas of the vehicle should be searched since the officer has probable cause to believe that a supply of narcotics remains in other areas of the vehicle, such as the trunk or glove compartment.

(2) *Scope of the Search.*

When an officer arrests a subject in or near a vehicle and he has probable cause to believe that vehicle contains fruits, instrumentalities, contraband, or evidence of the crime for which the arrest was made, only those areas of the vehicle which could physically contain that evidence shall be searched. Examples of the scope of the search are:

(a) *Vehicle Used in Burglary.* An officer has stopped a vehicle for a traffic spot check and has been informed by the dispatcher that the vehicle has been reported as being used in a burglary which occurred a few hours earlier in which a portable television set was stolen. Since it is generally known that most burglaries are effected by means of small tools, easily concealed, all areas of the vehicle may be searched for such tools, unless the officer has specific information that entry was gained in a manner other than by use of a small tool. In such a case, only those areas of the vehicle which could physically contain the portable television set or the object used to enter the premises may be searched because they are the only areas for which the officer has probable cause to believe that fruits, instrumentalities, or evidence of the crime for which the arrest has been made may be contained.

(b) *Vehicle Containing Large Object Used in a Homicide.* A vehicle is stopped, pursuant to a lookout, for a suspect wanted in connection with a homicide in which the deceased was struck with a tire iron which the assailant was seen carrying toward the vehicle. The officer should not search the locked glove compartment because the large object could not be contained in such a small space. The trunk, however, should be searched for the object. If, however, there is some other missing item of evidence (e.g., a blood-stained glove of the suspect), the locked glove compartment may be searched if there is probable cause to believe that the item is in the possession of the suspect or in the vehicle at the time of the arrest.

(3) *Time and Place of Search.*

The search of the vehicle shall be conducted as soon as the prisoner is placed in secure custody and ordinarily at the scene of the arrest. It is not necessary to keep the prisoner near the vehicle during this type of search. In those exceptional cases where it is not practical to conduct a search of the automobile at the scene of the arrest, the vehicle shall be removed to a police facility or other area where the search shall be conducted as soon as possible. In those cases where the search is conducted at a place other than the scene of the arrest, an officer shall remain with the vehicle to ensure a continuous chain of custody prior to the search. Examples of exceptional cases where search may be delayed are:

(a) *Keys to Locked Area not Available*. When the search of a locked trunk or glove compartment of a vehicle is not possible at the scene of the arrest because keys are not available, the officer shall notify the Auto Theft Section and request that a set of keys be sent to the location to which the vehicle has been taken. If the keys are not available, instructions shall be obtained from the Property Division as to the method to be used in opening the locked trunk or glove compartment. No search warrant is required, but the search shall be conducted as soon as possible.

(b) *Hostile Crowd or Inclement Weather*. When an officer believes it would be advisable to remove a vehicle from a public location prior to searching it because a hostile crowd has formed or because the weather is inclement, the vehicle may be taken to the nearest police facility and searched promptly without a warrant.

(1) *Search Warrant*.

When an officer arrests a subject in or near a vehicle and he has probable cause to believe that the vehicle contains fruits, instrumentalities, contraband, or evidence of the crime for which the subject is arrested, all those areas of the automobile which can contain such evidence shall be searched *without* a search warrant. In those exceptional cases where the search is not completed at the scene of the arrest and the vehicle is removed to a police facility or other area, the search shall be completed, as soon as possible, *without* a search warrant. In cases where there is adequate time to obtain a search warrant *prior* to the arrest of a subject in a vehicle, a warrant shall be obtained for the search of the vehicle. One example of the necessity for a search warrant is:

Adequate Time to Obtain Search Warrant Before Making Arrest in Vehicle. A subject has been under surveillance for several days because of the officer's suspicion that he is selling stolen property from his vehicle. If probable cause to arrest is gathered and the decision is made to obtain an arrest warrant for the subject, a search warrant for the vehicle should also be obtained because there is adequate time to do so.

2. *Searches Not Connected with an Arrest.*

General Rule. If an officer has probable cause to believe that a parked, unoccupied vehicle, whether locked or unlocked, contains fruits, instrumentalities, contraband, or evidence of a crime, all those areas of the vehicle which can contain such evidence shall be searched without a search warrant if the vehicle appears to be in such operational condition that it can be moved or easily rendered movable by minor repairs. If, however, a vehicle does not appear to be movable and there is adequate time in which to obtain a search warrant, such warrant shall be obtained prior to entering the vehicle. One example of such a search is:

An officer has been informed by a citizen that he observed a person place a sawed-off shotgun in the trunk of a vehicle one-half hour earlier. The citizen gives his name and address and accompanies the officer to the vehicle, which appears to be operational except for a flat rear tire. The officer may immediately search the trunk of the vehicle without a search warrant because he has probable cause to believe that the shotgun is in the trunk of the vehicle and the vehicle may be easily rendered movable by a minor repair. If, however, the vehicle has been completely stripped, including the wheels, the officer should obtain a search warrant prior to searching the trunk of the vehicle.

B. *Inventories.*

An inventory is an administrative process by which items of property are listed and secured. An inventory is not to be considered or used as a substitute for a search. Automobiles coming into the custody of the police department shall be classified for purposes of this paragraph relating to inventories in one of the following five categories:

Seizures for purposes of forfeiture.

Seizures as evidence.

Prisoner's property.

Traffic impoundments.

Non-criminal impoundments.

The officer's right to inventory an automobile and the time and scope of any such inventory depend upon the category into which it is classified.

1. *Seizures for Purposes of Forfeiture.*

    a. *Narcotics.* When an officer has probable cause to believe that a vehicle has been used to transport illegally possessed narcotics, he shall take the vehicle into custody and classify it as a. seizure for purpose of forfeiture *only if both of the following conditions exist*:

    (1) A substantial amount of drugs is involved.

    (2) The owner of the vehicle (not necessarily the user of the vehicle) is a significant drug violator.

No seizure under this paragraph shall be made without approval of an official of the Narcotics Branch. If a vehicle used to transport illegally possessed narcotics cannot be seized under this paragraph, it may not be inventoried unless it can be classified and inventoried under another section of part I, paragraph B of this order. An example of seizures based on narcotics violations is:

An officer stops an automobile and observes a glassine envelope containing a small amount of a substance which he has reason to believe is heroin in plain and open view of the floor boards. The driver (who is the owner of the vehicle) is arrested for illegal possession of narcotics. The officer contacts an official of the Narcotics Branch and is informed that because the driver has no previous narcotics record and the amount of narcotics seized is not substantial, the vehicle may not be seized for purposes of forfeiture. It may be classified, however, as prisoner's property pursuant to part I, paragraph B3 of this order and inventoried to the extent allowed under the rules contained in that paragraph.

b. *Gambling.* When an officer has probable cause to believe that a vehicle is being or has been used to conduct illegal gambling activities, it may be seized for purposes of forfeiture, irrespective of the age, value, or condition of the vehicle.

(1) *Authorization.* No seizure under this paragraph shall be made without approval of an official of the Gambling and Liquor Branch.

(2) *Examples of Seizures for Purposes of Forfeiture Based Upon Gambling Violations.*

(a) *Vehicle Used by Numbers Runner.* After surveillance, officers develop probable cause to believe that a person is a numbers runner and that a vehicle which he owns or used has been used to conduct the numbers operation. The officers obtained an arrest warrant and a search warrant for his vehicle. When the officers execute the arrest warrant during one of the runs, the defendant's vehicle may be seized for purposes of forfeiture if such seizure has been approved by an official of the Gambling and Liquor Branch.

(b) *Arrest for Possession of a Numbers Slip.* On a routine traffic stop an officer observes in the driver's wallet a single numbers slip and arrests the driver for its possession. If the evidence indicates that the driver was simply a person who placed a numbers bet rather than one who was involved in *conducting* a gambling operation, the vehicle may not be seized for purposes of forfeiture.

c. *National Firearms Act Violations.* When an officer has probable cause to believe that a vehicle has been used to transport a firearm possessed illegally under the National Firearms Act (49 U.S.C. SS 781–788), he shall follow the procedures contained in General Order No. 601.1 in determining whether the vehicle shall be seized for purposes of forfeiture under the Act.

d. *Procedure.* An officer who seizes an automobile for purposes of forfeiture shall completely inventory the contents of the automobile immediately upon its arrival at a police facility. The scope of that inventory shall be limited by the rules provided in part I, paragraph B6 of this order. Upon completion of the inventory, the officer shall obtain instructions from an official of either the Narcotic or Gambling and Liquor Branch or from an agent of the Alcohol, Tobacco and Firearms Division of the Internal Revenue Service, relating to appropriate further processing of the vehicle.

2. *Seizures as Evidence.*

When an officer has probable cause to believe that a vehicle is a fruit, instrumentality, or evidence of a crime, he shall take the vehicle into police custody and shall classify it as a seizure as evidence.

a. *Examples of Seizures as Evidence.*

(1) *Homicide in an Automobile.* A citizen is shot to death in an automobile. After appropriate on-the-scene processing by the Homicide Section, the vehicle shall be seized as evidence because it is evidence and, in addition, may contain evidence of the offense.

(2) *Vehicle Used in an Offense.* Two days after a bank robbery an officer locates an automobile which has been described by witnesses as the getaway vehicle. Whether or not an arrest has been made in the case,

the vehicle shall be seized as evidence because it is an instrumentality of the offense of bank robbery.

NOTE: Although whenever there is either a moving or a parking traffic violation the vehicle involved is technically evidence of that offense, vehicles shall *not* be seized as evidence simply because they were involved in relatively minor traffic offenses. However, if a vehicle has some evidentiary value beyond the fact that it was used to commit a minor traffic offense it shall be seized as evidence.

b. *Procedure.* An officer who seizes a vehicle as evidence shall completely inventory the contents of the vehicle immediately upon its arrival at a police facility, provided that such an inventory will not damage or destroy any evidence contained therein. The scope of that inventory shall be limited by the rules provided in part I, paragraph B6 of this order.

c. *Release of Vehicle.* Vehicles seized as evidence shall not be released to any person until the appropriate prosecutor has signed the proper release form indicating that the vehicle is no longer needed as evidence. In cases where a prosecutor is unavailable and application of this rule would result in hardship to an innocent party, verbal authorization may be obtained by telephone from an Assistant United States Attorney on emergency duty for the month or from any other available Assistant United States Attorney.

3. *Prisoner's Property.*

When a person is arrested in an automobile which he owns or has been authorized to use and the vehicle cannot be classified under part I, paragraph B1 or B2 of this order, that vehicle shall be classified as prisoner's property. One example of prisoner's property is:

Robbery Suspect. A liquor store owner has been robbed by a single assailant who fled on foot. Ten days after the offense the defendant is arrested on a warrant in an automobile. Since there is no basis for seizing the automobile either as evidence or for purposes of forfeiture, the automobile shall be classified as prisoner's property.

a. *Disposition of Prisoner's Property.* A vehicle which is classified as prisoner's property shall be disposed of in any lawful manner in which the person arrested directs. In any case where a prisoner requests that his vehicle be lawfully parked on a public street, he shall be required to indicate his request in writing. An example of disposition of prisoner's property is:

> *Robbery Arrest.* In the robbery example above, the defendant is accompanied by his wife at the time of his arrest. If the defendant so requests, his wife shall be permitted to drive the vehicle from the scene of the arrest. If the defendant is alone at the time of arrest and requests that the vehicle be lawfully parked pending notification of his wife, the request shall be honored, so long as he indicates his request that the vehicle be so parked in writing.

b. *Initial Procedure.* If a vehicle classified as prisoner's property is disposed of so that it is not taken to a police facility, it shall not be inventoried in any way. If it is necessary to take such a vehicle into police custody, the vehicle shall be taken to a police facility or to a location in front of or near a police facility. Immediately upon arrival at the police facility the arresting officer shall remove from the passenger compartment of the vehicle any personal property which can easily be seen from outside the vehicle and which reasonably has a value in excess of $25. After removing such property, if any, the officer shall make sure that the windows are rolled up and the doors and trunk are locked. Any property so removed shall be brought into the police facility and appropriate entries and returns made in accordance with General Order No. 601.1. No other inventory or search of the vehicle shall be made at this time.

c. *Procedure After 24 Hours.* If a person authorized by the prisoner or the prisoner himself, upon his release, does not claim the vehicle within 24 hours of the time that the prisoner was arrested, a complete inventory of the contents of the automobile shall be made by the arresting officer or an officer designated by an official. The scope of that inventory shall be limited by the rules provided in part I, paragraph B6 of this order.

4. *Traffic Impoundments.*

Only those vehicles which, pursuant to section 91 of the D.C. Traffic and Motor Vehicle Regulations, are taken into police custody *and* placed on police department property or at a location in front of or near a police facility shall be classified as "traffic impoundments." Vehicles classified as traffic impoundments shall be inventoried *only* in accordance with part I, paragraphs B4d and B4e of this order. If a vehicle is not placed on police department property or near a police facility, it is not a traffic impoundment and shall not be inventoried or searched in any way.

a. *Non-Impounded Vehicles.* Except as provided in part I, paragraph B4c below, whenever an officer causes a vehicle to be moved pursuant to the traffic regulations, the vehicle shall, if possible, be moved to a location on a public street as close to the original location as possible, consistent with prevailing traffic conditions.

b. *Procedure in Non-Impoundment Situations.* Vehicles moved but not taken to a police facility or to a location in front of or near a police facility shall not be classified as traffic impoundments and shall not be inventoried or searched in any way. However, the officer who caused the automobile to be moved shall make sure that the windows of the automobile are rolled up and, if possible, the trunk and doors are locked before he leaves the vehicle. In all cases where a vehicle is moved without the knowledge of the owner, the Teletype Branch shall be notified in accordance with General Order No. 601.1. An example of a non-impoundment situation is:

Illegal Parking on Main Arteries During Rush Hour. Illegally parked vehicles are disrupting the flow of traffic on a main artery during rush hour. The vehicles should be moved to a location as close to the original location as possible, consistent with prevailing traffic conditions. The vehicle shall not be inventoried or searched in any way.

c. *Impoundments in Exceptional Circumstances.* Only in exceptional circumstances shall the vehicle be impounded for traffic violations and taken to police property or to a location in front of or near a police facility. Examples of exceptional circumstances are:

(1) *Large Amounts of Personal Property in Plain View Within the Automobile.* A vehicle is unlawfully parked on Constitution Avenue during rush hour. Large amounts of clothing and a number of suitcases are in plain view on the back seat of the automobile. In order to protect the citizen's property, the automobile shall be impounded and towed to a police facility or to a location in front of or near a police facility.

(2) *Outstanding Traffic Warrants.* A vehicle is unlawfully parked in front of a fire hydrant. A WALES check discloses that there is a traffic arrest warrant outstanding for the registered owner in addition to 10 unpaid tickets. The vehicle shall be impounded and taken to a police facility or to a location in front of or near the police facility. The vehicle shall not be released to the citizen until collateral in the appropriate amount for the outstanding and present violations is posted.

In these circumstances, the vehicle may also be immobilized by use of a boot or other immobilizing device. If a vehicle is immobilized, rather than impounded and brought to a police facility, the vehicle shall not be inventoried in any way.

d. *Procedure in Impoundment Situations Upon Arrival at Police Facility.* Immediately upon arrival at the police facility, the impounding officer shall remove from the passenger compartment of the vehicle any personal property which can easily be seen from outside the vehicle and which reasonably has a value in excess of $25. After removing such property, if any, the officer shall make sure that the windows are rolled up and, if possible, that the doors and trunk are locked. Any property so removed shall be brought into the police facility and appropriate entries and returns made in accordance with General Order No. 601.1. No other inventory or search of the vehicle shall be made at this time. An example of an impoundment situation upon arrival at a police facility is:

Large Amounts of Personal Property in Plain View Within the Automobile. In the example above relating to large amounts of clothing and suitcases within the automobile, the officer shall remove the clothing and suitcases from the automobile *immediately* upon arrival at the police facility. He shall not examine the glove compartment, search under the seat, or make any other search at this time. The windows shall then be rolled up and the vehicle locked. Appropriate entries and returns shall be made in accordance with General Order No. 601.1.

e. *Procedure in Impoundment Situations After 24 Hours.* If a vehicle which has been impounded is not claimed by the registered owner or a person authorized by the registered owner with 24 hours of the time that the vehicle was impounded, a complete inventory of the contents of the automobile shall be made by the impounding officer or an officer designated by an official. The scope of that inventory shall be limited by the rules provided in part I, paragraph B6 of this order.

5. *Non-Criminal Impoundments.*

When an officer has taken a vehicle into police custody because there is reason to believe that it is abandoned, part of the estate of a deceased person, property of an insane person or a person taken to the hospital, or property turned over to the police at the scene of a fire or disaster, he shall classify it as a non-criminal impoundment.

Procedure. Since the vehicle may be in police custody for an undetermined period of time, an officer who impounds a vehicle as a non-criminal impoundment shall completely inventory the vehicle immediately upon its arrival at a police facility. The scope of that inventory shall be limited by the rules provided in part I, paragraph B6 of this order.

6. *Scope of Inventory.*

Whenever an officer has a right to inventory a vehicle pursuant to this order, the officer shall examine the passenger compartment, whether or not locked, and the trunk, whether or not locked. Any items of personal property which reasonably have a value in excess of $25 shall be removed from the vehicle and placed in secure custody. All items so removed shall be listed and recorded on a property return as provided in General Order No. 601.1. Any container such as boxes or suitcases found within the vehicle shall be opened and any items of personal property found in such containers which reasonably has a value in excess of $25 shall be listed and recorded separately. Immediately upon completion of the inventory, the officer shall make sure that the windows are rolled up and the doors and the trunk are locked.

(signed) *Jerry V. Wilson*
Chief of Police

APPENDIX H

Court Decisions Referred to Within the Text

McNabb v. United States, 318 U.S. 332 (1943)

Upshaw v. United States, 335 U.S. 410 (1948)

Mallory v. United States, 354 U.S. 449 (1957)

Mapp v. Ohio, 367 U.S. 643 (1961)

Escobedo v. Illinois, 378 U.S. 478 (1964)

Miranda v. Arizona, 384 U.S. 436 (1966)

United States v. Wade, 388 U.S. 218 (1967)

Gilbert v. California, 388 U.S. 263 (1967)

Stovall v. Denno, 388 U.S. 293 (1967)

United States v. Perry, 145 U.S. App. D.C. 364 (1971)

United States v. Ash, 149 U.S. App. D.C. 1 (1972)

United States v. Willie Robinson Jr., 471 F. 2d 1082 (1972)

United States v. Kenneth C. Simmons, 302 A. 2d 728 (1973)

United States v. Robinson, 414 U.S. 218 (1973)

INDEX